Thank you for your
service—

Phil

Thank you
for my dnah!
...esiong

JOB WON!

FOR AMERICA'S VETERANS

EVERY VETERAN'S GUIDE TO A SUCCESSFUL
TRANSITION FROM MILITARY SERVICE INTO NEW
EXCITING OPPORTUNITIES IN THE PRIVATE SECTOR

PHIL BLAIR

authorHOUSE®

AuthorHouse™
1663 Liberty Drive
Bloomington, IN 47403
www.authorhouse.com
Phone: 1 (800) 839-8640

Published by AuthorHouse 08/31/2018

ISBN: 978-1-5246-9728-0 (sc)
ISBN: 978-1-5462-0332-2 (e)

Library of Congress Control Number: 2017912186

Printed in the United States of America.

What People are Saying About
Job Won! for America's Veterans

"Congratulations Phil! I have not read a better book dedicated to supporting veterans making the transition into the corporate world. Phil Blair with over 35 years of Manpower and personal consulting experience and the author of the highly popular book "JOB Won!" has written a veteran transition masterpiece: "Job Won! for America's Veterans." In this practical guide, Phil details every step of the process with real life examples. As a San Diego resident, Phil has been a long-time supporter of the Navy and Marine Corps. This book is another way Phil Blair has given back to those who have served our great nation."

VADM (RET) Bill French,
Former Navy Region Southwest Commander and Former Commander, Navy Installations Command.

"Service members are a true asset to our nation, but most leave the military without private sector employment experience, which can be very challenging. Phil Blair's candid, conversational style and real-life examples in *Job Won! For America's Veterans* makes it an engaging read, and one that is packed full of great guidance and steps for success. This is a must read and a handy reference for service members before and after their separation from the military."

Sean Mahoney, CAPT USCG (Ret.), Executive Director of zero8hundred

"I wish I had a book like this back when I was trying to figure out my post-military future. They should hand this to every soldier as they exit the base for the last time. I can see this becoming an online class with a study guide."

Christina R., United States Army Reserves, Retired

"Every person has unique gifts,
and those gifts give him or her the power and the opportunity
to accomplish great things, if he or she learns how
to use those gifts and channel them in the right direction"
– Zig Zigler in "Born to Win"

Contents

Dedication xv

Acknowledgements xvii

Introduction... xix

- How to use this guide... xxi
- Start early xxi
- My definition of veteran... xxii
- Definition of private sector xxiii

phil-osophy 101   1...1

1.0   The Time is Now..3

- Setting appropriate expectations 6

phil-osophy 101   2...9

2.0   Long-Term Planning While Still in the Military.... 11

- Technical training 11
- Eyes wide open..11
- Be COOL 12
- College while in service 13
- Professional associations 15
- Financial planning 17

phil-osophy 101   3...19

3.0   Making a Career Plan.....................................21

- Your dream job...23
- Create your own dream job...................................24
- Taking action...28
- Example: 30-second elevator speech....................39
- Career options to consider...................................40

phil-osophy 101   4 45
4.0   Making the Leap 47
  •   Keep an open mind to all opportunities....................48
  •   Opportunity cost 49
  •   Start early 52
  •   Play the veteran card 53
  •   "Something in leadership or management"................55
  •   Government jobs..57
  •   If a government job really interests you.....................59
  •   Selling yourself... 60
  •   Selling "self" versus "team" 61
  •   Understanding the private sector employer mindset.......62
  •   Staying current..63
  •   Business 101..65
  •   Software... 66
  •   Education and saving your GI Bill 66
  •   Looks are everything 69
  •   Job search 69
  •   Activity tracker 70
  •   50 cups of coffee 71
  •   Structuring your time..71
  •   Getting inside a company 72
  •   How to work a job fair 77
  •   Other reasons we can't stand job fairs......................77
  •   Temporary staffing agencies......................................81
  •   Does no always mean no?..85
  •   Email etiquette 86
  •   Selecting your email address.................................... 86
  •   Subject headings 87
  •   Email content 88
  •   Cell phone voicemail..88
  •   Social media 90

phil-osophy 101   5..93
5.0   Networking 101 97
  •   Face-to-face: there is no substitute.......................... 99
  •   Body language 100
  •   Using names 101

- Is it Phil, or Mr. Blair?..101
- Business cards 102
- Make volunteering part of your transition plan 105
- Selecting the right volunteer opportunities...............105
- Staying in the game 106
- It doesn't have to be full time...nor should it 107
- Free training...108
- Safe environment in which to take some risks..........108
- Volunteering as an experience accelerator...............109
- Leveraging your volunteer experience into a nonprofit career...109
- Toastmasters (or any other public speaking training group/class)... 110

phil-osophy 101   6... 111
6.0   Résumés.. 113
- Many paths to success 113
- Getting started on your résumé 114
- Objective statements 116
- Availability date 119
- Learn to sell yourself.. 119
- Quantify, quantify, quantify....................................120
- Living document..121
- Key word searches 122
- Proof reading 122
- Keep it simple 123
- Other key details 123
- Plugging the gaps 125
- Awards and recognition 125
- Cover letters...126
- Résumé pitfalls 127
- Trevor's top 10 résumé slip-ups 129

phil-osophy 101   7..131
7.0   It's Time to Apply 133
- Inside the HR Manager's mind................................133
- Networking your way around HR 136
- Seven times the chance...137

- Job descriptions. 75% is close enough 137
- The hiring process flow 138
- Online applications 139
- Small to medium size businesses approach 143

phil-osophy 101   8 145
8.0   Interviewing 149
- Nobody likes interviewing 149
- Informational interviews 151
- Preparation 153
- Actual job interview 157
- Dispelling the rigid soldier myth 158
- Interviews formats 159
- Your interview checklist 161
- Identify your golden nuggets 165
- Interview questions you should be ready for 165
- More common interview questions 169
- Keep your answers brief 171
- Never badmouth in an interview 172
- Ask good questions 172
- Using your volunteer experience in an interview ... 175
- Virtual interviewing 176
- Body language 177
- The strong close 177
- Tips for acing the phone Interview 178
- Dressing for success in the private sector 181
- The job interview 183
- How to build a CAR 184
- The actual job interview 185
- Learn about the employer 187
- Interview questions 191
- Thought-provoking questions for all applicants ... 193
- Real (and really dumb) questions 197
- Checklist 198
- I want the job! 199
- References 200

- • Interviews from Hell 202
- • Real and really weird things said during an interview..203
- • And my personal all-time favorite............................203

phil-osophy 101   9..205
9.0   Polite Persistence to Job Offer 207
- • The other perspective – HR's 211
- • Hold your horses..212
- • WAIT! Negotiate!..213
- • Negotiating your employment package....................215
- • Salary negotiation 217
- • Making the hard decision..224
- • Your first day 225

phil-osophy 101   10..227
10.0 Keeping the Job..229
- • JobWon! Day one and beyond................................231
- • Surviving and thriving in the workplace 236
- • Dare I ask for a raise?..242
- • Playing nicely with others.......................................244

phil-osophy 101   11 247
11.0 Managing for Change in your Career 249
- • Know when to go 251
- • The new and improved you.....................................253
- • Keep your network active..256
- • When do I use my network? 258
- • And that's the way it is 258

Appendix...261
- • Insider scoop: The recruitment process..................262
- • How do companies really recruit?...........................263

Bibliography..267

Dedication

This book is dedicated to all of America's military men and women who have ever served in any branches of the military at any time. For the few who retired from serving and stayed retired, I congratulate you on your long term planning that allowed that to happen for you. But for the thousands of men and women who have served and, either because they now need to, or are retiring by their choice and are ready for a new challenge in life, are transitioning into a private sector career, we are here to help.

I know you may feel awkward at times in the process of transition. Everything you learned over your military career seems to be turned upside down when you approach the private sector. I have written *"Job Won! for America's Veterans"* for that exact reason. I see the confusion every day as our company tries its best to hire veterans for our thousands of private sector jobs. I could stand by and say I am sorry you are not qualified for the jobs I have open, or stand by and watch you interview for positions you are very qualified for and know exactly why you didn't get the job. I chose not to stand by but to get involved.

"Thank you for your service," just didn't seem like enough. This version of *Job Won!* is written specifically for our transitioning veterans and is dedicated to those same great Americans. I want to help you understand those of us in the private sector and how to play our game. I welcome you with open arms and am excited to add your skills and talents to the American private sector workforce!

Acknowledgements

Living in San Diego, one of the world's centers of military establishments, I have had the pleasure of meeting many Admirals and Generals including Vice Admiral Dixon Smith. I am often surprised that I have never seen them yell or lose their temper. At least not with civilians. I just assumed every officer was like a drill sergeant.

Manpower made me aware of the challenges employers are facing transitioning veterans into the private sector workforce. Vice Admiral Smith made me aware of the need for transition training from a military career to a private sector career. He would talk about all his "transitioning kids" in San Diego that needed private sector jobs and there didn't seem to be a place he could send them for assistance. Dixon had read *Job Won!* and easily convinced me I needed to write a military version to assist the service members who were entering my job market.

I know the private sector job market, but I sure didn't understand the transition from the military market. I was smart enough to reach out for help from lots of people who did know it. The greatest input was from Shawn VanDiver, who entered the Navy a 17 year old and spent 12 as an active duty Sailor. Due to his determination and very outgoing personality, he had very little problem transitioning into the private sector. You will learn more about Shawn as you read the book. Shawn was my eyes and ears to make sure we covered the key issues that so many of his counterparts struggled with. Thank you, Shawn, for all of your great input telling it like it is coming from the world you understood into the world of work outside the military.

Lots of other people were very helpful, too, and were quick to give input on any questions I might have. Trevor Blair, of whom I am the proud father, teaches transitioning veterans and is the number one resource for veteran transition panels. Although he never served in the military, his input was very helpful viewing veterans from the HR Department's point of view. Neil Zerbe, known as Cowboy by all of his counterparts, works for Manpower West's Veteran Division and is our key outreach into the veteran community and keeps us grounded on the needs and frustrations that veterans are feeling, and especially the road blocks they are hitting. Shane Smith, a racquetball buddy, was transitioning out of the Marines right when I was writing this book. He was, and still is, my go-to person to ask about realities and frustrations that both enlisted men and women, including himself, were feeling. Shane is my "Don't let them blow smoke up your ass" guy. And a special thank you to Nancy Mumford for spearheading this project from the very beginning. Nancy was very helpful with the original Job Won! version but, even after moving back east, was, and is, the stalwart that keep the For America's Veterans version going. Without her help it would never have happened. I thank you, Nancy.

I want to thank all the veterans I have talked to, some with smooth and many with challenging transitions into the private sector. I have learned something from all of you and hopefully have integrated your input into *Job Won! for America's Veterans*.

I am anxious to hear your feedback reading *Job Won! for American's Veterans*. Let me know at jobwon@manpowersd.com.

Introduction

Sniper! Really? Is that really what his résumé says?

Sitting on the other side of my desk was Zach, a very sharp young Marine looking for his first job in the private sector. He was the son of a friend of mine and he was doing exactly what he should be doing — using connections to network and get himself in front of decision makers who could point him toward potential job opportunities. So far, so good.

Before I asked to see Zach's résumé, we chatted for a few minutes about his past, and how his job search was going. He had been out of the Marines for six months and the job search was not going well. He was clearly frustrated by a total lack of response to the dozens of résumés he had submitted. There were plenty of jobs out there that he felt he was qualified for, both because of his education and because of his six years in the Marines. So I asked to see his résumé.

The page he slid across the desk explained everything. The lead caption was "Sniper." Wow! No wonder he wasn't getting any callbacks on all those résumé submittals! And no wonder his frustration was building to the point of despair.

Later that afternoon, I was speaking to a group of 150 HR professionals about the current state of the job market, and its effect on the increasingly larger number of veterans leaving the military each year. For a moment of levity, I asked the group for a show of hands: how many had hired snipers in the last three months? Lots of giggles, but no hands went up in the air. So I expanded: how many in the last six months, six years, six decades? Not a single hand. I then told them Zach's story, and you could hear the sigh of compassion for his challenge, and the tens of thousands of transitioning veterans just like him. How could a decorated United States veteran, with two combat tours, one in Iraq and one in Afghanistan, end up applying for private sector jobs using a sniper résumé? How did we let this happen?

Now, Human Resources folks are by their very nature compassionate people who want to go out of their way to help others succeed. That's why we got into the field. It sure wasn't for the periods of downsizing and firings that we dread being called upon to facilitate. I was ready to move on in my remarks, but I was stopped by a number of hands going up with questions. As I called on the attendees, they each had a similar story to tell, about their frustration at not having the time or resources to stop their recruiting project, call the veteran and invite them in for a résumé and job search tutorial. But they sure wish they could have.

That's when Vice Admiral Smith's comments really started to make sense. HR professionals and veterans were speaking different languages. I needed to take my *Job Won!* career guide, and create an all-new version specifically for Zach and the thousands of other veterans like him. My hope is that the strategies and experience provided here will prevent future generations of veterans from struggling as Zach has struggled.

This is how *Job Won! for America's Veterans came about.* I wrote this book, specifically to meet the needs of anyone who is either currently serving, or has recently served, in the armed forces. If your career needs a boost, then you've come to the right place. I hope by reading *Job Won! for America's Veterans* you will see the transformation we made with Zach from his military beginnings to a very successful career in the civilian sector.

How to use this guide

And yes, I call it a guide, and a book. Have a pen and maybe a highlighter in your hand as you read. Highlight, take notes in the margins, and reflect on how the content relates to your personal transition experience. The act of actually writing, as opposed to typing notes into a phone, tablet or computer, can be therapeutic. It also helps you better retain the content. Please don't just read this guide once through and put it on your bookshelf. It's designed to be small enough to fit in the glove box of your car, your laptop bag, or interview portfolio. You will want to refer to it regularly at different decision points. I can't tell you the number of times that a reader has emailed that they reread the chapter on interviewing right before the interview and "nailed" it.

Start early

I hope you have *Job Won! for America's Veterans* in your hands at least a year before your terminal leave begins. After the first read-through, you should, at a minimum, be ready to get started on your job search plan. Do not wait until you are assigned to attend transition classes. The ensuing months or weeks will give you some time to digest the content and reflect on the thoughts and ideas you wrote in the margins. More important, it will also give you an opportunity to test-drive many of the job search and networking strategies offered here before they really matter. Screwing up a networking opportunity when it doesn't really matter is acceptable, but it will provide valuable context for future networking opportunities. I suggest a second read after about four weeks. By then you'll hopefully have some early job leads, and the beginnings of your new private sector network of local professionals. Reading *JobWon! for America's Veterans* for the second time will probably validate some of your initial experiences, and also spark new ideas and insights you can implement right away.

> *Ron, one of my earlier veteran clients, still keeps several copies with him in his car trunk and gives them out like trick or treat to every veteran he runs into who is considering their transition to the private sector. He tells everyone, "I wish I had this resource when I was where you are."*

Your job is to put in the time and effort to identify a range of occupations and sectors that interest you and meet your requirements for location, salary, schedule, etc. Then, when a recruiter or professional contact asks the question, what kind of job are you looking for? You can respond with a thoughtful, targeted answer. Something like, "Thanks for asking. I'm interested in a couple of fields actually, both of which would enable me to draw on the skills and experience I gained during my time in the Marines Corps. I have a background in IT hardware and software support, and I'm also interested in using those analytical skills to start a career as a Business Analyst in the biotech sector."

You just eased into a 30-second elevator speech that doesn't pigeon hole you into just one field or occupation. And while those two careers are actually quite different, the answer is detailed enough to show you have already started thinking seriously about the next move.

My definition of veteran

For the sake of simplicity, we use the term "veteran" to include individuals who have actually separated from the military, as well as those who might still be on active duty and are contemplating their next career move. The concepts and strategies contained in this guide are also equally applicable to spouses of active duty military personnel and spouses of veterans, both of whom are often included under the category of "millfam/milspouse" (military family/military spouse — terms we use with respect and gratitude). I understand how important a military professional's spouse's support is to their successful completion of their goals in the military and development of their career outside the military. Our Manpower operation has been working in the veteran's transition space for a number of years now, and we are still surprised by the degree of inattention to milfam career needs. While the number of resources available to veterans is pretty substantial, solid career resources for milfams are paltry. A *JobWon! for America's Military Spouses* is the next project we'd like to undertake.

Mary, a Staff Sergeant's wife, may just be the favorite Manpower temporary employee in the whole United States. Like many milspouses, hers is the "trailing career." When they first met and discussed his desire for a career in the military, they were very aware that he would be transferred often to new posts. She gave up her profession as a sales person and became an excellent Executive Assistant, a skill in demand everywhere. Mary worked for our Manpower franchise and when relocation orders came, we forwarded her records to the Manpower office closest to their assignment, she was welcomed with open arms and she was working immediately. There's no telling how many Manpower offices Mary has worked for, but the system works perfectly for her as a milspouse with skills in demand.

Definition of private sector

Throughout this guide, we use the term "private sector" to refer to any job not associated with a government's military entity, including federal, state, county, city, and other levels. Companies such as Booz Allen Hamilton or Lockheed Martin, which derive the vast majority of their revenue from government contracts, and which often place their employees on work assignments inside government entities, are definitely still private sector businesses. Non-profit organizations, although not the focus of this guide, also fall into the private sector category, as they must still hustle and compete for their revenue every bit as much as a for-profit business must compete in its marketplace. And remember that the private sector is made up of some huge companies, and many middle size ones, but by far the most jobs are found in small companies that make up the backbone of the US economy. These small businesses are where the hidden opportunities lie because so often they are overlooked by job seekers.

Whether you just graduated boot camp, are debating reenlistment or separation, or are wrapping up a storied career and retiring, *Job Won! For America's Veterans* is for you. Let's dive in…

Let's start with the "challenging" news: Once you leave the service, it very well may not be as easy as you think to transition into a private sector career. In fact, most employers still don't understand the hard skills, and especially the soft skills, that come instilled in service members. For the most part very few have served in the military themselves and only two percent even know anyone close to them who has served. You are an unknown commodity to them. But they know you have probably been trained to fight and defend our country. When it comes to talking about your job experience, you speak a foreign language. The good news is that with training and practice you will wow them.

"The harder I work, the luckier I get." We've all heard stories about people who seemed to be the recipients (deserving or not) of incredible luck. They were at a party and heard cocktail chatter about a fantastic job opportunity. They fortuitously knew a guy who knew a guy, etc.

The first century Roman philosopher Seneca said, "Luck is what happens when preparation meets opportunity." A lot of folks have echoed that sentiment over the millennia. Luck favors those who don't depend upon it. Sure, some things are mostly about luck. Las Vegas for example. But mostly, we must make our own luck by taking advantage of every opportunity we recognize or create.

If you think you're lucky, you'll be lucky. The lucky guy who heard about the dream job at the party may have been lucky because he knew that party was a good place to pick up tips for new opportunities.

He was in the right place at the right time because he put himself there. Be that guy. Reach out to people. Attend events. Be seen as personable, interactive and maybe even a little aggressive (but in a good, non-threatening way). If you feel uncomfortable networking, know that you are not alone. It is an acquired skill. Practice it like you would any other skill that you have honed.

Just like when you served abroad on an assignment, you will pick up the lingo really fast and mitigate all these issues through planning and preparation prior to exiting the service. Just like you learned to speak a foreign language when you were on deployment, you will learn the language and habits of the HR and business owner world.

1.0   The Time is Now

If I accomplish nothing with this book but give you and your fellow men and women who have worn our country's uniform a wakeup call, then I have succeeded. It's a new world out there. It's an exciting world with lots of new parameters for you to embrace. But do not expect employers to come chasing you down with phenomenal job opportunities. Until about 10 years ago we would guide veterans during terminal leave to contact each and every defense industry firm they could find. Defense businesses were booming and they needed experienced veterans to join them on their side of the negotiating table. But those days are long gone and you will have to work for each interview and job offer you receive.

Whether you're about to leave for basic training or Officer Candidate School, are actively serving and thinking about leaving the military, or separating in a day, you should be thinking about transition. It is never too early to begin planning for your next career move. It's also never too late to make positive decisions that will help you succeed in your next venture. This is as true for private sector job seekers as it is for veterans transitioning.

> *Shane is a racquetball buddy of mine. He and I recently worked through his transition from Marine officer to a senior HR position. His first words of advice to every veteran he meets is, "Don't let them blow smoke up your ass! Anyone who tells you the job offers will come flowing in, the pay rates are much higher, you'll have your pick of jobs and be working within weeks of ending your terminal leave, has never made the transition."*

> *Take Shawn VanDiver, for example, the veteran who helped me write this book. He served for 12 years in the Navy as an enlisted Fire Controlman. He dealt with the missiles and guns on ships, and not put out fires, as this layman assumed! He entered service at 17 years old and took advantage of nearly everything the Navy had to offer in the way of education and life after service. He left the Navy with three degrees, six journeyman cards for the US Department of Labor, and 21 civilian certifications plus leadership positions within several professional organizations and a network of relationships culled through the various industries he touched both in and out of service. Shawn was walking into an appointment with the City of San Diego when he left service, but a major scandal in the Mayor's office erupted, the unexpected curve ball in life…and that job disappeared. He didn't think he needed a backup plan but he did have his network to lean on. Through connections Shawn swiftly landed a job with Sony PlayStation, one of the most well-known companies in the world, as the San Diego Enterprise Risk and Security Manager.*

Just as there was no one thing to point to that landed him that position; there is no "silver bullet" to finding your next big career. Shawn recognized early in his career that he needed to set himself up if he wanted to succeed outside of the Navy, so he worked really hard both in and outside the lifelines of the Navy. It took years of hard work in the Navy meeting and networking with lots of people and climbing through the ranks of volunteer positions within professional organizations that would eventually expose him to opportunities in his field. This is why I feel so strongly that military personnel should be aware how important it is to start preparing for their civilian job long before they decide to leave the military. Or worse, the military decides to leave them.

That first job when you get out is important. It can set the tone for the rest of your career. Ideally, and with the right preparation, you can take a step up in responsibility and pay when you leave the military.

It is important, however, to recognize that this is not the reality for many.

> *Kevin left the service after 12 years also. He made it all the way to Chief Petty Officer (Navy E7) in his short career and was certain that he would leave the Navy, immediately go to school, working full time, and prosper. But he didn't take advantage of the apprenticeship programs, college education programs, or any other programs outside of his day-to-day job in the Navy. Kevin left the Navy and applied online to every position he could find but rarely got a call back. He finally landed a position with a security company as a guard in his hometown. These days, Kevin has an internship with a software design company (he's studying computer science). His experience in the military is helping him climb the ladder faster than most, but the lack of a degree, coupled with his being new to the IT field means that he is starting over at or near entry level in his new career path. Because of a lack of preparation, Kevin is way behind Shawn in his new career.*

Starting over at entry level is a hard transition to make but not a bad thing. In fact, it's a great thing. You get to take all of those lessons you've learned in the military and apply them to your new exciting position in the private sector. An example I often use is that I am an ROTC drop out who is now in senior management in a HR company. If I went to the head of HR for the Navy and said I wanted to make a lateral move into being a Commander with zero Navy experience, how long would it be before I was laughed out of the room? I'd probably be told to enlist, survive boot camp, sign up for Officer Candidate School and come back in 10 years with naval experience. Well, it's the same concern going the other way. Unless your military skills tee you up for a lateral move into a private sector job then be ready to drop down a few notches and begin to work your way back up your new career ladder. I am convinced that with your military experience you will move up that ladder faster than your new civilian peers without your background, Shawn, above, took advantage of the different professional development and higher education programs, and was able to land a senior position when he left the service. Look for the opportunity and the growth potential before you routinely turn away any job prospects that seem beneath your current military status. This is especially difficult for high level officers. But remember you are in it for the long term, not for immediate gratification. Because of that, you may promote faster and higher.

Setting appropriate expectations

Before you go full steam ahead, you should stop and make sure going directly into the civilian workforce is the right move for you at this time. Maybe you should you go directly to school instead and earn the credentials and experience through internships that you missed out on in the military. A specialized degree and experience and connections, even as an intern or a part time job, may be essential to your career success in the private sector.

Remember Kevin, who we talked about before, was senior to Shawn while in the service, but because Shawn took advantage of the different professional development and higher education programs, he was able to land a more senior position when he left the service. If you are looking for a break from work to go to school after you exit the service, that's a great route. If you qualify for the GI Bill, you'll receive Basic Allowance for Housing (BAH) at the equivalent of E5 for your home and you'll be able to use GI Bill benefits to go to school for up to 36 months (which can equate to 4 years of school). You'll also have the latitude to land some internships in the civilian workforce while still in school to get a good idea of where your skills can lead you.

If, after analyzing educational options you want to dive right into the workforce, that's awesome, too. As I said earlier, you'll need to have realistic expectations about where you can land. Depending on what you do or did in the military, you may have a job that translates directly to the civilian world. Some examples are cook, personnel specialists /admin, electricians, mechanics, and commanding officers. Some jobs, like armored, special operations demolitions, or attack helicopter pilot may not translate directly so you'll need to consider what that means for your career options.

Sam was a submarine captain whom I met a few years ago. Talk about a challenging transition into private sector! How many companies hire captains for their submarines? And yes, full confession, I did make a corny joke about Disneyland having a submarine ride that maybe would be right up his alley. The captain did not find it humorous. But after a quick recovery we redefined his talents and experience as the CEO of a large firm with an annual budget of $400M and a rotating staff of very experienced and talented workers that hit their goals and metrics year after year with profound flexibility. Once Sam reoriented his skill sets to talk about them in a way the private sector could understand and relate to, he had a senior job in the shipbuilding industry within three months.

And it's also important to note that you aren't likely to initially make as much as a civilian as you do in the military. We don't provide base housing, danger pay, PXs, unlimited healthcare benefits, clothing allowance, and many other benefits you probably don't appreciate while serving. Want to join a health club to work out? Get ready to pay monthly dues. This is especially true if you are transitioning into a market with a high supply of military labor. You will be competing with lots of fellow veterans wanting to stay in the community where they and their families now live. And they have very similar skill sets to yours. We'll dive deep into these issues and more as we progress, but I want you to be aware so that you join this job market earlier and better prepared than your peers.

phil-osophy 101   2

All of us have turning points in our lives and our careers where going right or left will make a significant difference. We know straight ahead is not always the best choice. But how do we prepare ourselves for the big decisions that lay ahead?

Scenario one, for you, may be "been there done that." I have enjoyed my stint in the military, have either max'd out my retirement benefits (of not) and just don't have the fire in the belly for receiving new orders that take me away from my family for long stretches of time or force me to relocate my family again. It's your choice. Maybe you're burned out and you need to take the initiative to make a change. The military sure isn't going to ask you what you would like and make it happen.

Or your recent turning point may very well have been because you didn't get the next promotion, signaling that your upward movement in the military has probably come to an end. In the military, it is clearly an up or out dynamic. So it is decision time.

And third, you can be loving your career in whatever branch of the military you are, and at whatever level you are, and wherever you are currently assigned, but a BRAC (Base Realignment and Closure) comes along and the military needs more technology or ships and fewer bodies. Thank you for your service but your skill sets will no longer be needed. I especially see this in young recruits who finished high school, enlisted right away, and planned on a long, exciting, and stable career in the military. They got the exciting but not the long and stable part.

Each of these scenarios forces you to suddenly make a change. Just like I am adamant that no one should ever be surprised that they are getting fired, no one should be surprised that they are burning out, may not get a promotion, or that they are not assured a lifelong job.

Be aware that all of these situations can happen in the private sector just as easily. The message is the same. Prepare for the obvious and the unexpected. You have a Career Coach and soon it will be you. Make sure your contacts are doing the job for you that you need them to do.

Phil

2.0 Long-Term Planning While Still in the Military

If you've still got some time left in service, you've got ample opportunity to set yourself up for a successful life outside of the military. This chapter will cover some opportunities you are probably already thinking about as well as some you may not be aware of yet.

Technical training

Simply by virtue of being in today's military, you no doubt have a good deal of technical training under your belt. Make sure you keep all those certificates you have earned and that they make it onto your Joint Services Transcript. This will not only help you keep track of your training but will also be an official record for any employers or educational institutions later down the road. And know that we will check. We have been burned by résumé creep and downright falsifications of education and rank.

Eyes wide open

As you go through your military career, I encourage you to always have an eye on several career paths that might interest you when you decide to leave the military. You can change your mind 10 times but here are some thought processes to go through. And these steps apply to your military career too.

After you've finished your initial accession training and are at your first duty station, you will likely be very busy learning your new job and applying the skills you've just acquired. This initial qualification time is just as (and potentially more) important than the training you completed. The same will be true for your civilian career, but more on that later.

After you're qualified and proficient at your job, you'll have an opportunity to take on some extracurricular activities; most services call them collateral duties. If possible, do this with an eye toward potential benefits on the outside. You can ask yourself a series of questions:

1. Does this get me college credit?
2. Does this increase my skill set and make me a more attractive candidate for future positions in and /or outside of the military?
3. Will there be opportunities to expand my military and non-military network?

If the answer to at least one of these is "yes," then you should consider it a good chance to develop professionally.

You will also have an opportunity to attend other schools and trainings while in the military. As you know, these classes range from one day to several months, with the average being about a week in length. Most commands have a schools coordinator who can help get you placed and may help you receive education sought after both on the outside of the military as well as while you're in. Many of these courses can also provide direct or indirect college credit. "Direct," meaning they've been evaluated and will be reflected on your Joint Services Transcript and "indirect," meaning you can submit to an educational institution and make an argument that you should receive college credit.

Be COOL

No matter what job you're in, there is probably a civilian certification you are qualified for and you may not even know it. Moreover, the military will probably cover the cost of you getting certified while you're still in (but be aware usually not if you have less than a year left). If you are serving in the Navy or Army, there is a program called Credentialing Opportunities On-Line (COOL). The COOL program pays for civilian certifications while you're on active duty. Not only does this help you establish yourself as qualified for civilian employment long before you separate, it also may help you promote while you're in service. Shawn, the veteran helping me write this iteration of *Job Won!*, for example, was able to complete 21 civilian certifications through Navy COOL before he left service. He tells me that these certs were critical to landing his first job.

The United States Department of Labor also offers free journeyman certification for simply logging the hours you're already working through the Uniformed Services Military Apprenticeship Program (USMAP). These trades range from 1,000 – 8,000 hours (and some maybe even more), and for every year you have over the pay grade of E4 you are awarded 1,000 hours (up to half of the required hours).

Shawn tells me that not doing this program is naïve because it's free validation of your skills and doesn't cost anything but about 15 minutes a week. It will also help you stand out among your peers while you're still serving.

You will also, no doubt, attend at least one leadership development course during your time in the military. These are wonderful because they are often taught outside of your home command and offer you an opportunity to meet and confer with a group of folks from diverse backgrounds. The military offers some of the very best leadership training and, although it may seem like common sense, it is important to pay attention and hone your leadership skills at every opportunity. Those skills will come in handy when you transition and are starting a new career. It's also important to use these courses as an opportunity to network among peers at other commands. You never know when you might need a bucket of paint unavailable at your command or that rare part that one of your leadership school buddies has in his or her shop. And what better time to practice your networking skills and pay it forward than while still in the military?

College while in service

For many who enter the service, a driving motivator is the prospect of using the GI Bill or College Fund for free education when you get out. If you fall into this category (or the "I want to go to college" category") then you are in luck! The military offers a lot in the way of educational opportunities.

In addition to the college credit you can and will receive from the previously mentioned technical training, you can also attend courses while on active duty. There are many options including online, brick and mortar, and hybrid. Many units even hire professors to teach courses during deployments overseas. Some units also offer courses through local community colleges. The possibilities are endless and it's not unheard of these days for Sailors, Soldiers, Airmen, Marines, and Coast Guardsmen to enter the service with a high school diploma/GED (or equivalent) and leave with a Master's degree. If you have time on your hands, put it to good use. You not only will be able to impress your interviewer about how diligent you were to get your degree during service, but also save two years of earning power by not having to go to school full time when you get out. Even if you don't finish your degree, it can make a huge dent in the time it will take to get the degree, post service.

I would encourage you to seriously consider attending college, no matter what field you would like to go into. And not only because education is the key that unlocks doors aplenty, but also because of the opportunities that will inevitably stem from it. "You have too much education" is a phrase you would like to hear versus "this job demands a degree for applicant consideration." More later on how to negotiate the over-educated push back.

When you step out of your military unit and into the world of academia, rank disappears. Ideas, attitude and interpersonal skills are what really matter. You can hone your communications skills, meet people you otherwise would never meet, and learn about things you'd never considered. The personal and professional benefits are endless.

If you choose to go the formal education route, you should research the schools available on your base and/or in your area. Every service has ample resources dedicated to making college accessible and affordable for its members. The basic steps to getting enrolled in college, if you've not yet attended, are:

1. Identify the school you'd like to attend
2. Apply online (be aware that many schools have strict application deadlines [SM1], but several do cater to the military and may have year-round enrollment)
3. Unofficial transcript evaluations (you'll need any previous education plus your Joint Service Transcript)
4. Begin classes

Remember, as you progress academically, you'll want to track your progress through the school's online portal and make sure that you don't have any unexpected surprises. Sometimes requirements change and you'll want to be on top of that.

When you hit your third or fourth year of college, and if you have the professional bandwidth, you should begin looking for a part-time internship in your field of choice.

Professional associations

Whether you decide to go back to school or continue down the technical path, every industry has professional organizations. These are the rooms where go-getters mingle with other go-getters and drive their field forward. These are also the rooms where jobs are made known first and never posted jobs are first discussed.

> *Bill left the Army after serving 24 years. Before he got out, he joined ASIS International, a professional organization focused on the security industry. Through his involvement on the local chapter board and at the national and international levels on ANSI standard writing bodies, he was able to meet security professionals from all over the world. He also earned their flagship certification, which tells the world that he knows what he's talking about. One of his contacts within ASIS let him know about a job in Amsterdam that seemed right up his alley. The American company was looking for someone to come be the Director of International Security in*

the European offices. Well, Bill happened to know the retiring previous director through ASIS and he and his wife are now retired from the military and living in Europe doing something he loves. He landed the job two months before he left the military and has been hard at work there for five years.

Along with the membership, many of these organizations also offer civilian certifications that will help show your experience when you're applying for jobs. The difference between a certification and a degree is that degrees show education and certifications show practical experience. The Holy Grail is to have a mixture of both.

Joining these associations while still on active duty will help you establish yourself as a professional in the field before you are looking for a job. Developing relationships with potential employers / coworkers prior to transition will go a long way toward helping you make the cut when the time comes to begin your nonmilitary career. This is also where you can use the uniqueness of being in the military to your advantage. You are surrounded by civilians and that makes you different and special. Use it. Accept all the "thank you for servings" you can get. Use it as a way to start a networking conversation. Most firms have veteran outreach programs so ask your new peers about what their firm provides. Don't be hesitant to talk about the professional groups area of focus and it is different and the same in the military version. Offer to be the speaker at a meeting. This is a rare opportunity for you to get in front of lots of folks that are active in your field of interest and let them know exactly what kind of job you are looking for when you get out. Get names and collect business cards for later follow up.

Many of these organizations struggle to find leadership for their boards of directors. If you can land a spot on the board of one of these organizations, you'll be head and shoulders above the competition as you search for that perfect job.

Finally, these professional organizations can help with the internships we mentioned in the section on college.

Networking while you're still inside the machine

We'll cover networking in its own chapter, but I wanted to make a quick note about ways to maximize the unique environment that the military offers. In our day and age, it is incredibly easy to stay connected to folks we meet, if even for a brief minute. Whenever you attend one of those technical schools, college courses, drills, leadership development courses (those offer college credit too!), or any other event or training outside of your home unit, make sure to connect with the folks you meet over LinkedIn or email. You never know what may come of the relationships you develop. The easiest way is to always have your business cards with you and offer yours and ask for theirs. You will be amazed at the contacts list you can quickly develop.

Financial planning

While you're still in, you should be planning for your financial future. The military is a unique employer because they provide you with a place to sleep and three square meals a day, if you want them. Shawn tells me that many service members end up renting or buying a place in their local communities and shopping at the commissary to prepare their own meals. It goes without saying that if you have a family, you're already doing that.

Planning for your financial separation for the military is more than just ensuring you have the money to cover expenses for housing and utilities. You'll also need to make sure that you're financially solvent enough to survive on the small unemployment check that you'll be eligible for after leaving service. Be very aware of what is free in the service and you will have to pay for on the outside. Know what additional pay, on top of your base pay, will disappear when you leave and most important, depending on your career choice, be very aware that you may be taking a step backward (earning wise) to take many steps forward as you progress in your new career.

There are veteran friendly pro bono financial literacy services to help you and your family prepare a realistic post military earnings based budget. One example is San Diego Financial Literacy Center (sdflc. org) and they have branches throughout the country.

Healthcare costs can be surprising, so can many of the other costs the military picks up.

> *Jeff, who left the Air Force as a Technical Sergeant, thought that he was all set when he was getting out because he found a job that paid the same as his Air Force job. He didn't take into account that groceries would cost 33% more or that healthcare costs for his family of four would cost $500 a month. Jeff and his spouse struggled until he eventually got promoted. But it was an unexpected struggle. Don't be Jeff.*

Do not treat the financial transition issues lightly. From taxes to savings, IRAs, 401Ks, and many more very important decisions need to be made. I strongly encourage you to get professional help as you begin to make your transition. Much of this assistance may be available at no cost from nonprofit organizations in your area.

phil-osophy 101   3

If you think you're lucky, you'll be lucky. The lucky guy who heard about the dream job at the party may have been lucky because he knew that party was a good place to pick up tips for new opportunities. He was in the right place at the right time because he put himself there. Be that guy. Reach out to people. Attend events. Be seen as personable, interactive and maybe even a little aggressive (but in a good, non-threatening way).

Odds are, you won't get lucky finding a job sitting at a computer all day scrolling employment listings. Computers don't hire people. So put yourself out there. It may be uncomfortable or awkward, but truth be told, it is for almost everyone. Not every outing will pay off immediately or at all. Some ventures will feel like a waste of time. Some might be. But work every opportunity as best you can. It will eventually pay off. The harder you work, the luckier you will get. If you don't know that by now, ask your Career Manager.

3.0   Making a Career Plan

"When it comes to the future, there are three kinds of people: Those who let it happen, those who make it happen and those who wonder what happened."
JOHN M. RICHARDSON

"I look to the future because that's where I'm going to spend the rest of my life."
GEORGE BURNS

A veteran starting a new career in the private sector can probably relate to one or more of these scenarios:

1. You're out and getting ready to start college and need to pick a major, or you've just finished college and need a job.
2. You've been fired (for cause) or laid off (right-sizing). Sure, you feel like you've been gut-punched. After all, it wasn't your idea, but, in a way, you may be pleased because this forces you to make a new start you didn't have the nerve to begin on your own.
3. You're in a job or field that's disappearing. Technology, automation or a reduction in forces are eliminating thousands of military jobs. Your skills may have become obsolete, or soon will.
4. You are bored. Your military job holds no meaning or gives no fulfillment. You have a pervasive sense of emptiness and discontent because work doesn't satisfy your fundamental desires or personal needs.

5. Your job is just a paycheck. You do your job well. You're successful at it, and you feel secure. But there is no upward advancement. The thought of doing this job for another 10 or 20 years is depressing.

If any of the above describes you, then you need a Career Plan. The best thing about working on your Plan is that you begin to feel like you're taking control of your career and your future. As I mentioned earlier, one of the worst aspects of being either jobless or unhappy in your job is the sense that your life has spiraled out-of-control. Your Career Plan is the most effective way I know for you to get that control back.

You might be thinking, "That sounds nice, Phil, but I need a job, like, yesterday. I don't have the luxury of making a long-range plan. I've got to pay the rent next week."

I consider myself a very pragmatic person and I understand it's hard to think about the future when current circumstances are weighing you down. Immediate issues can be lack of a nest egg, a car payment past due, or what you feel may be a lack of skills to get any job. I understand that and we need to work within those parameters.

First, get a job, any job. You need to keep a roof over your head while you work on your future. You will find that people can put up with the hardest, most boring and lowest paying job *if* they have a plan that leads to a way forward. Always remember the temporary staffing industry may help you find fast work that could lead to that permanent job you really want. While you are taking care of very short term needs with a job, you will find the job very tolerable if you know it is short-term and you know you have a plan to get out of that job.

Now that the world is not falling in on you, it's time to get back to your Career Plan.

Your dream job

I make frequent public presentations, discussing the job market and giving job search tips. Whether I am talking to one person or hundreds of people, I ask them to do this exercise: Take out a pen and a sheet of paper and write down your dream job. Forget about how much the job might pay or how much money you need to support your desired lifestyle. Family concerns aren't an issue; neither is geography. There are no constraints of any kind. In this moment, you have the freedom to imagine.

Often, when I give people these instructions, they look back at me perplexed. They don't understand. So I give them an example: My ideal job is to host the Today show on NBC. Yes, I know the job is filled by Hoda Kotb and she does a fine job. Still, in my mind (and mine alone), I'm convinced that if NBC hired me, Katie Couric would quit her job in a heartbeat and return to NBC as my co-host. All the other details are not important, like having to get up at 3 a.m. every morning or being casually conversant on Middle East politics or the New York art scene. This is my dream and I get to control it! This is my ideal job—at least right now. It could change tomorrow.

After I give my example and people have a few minutes to ponder, some begin writing furiously while others wait for inspiration to pop into their heads. For the latter, nothing actually comes to mind.

The real action begins when I ask participants to shout out their ideal jobs and why. Soon, others in the room begin to take parts of what they hear and cobble together their own ideal jobs. That's perfectly acceptable; others inspire us all the time.

What's not okay is simply adopting someone else's perfect job as your own just because it sounds good. Unless you truly feel the same passion for the job for the same reasons, it's a formula for failure, not unlike the notion of arranged marriages. A job or career defined for you by external influences (i.e., your parents, friends, boss) is bound to end badly. Avoid it at all costs. This is your time to fantasize, don't let other people do it for you.

Often people respond by citing a sport they love, usually adding that they'd also like to earn millions playing it. Usually it's golf. Or they say it would be to work for a charity helping abused children. Or they want to own their own business; be their own boss.

The details really don't matter. The point of the exercise is simply to get people thinking, to expand ones options, to dream big.

Create your own dream job
Now I'm going to ask you to engage in another bit of fantasizing. I want you to think "outside the box," to brainstorm without boundaries.

What is your dream job? This isn't just a fun exercise. As children, most of us have fantasies about what we'd like our lives to look like. We fantasize about where we'll travel, whom we'll marry, what kind of house we'll live in —and what kind of work we'll do. They help to shape what kind of person you'll become.

But many people, whether they realize it or not, begin early in their lives and careers to chip away at their dreams. Often, it's a process driven by harsh realities, but sometimes people simply lose confidence in their ability to make dreams happen. They become prisoners of their own reduced expectations.

Generally speaking, 40% of workers like what they do for a living. They don't mind getting up in the morning and usually come home feeling great.

Another 40% of workers stay in their jobs because it pays the bills.

The jobs are boring and unsatisfying. It's a paycheck and little more. Work is tolerable, but they live for five o'clock.

The last 10% simply hate what they do. Getting up in the morning to go to work is a conscionable act, a force of will. There are often feelings of resentment and conflict. The workday stretches on forever; they are bored to tears and may be under intense pressure.

These negative emotions affect both their work and personal lives. The job sucks and the weekend can't come soon enough.

But to be in the top 10% of career satisfaction with people who love what they do, who don't think of work as work, isn't mere good fortune. I'm a strong believer that "you make your own luck." Good times are the consequence of hard work. And hard work begins with a realistic and complete self-assessment, an examination of your values and attitudes and a readiness to change.

What career path do you think has the most people in the bottom 10%?

Manual laborers? Data entry clerks? Security guards? You would be wrong. It is attorneys. How can that be? Fancy title, well respected, highly paid? When I talk to them about their career choice, I hear very similar issues. "I went into it because it paid really well and there was nothing else I wanted to do. But now all I do as a corporate attorney is extremely boring contract work reading pages and pages of legal documents looking for loop holes." Or, "As a litigator, I do nothing but fight with people all day long. The pressure to win on behalf of my clients is intense and even when I do win, they are mad when they get my bill."

In both cases, these attorneys feel they are making way too much money to drop out of a legal career and start over. They feel trapped and can't get out.

Values are principles, standards, or qualities that are inherently held to be desirable. Values motivate and fulfill. They imbue work and life with meaning. Attitudes describe your feelings, perspectives and state of mind regarding people, places, ideas, or things. Attitudes can be positive or negative. A healthy, successful person embraces the former.

We don't all hold the same values, or to the same degree. Below, I've listed 99 common values. Mark those that resonate with you, that you feel are vital to a good and fulfilled life. My list, culled from many sources, is far from complete. Feel free to add other values.

■ Achievement	■ Dignity	■ Intensity
■ Adaptability	■ Discipline	■ Intuition
■ Altruism	■ Discretion	■ Judiciousness
■ Ambition	■ Education	■ Justice
■ Assurance	■ Efficiency	■ Kindness
■ Audacity	■ Empathy	■ Knowledge
■ Beauty	■ Energy	■ Leadership
■ Benevolence	■ Experience	■ Logic
■ Bliss	■ Fairness	■ Loyalty
■ Bravery	■ Family	■ Maturity
■ Charm	■ Ferocity	■ Modesty
■ Cheerfulness	■ Fitness	■ Obedience
■ Cleanliness	■ Flexibility	■ Open-mindedness
■ Comfort	■ Friendliness	■ Organization
■ Commitment	■ Frugality	■ Perseverance
■ Compassion	■ Generosity	■ Persistence
■ Composure	■ Harmony	■ Persuasiveness
■ Confidence	■ Honesty	■ Playfulness
■ Consistency	■ Honor	■ Poise
■ Courtesy	■ Hopefulness	■ Practicality
■ Decisiveness	■ Humor	■ Pragmatism
■ Decorum	■ Hygiene	■ Professionalism
■ Deference	■ Imagination	■ Prudence
■ Dependability	■ Inquisitiveness	■ Punctuality
■ Determination	■ Intelligence	■ Reasonableness
■ Recognition	■ Sacrifice	■ Traditionalism
■ Recreation	■ Self-control	■ Utility
■ Refinement	■ Simplicity	■ Vitality
■ Reflection	■ Sharing	■ Warmth
■ Resilience	■ Spunk	■ Wisdom
■ Resourcefulness	■ Teamwork	■ Wonder
■ Respect	■ Thrift	■ Youthfulness

Readiness to change is exactly that. Most people don't like change. They think it is often difficult or uncomfortable. It means swapping the known for the unknown, the familiar for the unfamiliar, the comfortable for the uncomfortable. Your readiness to change is measured by your tolerance for the unknown, the unfamiliar, and the uncomfortable.

People want their job to reflect their values, to mean something — to themselves, to others, and to their community. The measure of success for most people isn't merely money and prestige. If your singular ambition is simply to make as much money as possible in a job with little or no relation to your quality of life, then okay. Go be an attorney. But I can guarantee that it won't bring lasting satisfaction — even if your earnings and "toys" are the envy of all around you.

In college Fred didn't know what he wanted to do. He was smart, however, and saw that a career in medicine or law could be both prestigious and lucrative. He chose law and for the next few years, worked hard to get through school and become a successful attorney.

Becoming a lawyer wasn't Fred's passion, but he landed a good job out of law school and was making $150,000 after just two years. After 10 years, his salary had doubled and he was a partner. And he was miserable.

Fred would complain that being a lawyer meant day after day of cut-throat competition and negativity. He was always in battle, usually with lawyers representing the other side, sometimes with his colleagues. He hated it, but what could he do?

His family (and to be honest, himself) had grown accustomed to a rather cushy lifestyle. He would complain and his wife would say, "Okay, what is it you want to do? And how do you propose to do it?" Fred had no answer. Charging clients $350 an hour proved to be poor compensation for interminable misery, but Fred was stuck. And the unfortunate thing about Fred was that after we met several times he didn't want to do anything about it, except complain. His wife was not *supportive of a life style change. In fact, he was afraid she would leave him. He was old and tired before his time and had given up.*

Please don't ever let yourself become a Fred.

Taking action

Julie Jansen, the author of *I Don't Know What I Want, But I Know It's Not This: A Step-by-Step Guide to Finding Gratifying Work*, says there are different types of meaning as it relates to work. These types vary in importance, depending upon the person. Some people seek jobs rich in rewards and challenges. Others want their work to be interesting, an expression of their personal ideals and values. Some people work to make a difference in people's lives or in their community. Others, because they like solving problems. Jobs can be attractive because they permit a certain lifestyle, promote a cause, or foster creativity or learning. Or simply because they pay well.

Jansen advises thinking about each of these aspects of meaning and ranking them in terms of importance. Doing so will say much about you and help refine the kind of job and career you should seek.

There are many ways to conduct a self-assessment. You can seek professional consultation and guidance. You can buy books or step-by-step guides on the subject. There are countless Websites dedicated to self-analysis.

Or you can just sit down with some paper and a pen and ask yourself some questions. The key is to be honest. You want the answers and results to match you, not some idealized notion of yourself.

Richard Bolles in *What Color is Your Parachute?* suggests asking yourself what kind of outcome you want from your work (and by extension, your time on Earth).

- Do you want to focus on contributing to human knowledge, truth, or clarity?

- Are you concerned with human health, fitness, and wholeness?
- Are the arts important to you, such as theater or music?
- Do you want your legacy to emphasize love and compassion, or morality and justice?
- Do you want to leave behind a legacy of laughter and entertainment?
- Do you want the Earth, the planet itself, to be better for your existence upon it?

One book that I've found useful is Dr. Victor Frankl's classic *Man's Search for Meaning*. In it, Frankl poses some simple questions, though the answers may be complicated:

- What were you doing when you last lost all track of time?
- What do people say you are very good at?
- How would you answer if a seven-year-old asked you, "What are you most proud of in your life?"
- Who is living the life you most envy?
- What job would you gladly do for free?
- How do you want to be remembered?
- What would you tell your great-grandkids is most important in your life?
- What excites you?
- What angers you?
- What can you do about both?

Mel and I started Manpower in San Diego on something of a whim. We were both jobless. He was "separated from his job" and I quit (a difference I lord over him constantly, but if the truth be known, I quit right before they were going to fire me) from management positions with a major chain of upscale department stores where we were buyers. The reality was we were lousy managers. We had lost interest in the business, didn't care and goofed off. Mel's father had a temp agency in Las Vegas. Standing in a swimming pool in Phoenix, where our families lived at the time, pondering the vastness of our unemployed vistas, Mel and I decided this temp stuff was something we could do, too. We thought if his dad could do that, imagine what we could do! In truth neither of us had any relevant experience or even a clue. But we did have an overabundance of confidence.

Living in Phoenix, the one thing we did know was that we wanted to live in San Diego. We researched ice cream parlors, pinball machines, tour guides, and all sorts of far-flung ideas. But we kept coming back to temporary help and Manpower franchises. We spent a few days with Mel's father in Las Vegas learning how to write payroll and run a temp agency. Then we went out and partied and wound up sleeping off hangovers in his father's conference room. Mel's father shook his head in dismay, but apparently his lessons stuck.

We took over a sad and sinking branch of Manpower in San Diego and built it into a thriving enterprise. It wasn't easy but we didn't know it at the time. We loved what we did, were completely challenged, and everything was new every day. There were long hours and days and plenty of crises. Once, a big local electronics firm cancelled 40% of our business over just two weeks. A crisis indeed, but it just meant we had to double down, to work even harder.

We loved it.

Answering these kinds of questions are merely prompts to get you thinking, to help you start a reflection process that will provide you with clues and cues to what you want, what to do, where to go and how to get there. More than that, they help you define and refine your life outside of work.

The goal, of course, is to find the ideal job. But what does that look like? Let's do a little job diagramming using my fantasy of hosting the Today show as an example. Here are my values from the previous exercise:

- Achievement
- Acknowledgement
- Ambition
- Cheerfulness
- Confidence
- Dignity
- Family
- Fitness
- Humor
- Intuition
- Knowledge
- Open-mindedness
- Pressure
- Professionalism
- Self-control
- Variety

What is it about the Today Show job that makes it so desirable to me?

1. The job is in New York City. Not my all-time favorite city, but indisputably a great metropolis and one of the most exciting, vibrant places in the world.
2. The job pays extraordinarily well. I once read a Reuters story that said the current host earns $16 million a year. I could live on that.
3. Every morning, the host of the Today show wakes up knowing he/she will be meeting and interviewing the most fascinating, interesting people in the world: the President of the United States, movie stars, Super Bowl-winning quarterbacks, the guy who ate 54 hot dogs (with buns) in just 10 minutes! It's hard to imagine getting bored at work.
4. Often the Today show crew has to travel to where the stories are, which means a certain amount of travel, some of it international.
5. I'd be on national television, in front of millions of viewers. It's a chance to make a mark, to be widely influential in a very positive way. And it's live, which means I'd have to be on top of my game every day, every minute.

So for me, these are the elements that I need to incorporate into my ideal job search:

1. I like living in a big, vibrant city.
2. I like meeting interesting people.
3. I like being challenged to have meaningful interactions with them.
4. I like traveling the world.
5. I like earning lots of money.
6. I like being kept on my toes at all times.

I am making progress toward defining career paths that will be of interest to me. I have my six points that I feel are very important to my satisfaction with a career. So what careers could most likely provide me these attributes?

Let's get pragmatic. There is almost zero chance I will ever host the Today show. There is little chance any of us will ever get our ideal job, one with 100% of the components we desire. But we can look for jobs that offer the maximum number of components. To see what the real world looks like, we'll have to do some research. Since this is my exercise, I would perhaps be drawn to researching jobs in the "marketing" field:

- Products that I think make the world better, make people's lives easier or help them feel better about themselves.
- Positions at a large company, preferably an international company that includes an acceptable amount of travel, some of it to foreign countries.
- I might also research jobs in "sales." The sales field is similar to marketing, but with some different features. I would look for sales jobs that include:
  o Payment on commission. I'm comfortable with a commissioned-based position since I find my pay being directly related to my production motivating, not intimidating. For me pressure is energizing.
  o High-end products or services. High-end buyers are more likely to become long-term customers,

thus facilitating the building of long- term working relationships.
o   Face-to-face presentations, either one-on-one or in front of groups.

Because I enjoy teaching, sharing my experience and, most especially, motivating people, I might look at becoming an "author/ motivational speaker." This involves having a product that I believe in (my book, video or CD), one with multiple purchasers, and one whose sales are dependent in a large part on my personal presentation of the topic. I would develop and own the product and be responsible for its success or failure.

Another possibility is "Human Resources." I could help people find the work that will support them and fulfill their lives. It involves the meaningful interactions and daily challenges that I listed as part of my ideal job.

There are also jobs that came out of this exercise that do not interest me:

- Advertising/public relations
- Minister for a church
- Elected official

There are two important topics that are pervasive in considering career paths: pressure and the importance of money.

Let's start with pressure. I find it very motivational. "If you want something done, give it to someone with too much to do." I think this is a very valid statement. If we have a lot of time, with no deadlines, we all tend to procrastinate. If we have a 40-hour job and only 20 hours of work we will stretch it out to fill the full 40 hours. But give someone like me 50 hours of work and 40 hours to do it; I will be done in 35 hours. When I have a deadline, I get motivated and energized as the deadline nears. That doesn't mean someone like me doesn't think about it for days and contemplate my approach. I will not have it done two weeks ahead and feel the relief of a finished project. This drives my wife crazy and her finishing project weeks early makes me wonder if another good idea might not have come to her if she had not finished so early. We will never know who is right and wrong, and maybe the truth is in the middle.

But I know my style, what works for me and what I am comfortable with. This allows me to do my best work. So have a talk with yourself. What parameters allow you to do your best work? Is it well planned out or finished well before the deadline? Are you motivated by having pressure coming down to the wire?

Often related to pressure is the importance of money. How important to you is earning potential? On the scale of "I love my job and could care less what it pays" to "I want to earn as much as I possibly can and will do anything legal to get it," where are you? Granted, it is not one extreme or the other. Like most things there is a continuum, but you have to have an idea of where you are on the range.

I have friends who grew up poor and are determined to provide better for their family, and in fact leave a legacy in their estate for generations to come. They are much less concerned with finding their passion in their work as they are with how much they can earn. These people tend to end up in highly commissioned sales, such as commercial real estate sales or entrepreneurship. Either they start a new company or jump on board a startup. Often success is a roll of the dice; whether it will be feast or famine, they are comfortable taking those risks to gain the reward. Others I know are risk adverse and just put their head down and work very hard to earn as much as they can, without risking losing it all on a failure. Both feel they can handle pressure very well and are willing to pay that price to gain wealth.

And I have as many friends with passion in a field that doesn't pay all that much — teaching, child care, and nonprofits. They go to bed every night thrilled about what they accomplished helping others or working for the greater cause.

As you look at positions in the private sector, be thinking about both pressure and earnings. Where are you on the continuum? I know that pressure motivates me, but I am not willing to wake up in the middle of the night worrying about hitting deadlines. I am motivated by money and find it an excellent score card of my progress. But I have to wake up every morning anxious to go to work, doing something I am passionate about that I feel good about. You will need to find your comfort zone and use it to analyze each job opportunity and whether or not it fits into your criteria that will make you happy.

Overriding all of these choices is the desire to control my own destiny. As I said earlier, I am one of those people who is motivated by pressure. I often go out of my way to put pressure on myself, to get my heart beating and my blood flowing. This energizes me and spurs me on to do a better job, whatever it is. As a result, I would also start researching entrepreneurial opportunities. Estimates are that 45% of veterans end up starting their own businesses. If that interests you, be sure to explore it as an option.

So now I've expanded my job search to include four main areas:
- Marketing
- Sales
- Author/Speaker
- Human Resources

Let me draw you a map of what we've done so far:

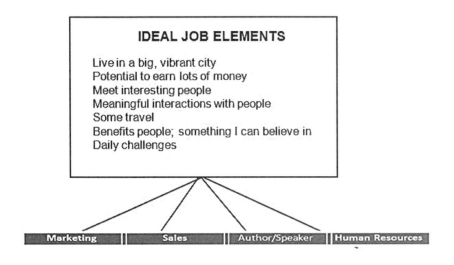

IDEAL JOB ELEMENTS

Live in a big, vibrant city
Potential to earn lots of money
Meet interesting people
Meaningful interactions with people
Some travel
Benefits people; something I can believe in
Daily challenges

| Marketing | Sales | Author/Speaker | Human Resources |

Let's continue with my example, using the Human Resource path since that's where I found success.

I research job boards, advertisements, corporate websites and talk to a lot of people. The HR positions that I uncover and decide to zero in are:

- Qualcomm: HR Supervisor
- Hewlett-Packard: Senior Recruiter
- Scripps Hospital Group: Employee Benefits Manager

Now the fun begins. I rewrite my résumé to highlight my education, talents, accomplishments, and experiences for each of the positions listed above. When I'm done, I'll have three different résumés. Then I write my cover letter for each position to introduce my résumé. But I don't send them anywhere. If I do, my résumé and cover letter are going to wind up on some stack, or in someone's desk to die a slow death. Remember, that's an employer's least favorite way to find people.

Instead, I ask myself, who do I know who works at Qualcomm, HP, or Scripps? No one? Okay, do I know anyone who knows someone who works at one of these places? A friend of a friend? You might think you don't have any contacts in the places you'd like to work, but I'm willing to bet you're wrong. My guess is, in our own communities, we are only two or three people away from just about anyone we'd like to meet. Give it some thought, go through your address book, ask your friends and relatives, use Google, Facebook, or LinkedIn. Someone will come up with a name you can use.

This is the very first step in building your network, a process we'll explore in detail in Chapter Five.

So I start going through the contacts in my address book and bingo! I see the name of a person whose father works at Qualcomm. I call my person and ask him some questions about working at Qualcomm. Notice I don't say I want to go to work there. It's possible I don't even qualify for the job. I'm looking for information. I call the person and ask for an informational interview. It is a powerful and important tool for you to use in your job search. When the person answers, I mention that I know a mutual acquaintance and that I'd like to ask a few questions about working at Qualcomm. People almost always say yes to such a request because there's the implied endorsement and there's no risk to them in granting such an interview. Usually, they are flattered that you're asking for their help and welcome an opportunity to share what they know.

I show up for the interview — on time, properly dressed, with my questions ready. Now when the person asks "what job I'm looking for," do I say, "I dunno?" Of course not. Instead, I'm very clear about the field. I'm interested in and what I'd like to do. I ask my acquaintance's father about Qualcomm: How does he like working there? What is the company's future? I ask whatever I'd like to know. Before the interview is over, I ask him for the name of someone in HR department. In a perfect world, he will happily take me down the hall and introduce me to this person, who happens to be the Vice President of Human Resources. Should that happen, I'm on my own to sell myself as the absolute best candidate for the HR job opening.

More realistically, my contact would probably just give me the name of someone in HR. But that's okay. I call that person, using the name of the acquaintance and ask for another informational interview. I do this a few times and it won't be long before I'm talking to the person with the authority to hire me. At this stage, you have maneuvered yourself in front of some who can make the hiring decision to make or break this stage of your job search. Now you need to wow them during the interview process. This is where Frank stumbled and lost the job opportunity. Don't let this happen to you.

Most job seekers assume that employers recruit for new hires. That is exactly opposite of how most employers recruit. Employers prefer:

- Hiring from within — promoting current employees or hiring a current temp, contractor or consultant who is a known commodity.

- Hiring applicants who bring in verifiable examples of their work that shows their capabilities.
- Hiring a referral from a current employee or a trusted friend or vendor.
- Using a staffing agency that they trust and have experience with, typically a temp to perm assignment or a permanent placement.
- Placing an advertisement in social media.
- Pulling résumés out of their database of unknown applicants

Applicants think employers go to their data bases first and seek out applicants résumés from the thousands, or hundreds of thousands of résumés they have collected over the years. Many of the resumes are clearly old and stale.

You can see the mismatch. Employers start at the top with current employees or current temps, contract employees or consultants that already work for them. Therefore you need to find a way to get a temporary assignment or a consulting gig at the company. That gets you behind the iron wall and you can network your way to HR, the manager of the department of interest or to the owner of a smaller company. It does not matter what temp job you start at, it is how you work the system from the inside to get noticed.

So working backwards:

1. You have to submit your résumé to the database but you don't have to stop there.
2. Always respond to any adverts you see, but you don't stop there either.
3. Find out what staffing firm(s) the company uses. Yes just call them or stop by; receptionists know everything. Check the staffing firm(s) website for open assignments and get yourself placed on just about any temp assignment that will get you inside the company. Now you begin to prove your value.
4. Network like crazy to find someone/anyone that will walk your résumé down to the hiring decision maker and will vouch for

you. It's who you know that knows someone, who knows someone, who knows someone. If you can get someone to walk your résumé down the hall, you have seven times the chances of landing the job.

5. Bring in samples of your work if possible or reference letters that clearly speak to your capabilities.
6. Remember: it's hard to get promoted into the job you want if you don't work there!

Example: 30-second elevator speech

When I teach at the college level, I stand in front of the classroom that has an auditorium style set up at the base of the steps and pretend I am standing in the elevator. The students have to wait for the elevator door to open to see me. Not noticing who they are, they have to step into the elevator, see me, get my attention and then the scenario begins.

Hello Mr. Blair. My name is Fred Smith and I was in a TGPS you addressed a few months ago. Nice to see you again.

Hi Fred. How are you doing?

Really well. I am in the middle of my civilian job search and am using a lot of the tools that you talked about.

What kind of work are you looking for?

I'm really interested in the Human Resources field, especially, comp and benefits. During my 20 years in the Navy, I spent most of my time running administrative operations and finance for the supply department aboard cruisers and destroyers. While getting my MBA, I found I really enjoy helping people understand their benefits options. Three companies that I am especially interested in are Qualcomm, Carefusion and Illumina. Here's my card. Would it be okay for me to contact you to see if we can meet and I can get your input on my options?

Look at all the information you have communicated in that 30 seconds:

- You remembered me, by name, from my presentation
- You have an MBA, HR interests you, especially comp and benefits
- 20 years in the Navy — played the veteran card
- Almost 20 years of HR experience: you like helping people
- You identified three companies you are interested in
- I have your business card; and hopefully I offered mine
- You asked if we could meet. (You respect my input and opinion. A little flattery goes a long way.)

Not bad at all for 30 seconds!

You will have three or four career paths you are considering at all times, so be sure to have a concise 30 second elevator speech ready for each one. And as you add and drop career paths the first thing you need to do is write a fresh speech for that new path....

If you unexpectedly meet up with someone and don't know which speech to give, blend them all together:

> *Yes I am doing well. I'm in the middle of a new job search. I am anxious to use my 20 years in the Navy and my MBA in the Human Resources, Marketing or Sales field. And I'm especially interested in positions at Qualcomm, CareFusion and Illumina. I'd really like to get your opinion on some choices I have. Can I give you a call and meet up to discuss over coffee?*

Career options to consider
Entrepreneurship
Fact: veterans start their own businesses at a much higher rate than their civilian counterparts. Earlier I said explore it as an option. Maybe it's because they yearn for the freedom of being their own boss, after years within the armed forces hierarchy. Or maybe it's because the military provides them with the determination, toughness, and

self-reliance that makes for an entrepreneur. Either way, embrace your entrepreneurial zeal, but try working for another company when you first leave the military.

I'm not asking you to put your dreams on hold indefinitely. Although I'm strongly suggesting that you get a hands-on education in the private sector business world first. Working for another company actually pays you to get that experience, and just 24 months will pay big dividends. You need to be aware of how many new ventures fail in the first five years – give your future business its best chance at survival by gaining some experience inside another company. You'll be very glad you did.

Careers in business development

What's the first thing that comes to mind when you think of sales jobs? Is it the cheesy used car salesman with the bone crusher handshake? My experience has been that most veterans avoid job opportunities in sales because the idea of cold calling scares the heck out of them, and they can't get over a bad salesman experience they may have had in their past.

The following section is an attempt (and hopefully you find it to be a very effective one) to dispel all the negative notions about sales. For starters, we really should be using the term *business development* instead of *sales*, as that's exactly what this function does. You are developing long-term strategic business relationships and opportunities, not conducting a one-off transactional sale. There are two main areas of sales, and you may already be familiar with these terms:

1. Business-to-Business: commonly abbreviated as B2B sales. This is what my team here at Manpower does when we are trying to win new corporate clients for our staffing and executive search services. It is one business selling to another business.
2. Business-to-Consumer: commonly abbreviated as B2C. This is where the client is an individual person, not a company.

Consumer products and services from companies such as Nike, Sony, and United Airlines are all examples of B2C.

In my experience, veterans are often well-positioned for a lucrative career in this arena, because they already possess many of the key attributes of good business development professionals:

- Mission focus – also known as "stick-to-it-tiveness," or tenacity. Veterans know how to stay focused on the end goal, and will do whatever it takes to achieve it. You can close a deal.
- People skills – you were surrounded by people at all times during your military career. Business development is all about people and relationship building. You enjoy being around people, and after reading this book, know how to develop your likeability.
- Ethics – the military is founded on an incredibly strong code of honor, and you continue to live your life by this code. People recognize this in you, and they trust you.
- Self-reliance – business development is not for the faint of heart. There are tremendous highs and lows (although hopefully more of the former), and more likely than not the end result is dependent almost entirely upon you.
- Hunter instinct – you know how to sniff out an opportunity and pursue it to completion. You have a natural competiveness for success.
- Self-motivated – you don't need someone else to keep you focused and on-task. It naturally comes from within, and from your focus on the mission.
- Organized – good sales professionals are incredibly well-organized. They know exactly what needs to be done, and at exactly what stage. Without strong organizational skills, you could easily become overwhelmed, trying to chase everything at once, and not actually seeing any leads through to completion.

Here are a number of reasons why you should seriously consider a position in sales – at some point in your career and the sooner the better. These are attributes that will serve you extremely well over your entire career, no matter what industry you land in:

- Job security: more often than not, the sales or account manager has the closest relationship with the customer, because they made first contact, and developed the account over time. Smart companies are very reluctant to let go of the staff who actually "own" the customer.
- Income: sales positions usually have a low base salary, but often more than compensate with enormous earning potential through commissions. In a high performing company, the best paid position is often not the CEO, but the VP of Sales. The more you sell, the more you earn, and often there's no cap to the commissions you can make.
- Recognition: whomever makes the customer the happiest makes management happiest. Pretty simple.
- Career portability: no product or service can sell itself. Every company in every sector needs salespeople. The skills you'll use to sell defense contracting services are actually very similar to selling staffing services, for example. Even in a slow economy, good sales people are always in demand.

The other thing to know about sales is that we all have a unique style to the way we identify prospects and build relationships with those people. The key to being successful in sales is to identify and cultivate your natural style. You shouldn't really feel like you're selling, even when you're selling. OK, so prospecting and making that initial cold call might feel like selling, but after initial contact, it should begin to feel somewhat natural. I think most people get turned off by sales after just a short stint because they're using a style that isn't true to them. There's nothing more uncomfortable than trying to be something or someone you're not.

One of my favorite authors on sales and business development strategies is Jeff Gitomer (https://www.gitomer.com/). His strategies are very simple, tactical, and effective. Jeff's *Little Red Book of Selling* and *Little Black Book of Connections* are great reads for every business professional, whether you're in a frontline selling position or not. The thing about sales is that there is only so much reading you can do – ultimately you just have to get out there and try it. It is truly a case of learning by doing, containing equal parts art and science.

In addition to the benefits listed above, such as a large earning potential, job security, and career portability, there is another important reason I highly encourage all aspiring professionals to get some experience in sales. If you eventually want to lead a company or start your own business, your job will depend on your ability to sell. CEOs and corporate presidents are out selling their companies' brands and products or services every day – perhaps not directly calling on accounts, but they are convincing other businesses, financial markets, consumers – you name it – that the company they lead should be taken seriously. And more important, they need to know how sales and business development works, because they are responsible for managing the company's sales force. If you don't have a clue about business development, how are you supposed to effectively coach and manage your sales team?

One final word about sales and business development: I bet you already have some hands-on experience in this field, without realizing it. Most of us are actively selling every day, whether we know it or not. Every time you suggest an idea, pitch a solution, trouble shoot/ problem solve, or negotiate, you are using sales skills. You are identifying a solution, building a case for it, and implementing it. That my friends, is business development in action!

phil-osophy 101   4

If you look to your right and left in any training, class, or assembly you are looking at your competition for the perfect civilian job once you get out. What makes you better equipped, trained, prepared, and experienced than all the other transitioning folks beside you? I realize that in the military it's always a team effort, no man left behind and all for one. But not during your job search. Be sure you prepare yourself with better education, training, search resources, appearance, and interviewing skills than all your peers. You will hear me emphasize that I hire the person, not the team they came from.

This is especially true if you are considering staying in the area where you are being discharged. Huge military bases have hundreds if not thousands of sharp skilled people who are preparing to leave the military and don't want to uproot their family by moving to a new area. Be very aware that lots of men and women with your similar skill sets, and playing the same veteran card, will be looking for the same jobs as you at the same time. What makes you different? What make me want to hire you and not the others? Read on!

4.0   Making the Leap

As you plan your exit from the military, you'll have a lot of competing priorities. You'll need to make sure that you're tying up loose ends for your work, that your medical and dental records are complete, that you've got all of your important documents digitized and hard copied, and that you're checking whatever boxes you must. This includes Transition GPS (Goals, Plans, Success) or Transition Readiness Seminar (TRS), which is also called TGPS by other service branches, the DoD-mandated transition planning course to become a civilian. It is incredibly important to pay attention during this course and do your best to come fully prepared. It is also important to understand that TGPS/TRS is not going to find you a job and that with up to 100 people per class, there isn't enough time to do one-on-one in-depth job transition preparation. Alas, hope is not lost. You've already taken the first step toward bolstering your transition success by reding this book. The next step is understanding that your transition class will provide a lot of tools for your toolkit and how to use many of them.

Having spoken at many a TRS class to make transitioning folks aware of the real world of work, I realized the importance of *Job Won! for America's Veterans*. I find attendees are excited in the beginning but there is so much boring paperwork that by the time it gets to the career transition part they are turned off and daydreaming. My goal is to bring some excitement to the class and for the first time be the face of their new private sector boss. And I also play the role of the HR Manager or business owner that they have to get through and impress to get the job offer they desperately want. Either way, it is very valuable role playing and one newly transitioning soldiers need to hear. The combination of Transition GPS, with the tool of *Job Won!*

in your hands, gives you a huge head start on your competition. I have often thought *Job Won! for America's Veterans* should be the textbook for all Transition GPS classes, but maybe I'm a bit biased.

Be open to the many transition class opportunities in whatever community you are in. Transition GPS is just one opportunity. Make yourself aware of the many other classes that are offered typically free to veterans through Community Colleges, Chambers, United Ways, and many more. Also be sure to not limit your participation to only classes for veterans. You need to hear what private sector job seekers are hearing too. They just may be learning about how to sell themselves when competing with a veteran for the same job!

Keep an open mind to all opportunities

There's a very good chance you will ultimately land a job in a field totally unrelated to the careers you were targeting at the outset of your job search. And that's perfectly OK – so long as the work is fulfilling, meets your financial needs, and offers room for advancement. As you embark on your transition to civilian employment, you are diving into a great unknown. You need to be on the lookout for opportunities that will pop up unexpectedly, and that at first pass, might seem like a diversion from your chosen path. Don't dismiss these new options without first investigating – so long as they meet your career criteria, you can only gain from exploring them. Your eyes could be opened to a career field you never even knew existed.

Get ready for change. In the military you pretty much knew when you would be changing jobs and domiciles – it happened at fairly predictable intervals. The civilian world of work could not be more opposite – career changes often happen in rapid succession and unexpectedly. The average American college student today will change careers five to seven times in their lifetime. Not just change jobs, but change entire careers. From my experience I can tell you the premise holds true: people change careers, not just jobs, all the time. This flexibility in our labor force is one of the main reasons the US economy is so strong and competitive – our workers follow the opportunities. Learn to embrace change.

Opportunity cost

If you've ever suffered through an Economics 100-level class, you've come across the concept of Opportunity Cost. That's the value you forgo by choosing one option over another. With regards to your career transition, it's the cost you choose to incur by passing up attainable job opportunities while you hold out for that dream job you feel you deserve. Although opportunity costs ultimately come down to money, it has a number of factors in terms of your career. Here's how passing up that job today impacts your prospects for tomorrow:

- Weaker skill base: not only will you have lost time that you could have been building your non-military skills on the job, those relevant skills you do bring from the military are going cold with each passing day. I don't need to remind you how fast technology moves today.
- Smaller network: time lost that you would have been making connections inside your new company and industry.
- Lost promotion: the more time you spend out of work, the longer it will be before your first promotion.
- Lower employability: numerous studies have shown that the longer you are out of a job, the harder it becomes for you to finally gain employment – also known as a negative feedback loop.
- Lower starting salary: here's another fact – the longer you are unemployed, the lower your starting salary is likely to be, once you finally land a job.
- Diminished self-esteem: it doesn't feel good to be unemployed. We all derive immense value from work, even if the work is not our ideal job.

We can even put some numbers around all this. For example, if you pass up a job opportunity at $60,000 because you feel you are actually worth $75,000, here's how that choice will impact you, assuming you hold out another four months:

- Four months lost wages = $20,000

49

- Four months of COBRA healthcare coverage at up to $500 per month = $2,000
- Four months longer to get to your next promotion at another $2,000 of foregone income

As you can see, it adds up pretty quick. In this example we're already at $24,000 after just 120 days…and we've only put an economic value on three of the six factors listed above. The true cost to your career may be as high as $41,000, once these are all factored in. Remember, the network you build through employment also has a big impact on your future earnings.

The first job you take out of the military doesn't have to be your dream job – it just has to be a good starting point. Again, the mantra we teach:

- Get a job
- Get a better job
- Get a career

Don't get hung up on titles, they matter much less in the private sector than they do in the military. Focus instead on the job description, and think about how this job might be a springboard to the opportunity you *really* want.

Here's a case in point: a Navy O3 came to us for some career help. His goal was to land a job in financial services with one of the big banks. However, he was terrified of sales and had zero experience. Sales (also known as business development) skills are a key part of most financial services jobs. How did he overcome this skills deficit? He swallowed his pride and took a position as a sales team leader in the furniture department at Sears. No joke. Turns out, he had some fun with the job, built a great team, and his store knocked it out of the park. Six months later he started his new career as a banker, because of his business skills.

And here's another example that didn't turn out so pretty.

Tom served 20 years as a Naval Intelligence Specialist, before switching careers to become a Communications Analyst with a large defense contractor. However, his company downsized and Tom was eventually out of a job. He came to Manpower to acquire the networking and career management skills he needed to move into a non-DoD related career. After he completed our program, we got him out on several interviews with fast-growing technology companies. Although the positions were in his chosen field and area of expertise, he kept turning them down, as he saw them as beneath him. True, these were entry-level positions, but these were some of San Diego's most promising companies, offering a fast career path into bigger roles. Even so, Tom couldn't let go of the image of his last position, with its fancy title and salary. Despite our best efforts, he failed to understand the opportunity cost concept, and his career went into a tragic downward spiral. He spent the next 12 months adrift and unemployed. The last time I had contact with Tom, he was back to working the night shift as a security guard at minimum wage. It had been two years since he was laid off, and the skills and industry contacts he had from his prior job had all gone cold – he had no job leads on the horizon and his self-esteem was at an all-time low.

In the private sector you will likely change jobs and industries numerous times. Get comfortable with change, and get yourself skilled at using it to your advantage. You didn't need to worry about career moves in the military – much of that was decided for you.

In the private sector, the only person responsible for looking after your career is YOU.

After all that depressing stuff I just threw at you, here comes the good news: this is an exciting and potentially very lucrative journey you are embarking on. Benefits of transitioning to the private sector include:

- Control over your career

- Higher ultimate earning potential
- No more deployments
- No more relocations
- Choice over your work attire

And although your first job out of the military may come with a cut in rank, you will most likely make up that lost ground very, very quickly. Our experience has been that veterans tend to get promoted more quickly than their civilian counterparts, and each promotion comes with a nice little bump in salary. Your first job out the military is exactly that – your *first* job, not your *final* job. Look at it as a refresher training course, something to get you acclimated to the private sector. You'll pick up a few new skills, perhaps sharpen some existing skills, and meet a bunch of people who will be helpful to you when it comes time to landing your next position. And it's an opportunity to get some cash flow, even if the salary is far below what you had hoped for. With a little time and good performance on the job, it will come.

Your focus right now should be less on job titles and status, and more on the content of the position, experience you will gain, and the connections you will make. Get out there and start interviewing for lots of different jobs you are qualified for – as you learn more about these positions and sectors, you will also gain a tremendous amount of self-knowledge that will serve you well. And remember, the only person responsible for looking after your career is you.

Start early

It's never too soon to start thinking about your transition career move. For those of you still on active duty, one or even two years ahead of separation is the right time to start your job hunt. This isn't something you want to rush into – take time, do your research, think it through, and lay the groundwork for your transition before you leave the service. We find the highest caliber candidates are always the ones who took the time and effort to plan ahead and prepare. Do not put it off "until you have time."

Play the veteran card

America is still awash in post-9/11, Iraq, and Afghanistan patriotism and goodwill toward our military. But it won't last forever. Leverage this sentiment to your favor as much as you possibly can. People want to help active duty and recently separated veterans. But the longer your time gap becomes between after leaving active duty and seriously starting your job search, the harder it becomes to tap into that patriotic sentiment. And if history is any kind of indicator, we know this sea will recede. Need proof? Look at the euphoric reception the Greatest Generation received after coming home from WWII, compared to the treatment of Korean veterans just eight years later.

What does this mean in terms of your entire approach to both your transition and your career? I call it "playing the veteran card," and while that might initially make you squeamish, you're doing yourself a serious disservice if you don't. Besides, you made huge sacrifices to serve your country; you've earned every advantage you can get from your veteran status in the job market. You'll notice many of the networking strategies outlined in this book play up your veteran status. If you are in transition, or recently separated from the military, you need to be comfortable making folks aware that you are in the job search mode. It will help melt the ice and potentially open some doors for you.

In the private sector it is always risky to begin looking for a new job while you are working. Some companies have a policy that once they hear an employee is searching they feel the loss of loyalty, are concerned he/she will go to a competitor, and will fire the employee immediately. This seems extreme, but it is quite common. In the military it is quite different and instead of being fired, word of your search may result in loss of a promotion or referral to additional training. It's your call whether to stay clandestine in your search or be comfortable being public about it. Clearly the sooner you start before your release and the more public you are about it, the better. Often a sincere conversation with your commanding officer can help you make the decision.

Many military personnel have a large repository of unused leave time, which they must use to "run out the clock" before they can formally separate from the military. This terminal leave period is not the time to mentally check out, have some fun, start on the long list of honey do's, or take an extended vacation. This is one of the most obvious mistakes I see veterans make.

I have to confess here my first experience with the phrase "terminal leave." I was talking with a friend about his friend who was on terminal leave and looking for a position in the private sector. Now in my world terminal has to do with death, usually in the near future. I naively, yet very concerned, asked why he was looking for work if he is terminally ill. I think the military needs to come up with a much more positive sounding phrase for what the private sector calls burning out your accrued vacation time.

If you're still on active duty, the ideal time to begin this process is 12-18 months prior to going on terminal leave. In a perfect world, you would use this time to research and identify a couple of target careers, make some useful contacts in those industries, and start honing your interviewing skills. Then, once you go on terminal and are still drawing a full paycheck, you can hit the ground running and start racking up practice and serious interviews. Ideally you'll have a job offer in hand before your official date of separation. The result: your career momentum continues and your income is uninterrupted. And if you're really lucky, you might start that new job *before* your terminal ends, during which time you'd be collecting two paychecks. How sweet would that be?

You'll notice I qualified that scenario with the statement "in a perfect world." Most transitioning veterans aren't quite that lucky. But with some planning and hard work, you can minimize the gap between your date of separation and start date in your new position in the civilian world. Unfortunately, far too many veterans wait until it's too late, separating within a month or less, have absolutely no idea what they want to do after the military and haven't invested a single hour of time working on their transition. Please don't let this be you.

I hear from veterans, surprisingly often, that they are nonchalant or even offended when civilians say thank you for your service. As a layman I can't understand this thinking but I am sure there is a deep-seeded reason. But instead, make every opportunity to interact with civilians a networking opportunity. Know your 30 second elevator speech by heart and share it every time you can.

> *Donald was a salesman when my wife and I encountered him on the lot of a car dealership. He very appropriately stuck his hand out to introduce himself and the first words out where not his name but were, "Hello, I am a veteran of the United States Navy, fought in Iraq for our country's safety, and my name is Donald." Even in an extremely pro-military town like San Diego I thought that was a little affected. But dear Donald kept mentioning his military career and asking about mine, so many times that he could not have given us a car for free for me to deal with him. Well maybe free. Don't over play your veteran card. If they bite, go with it, if not drop it and keep the conversation moving forward.*

"Something in leadership or management"

Here's my next rant: when someone asks you what kind of position you're looking for, *please* (note use of italics), *please* (note second plea here…you know this must be a really important tip coming up) don't say, "I'm looking for something in leadership or management." Without fail, at least one candidate, but more often than not, several, will give me this answer at every single veterans event I attend. And the first thing I think: this guy has no clue what career he's looking for, and is woefully unprepared for his transition.

After leadership, when we ask about career interests, we hear leadership, teamwork and logistics. Does the military really move that much equipment around the world that every veteran is experienced in logistics?

What job could possibly be described as "no need for leadership skills or ability to manage people?" Or "no need for this hire to work well with a team of coworkers?" These skills are innate in every job at some level so to repeat them as your job goal means nothing and shows you have no clue what skills you have in the civilian job market. And let's add "logistics" to the list of job skills every veteran says they have.

We do our veterans a huge disservice by pumping them up to believe that employers will snatch them up immediately after separation because of their leadership skills and mission focus. How do we know? Well here in San Diego County, Manpower receives about 300 new job orders every week. Guess how many companies call us and say, "I've got a new job opening, and the title is *Leader*. Can you send me some résumés to screen?"

> *Matthew spent 20 years in the Navy in San Diego. He was a talented procurement officer for many of those years and knew that a purchasing agent in the Navy was very similar to a purchasing agent in the private sector. Matthew also had an outgoing personality, not usually seen in any purchasing department. All his civilian suppliers, while he was buying, told him about the great jobs available with their company whenever he was ready to transition. Matt really bought into it — literally and figuratively. But how much was hype to get on his good side as their customer and how much was sincere at the time? But the reality of thousands of veterans transitioning immediately into well-paying jobs in the defense industry has passed. The defense "machine" has declined with the military's budget and instead of ramping up each year they are cutting hiring as fast as or faster than the military is cutting its budgets. That leaves the non-defense private sector, which is not nearly as smooth a transition for veterans.*

Employers hire for specific skill sets to fill specific needs – generic qualities such as leadership and the ability to see a task through to completion. These are important attributes, but they are not hard skills. While high-performing employees must possess these attributes, they alone will not get you hired. Want more proof? Jump on one of the job boards and do a quick search for the title "Leader" or

"Manager," and see how many pop up with just that nonspecific title. You'll find plenty of postings for "Team Leader of XX" and "General Manager for XX" and more than a few "Director, XX". There will always be an XX in the title and requirements. The employer has an opening for a team leader for a specific function, like "Team Leader, Customer Service" or "Director of Development," the latter referring to fundraising, sales or business development. Most companies develop their leaders and managers from within their ranks. These are people who have a few years of experience inside the company and its industry. Management level staff aren't hired from the outside at random. You need to land a job inside a company first, and then position yourself for promotion into that leadership role.

Your job is to put in the time and effort to identify a range of occupations and sectors that interest you, and meet your requirements for location, salary, schedule, etc. Then, when a recruiter or professional contact asks the question: what kind of job are you looking for, you can respond with a thoughtful, targeted answer like:

> *"I'm interested in a couple of different fields actually, both of which would enable me to draw on the skills and experience I gained during my 20 years in the Marine Corps. I have a background in IT hardware and software support, and I'm interested in using those analytical skills to start a career as a Business Analyst or Project Manager in the biotech sector at companies like Carefusion, Pfizer, or Bayer."*

By the way, you just gave your perfect 30 second elevator speech! You must have attended one of my trainings.

You'll see that this answer doesn't pigeonhole the respondent into just one field or occupation. And while those two careers are actually quite different, the answer is detailed enough to show this candidate has already started thinking seriously about his next move.

Government jobs
Each year our recruiters attend dozens and dozens of veterans' employment events, sit on panels, give talks, and host workshops.

Suffice to say, we talk with a lot of veterans and transitioning active duty. And hands-down one of the most common questions we get asked is, "Do you have any government jobs?"

We certainly appreciate why a government job might initially be appealing for veterans, particularly for active duty who have yet to leave the service. Many government agencies allow you to retain some of your benefits, and count your time in the military towards your employment tenure with that agency. The agencies underneath the Department of Homeland Security are a good example. If you served two enlistments, and are then hired by one of these agencies, you would start your first day on the job with eight years of service under your belt. While government salaries are often below market initially, these jobs are notorious for lots of vacation time, health care benefits, employment protection, and other perks. My concern is that jobs in the government sector may be way too similar to military jobs. This should be an exciting time for change from what you have been doing for the last 20 years, not looking for a position that will continue that same job for another 20 years.

> *David retired after 24 years in the Army as a cook. He took a job cooking in the civilian world in a very good hotel in his hometown. What a nice smooth transition. But after about six months of that, he realized he was bored cooking in the Army and now it was just as boring to cook in a hotel. What he really wanted to do was pursue a career in business, taking the lessons he learned from more than two decades of service working with tough logistics problems. David had taken the easy way out, admitted it and did something about it. Today, David is the Senior Director, Supply Chain Management for a major national corporation.*

However tempting an easy and smooth transition to a government job might be, I encourage you to look farther afield, at jobs in the for-profit business world. As any economist will tell you, the vast majority of all new job growth will occur in the private sector, not government. If you're looking for a challenging, exciting, and potentially more lucrative new career, chances are you're going to find that opportunity in the private sector. We live in extremely exciting times, with change and progress happening 24/7, and it's all driven by technology and innovation coming out of private sector companies.

I mentioned earlier that I was going to be extremely frank with you: when a veteran comes up to me at a networking event and asks "does Manpower have any government jobs," I immediately think, "This guy is just looking for easy street. Next candidate please." I think you are looking for civil service positions, not highly thought of in the private sector because of the legal protections weighted toward the employee. Civil service may be a system that long ago became antiquated and burdensome. The companies Manpower serves are looking for talented, motivated individuals who want to get in there and make things happen every day. If you are only looking at government jobs simply because you came from government and haven't considered other options, then you clearly haven't put much time, thought, and effort into your career transition, and I encourage you to broaden your search.

Your job search should be driven by a genuine interest in your target occupations and industries, and the challenges they will provide you. If your dream job happens to land you with a public sector entity, that's fine, but *do not* let the "must be in government" check box drive your career transition. Doing that will only waste your talents and limit you to an extremely narrow field of options. If you'd like to verify all of this, take a few minutes and go on www.usajobs.gov, and start filling out an application. You'll still be filling out that application and working on page 607 of the federal jobs résumé template by the time the other guy has already landed a job. Expand your horizons and look beyond government!

If a government job really interests you...

Realize that the typical government agency's hiring process moves about as fast as their online application and résumé requirements are long. Law enforcement academies and fire academies can often take often take 18 months or more from the time your application is accepted until a place opens up for you in the next class. Also keep in mind that there may be a daunting array of background checks and physicals (although some federal agencies make exceptions for active duty), which also take an inordinate amount of time.

In the meantime, you need to keep your life moving forward, and probably some cash flow to live on. If you are dead set on a government job, you will need to conduct two job searches in parallel, one for government and the other for private sector opportunities. Ideally you'll get your USAJobs application submitted and then continue pursuing other opportunities in the private sector simultaneously. If all goes well, you'll land a fulfilling private sector job in the near-term, which will help pay the bills and gain you valuable business experience and contacts. All while you wait for that spot in government to open up. And don't worry about leaving a new role after just 18 months on the job – smart companies are much happier to get one or two good years out of an A-player, than to have a B or C-level plodder sitting on their payroll for five to 10 years. In addition, your boss will probably understand your desire to continue serving your community or country. And be sure to look at staffing agencies as another way to productively fill your time with temporary work while you wait out the government application process. As we discuss in a later section, you'll be amazed just how much benefit you can get from "temp and temp-to-hire jobs."

Selling yourself

What are the three main deficiencies holding veterans back from the jobs they want? They are an inability to:

1. Hunt – identifying industries, sectors, and jobs that are a good fit, and then executing a successful strategy to get themselves in front of the right people who hire for those jobs.
2. Connect – once in front of people who can assist in the hunt, veterans often lack the communication skills or employ the wrong strategies to make a strong human connection with decision makers. Common communication errors include:
   a. Not persistent enough with follow-up
   b. Personal presentation is off
   c. Rigidity/lack of flexibility

    d. Lack of passion and curiosity

    e. Failure to project energy and enthusiasm

3. Sell – no matter who you are or what you do for a living, we are ALL in sales. You are selling every day, most of the time without evening knowing it. Selling isn't just about the purchase of products and services. It happens all the time, both at work, and in our personal lives. For example, you sell an idea every time you assert a position, make an argument, or ask someone to do something. Selling happens explicitly and implicitly, and it's occurring all around us, every day, and most of the time without us ever perceiving it. Think about when you are negotiating to get your teenager to clean their room. You're selling and she ain't buying!

Bill had been retired from the Marines for a little over a year and was in his first civilian job when he was introduced to me by one of our recruiting managers as a candidate to join our team. In our company I empower my staff to select their staff but I do like to meet final candidates before they are hired and I do reserve veto rights if I feel they are not a culture fit. During our entire discussion, the interviews had already taken place, Bill kept saying "Yes Sir" and "No Sir" to every question, I called his potential new boss in and told him I was concerned that Bill could not relax, was too uptight and structured, never smiled or laughed, and would not fit into our very gregarious, fun-loving staff. The manager talked me out of my veto and knew that he could work with Bill to relax. To this day I still am surprised when my HR Director tells me how intimated people are when they first meet me. By the way, 31 years later Bill is one our top management staff and has excelled at everything he has done for us.

Selling "self" versus "team"

In the military, selling oneself or one's accomplishments is strongly frowned upon. The military is based on a superseding team ethos – there is no self, only your unit/team, and the mission. Period. You've lived by this code your entire military career, and now we're going to flip everything upside down on you.

Companies hire individuals, not teams, units, or missions. When you are in an interview or a networking situation, it's not about the team or mission. It's about you. That requires you to sell yourself. This means selfishly talking up your skills, abilities, and most of all, your accomplishments. Don't talk about the unit, talk about your specific role and contributions to make the mission happen. And be sure not to get carried away with all the technical details about the mission itself and the equipment you used. Hiring managers don't care about military hardware – they care about identifying potential employees that have the skills their business needs to operate. And they want to hear about specific accomplishments and results demonstrating you have those skills. Think of accomplishments as evidence. Evidence is what wins people over and will get you hired (conviction and passion also help tremendously but are not enough alone). In short, get comfortable with the term "I," and make sure you use it frequently in describing yourself and your background.

> *Mark, retiring after six years in the Army, was interviewing for a sales position with a commercial real estate broker. It was independent work and closing sales deals was dependent almost solely on his efforts as the agent. It was high commission and very much an "eat what you kill" environment. During the interview process, Mark kept answering questions with "when we;" "our team," and "the unit accomplished." Finally the Manager said, "Listen, I'm not hiring the team, the unit, the we!" What did you do? Mark was not able to recover and did not get the job.*

Understanding the private sector employer mindset

Roger Cameron, author of *PCS to Corporate America*, puts it bluntly: "Remember that in corporate America, no accomplishment is considered significant, unless it impacts the bottom line."

That's a pretty powerful statement, and on the whole, I think any recruiter would be hard-pressed to disagree with it. When you boil down the hiring process to its most simple elements, all organizations, even not-for-profits, are driven by just two basic things. How is this candidate going to:

- Make us money: increase productivity, secure new customers
- Save us money: reduce costs, increase efficiency

That doesn't mean every line on your résumé has to be quantified with a dollar sign. It does mean however that everything listed on your résumé, and cited in your interview responses, must point to at least one of these value-drivers in some way, and the more directly, the better. For example, when listening to your response in an interview, the hiring manager can't be left thinking: well that was a really interesting story, but so what? She never told me what value she brought to the job (code for to the bottom line) If that's the case, your chances for that job are fading quickly.

Staying current

You're going to need to learn a whole new language as you transition out of the military – the language of business. That begins with speaking succinctly and eliminating acronyms from your vocabulary. For example, start asking "what do you do for work," instead of "what's your MOS (or rate)?" As another example, you should say, "I'm currently undergoing a career transition," not "I'm going to PCS." Also, it's 4:00 pm, not 1600, and start signing your emails with a simple "Thanks," not R/T or V/R. You get the point by now I'm sure… time to start talking and acting like a civilian. Have your family and friends help you with this. They need to call you out every time you use military jargon from your previous career.

I mentioned curiosity above. Employers want to hire candidates who are hungry for knowledge, and who want to learn more about people and the companies they work for. Read as much as you can, but make sure you're reading the right sources. At a minimum, read your city's most reputable local paper every day. If your city doesn't have one, then the *New York Times* or *Wall Street Journal* are good substitutes. In fact, I always recommend the WSJ for every transitioning veteran. You can actually get through it pretty quickly, especially if you just skim the headlines of the Money & Markets section. Unless you want to be a bond trader or hedge fund manager, this is way more financial detail than you'll ever need. The rest of the paper, however, is extremely useful for learning current business lingo and getting a feel for the economic and business landscape. Start learning the names of leading companies in big industries and what makes them successful. And always be thinking if that company, that industry, or that job you just read about might be of interest to you. Is it one you should explore more seriously?

Many large cities also have a Business Journal as well. For instance, here in San Diego where I live, we have *The San Diego Business Journal*. While some of the articles are self-serving PR placements, journals like this do offer detailed insight into the local economy, particularly with regards to which companies are growing and which companies might be moving into your area. Make sure to read your local business journal weekly. It would also be a good idea to read *Forbes, Inc.*, and *Fast Company* magazines every month or so as well.

If you have already made one hard decision, where you are going to relocate your family, then start subscribing to the local newspapers as you are finishing your last assignment. This way when you get back home, you will be knowledgeable and up to speed on local issues and companies. You will know which ones are growing and prospering and those to stay away from. This can save you lots of serious pitfalls. It also shows your commitment to the new city. There is always a bias in every city for employers to hire local residents before new arrivals. Here is where you can play your veteran card. Convince the interviewer, with your best sincerity, that after moving to new assignments for many years you have chosen this city to put down your roots and raise your family. Anyone proud of their hometown will love hearing that. And after traveling the world defending our country, they may feel they owe you the job that will let you and your family settle down in your new hometown.

I also highly recommend reading a few business books that are quickly becoming some all-time classics. This would include: *Good to Great* by Jim Collins, *The Lean Startup* by Eric Ries, and *The Innovator's Dilemma* by Clayton Christensen. These will provide a good overview of what makes for a competitive organization in today's economy, and also immerse you in important business concepts and lingo. I also recommend reading Mike Grice's tongue-in-check but very informative *Orders to Nowhere*. It's a fun read.

Audio books are also extremely effective. You can turn every minute spent commuting, waiting in lines at medical, or sitting in the car into a powerful learning moment. Companies want to hire candidates who are naturally curious and hungry to learn. They are impressed by veterans who have taken the initiative to educate themselves on business issues and can talk comfortably with interviewers about concerns facing their industry or firm. It is very impressive to the interviewer because this knowledge is rare, veteran, or civilian, and you will stand out.

Trade journals and other industry magazines are also gold mines when it comes to researching companies and getting yourself up-to-speed on industries that might be of interest to you. You will be amazed to see just how many resources are out there – every industry, no matter how niche, has its own association and trade publication. For example, if you are interested in using your aviation background in some kind of technical field, you'd definitely want to check out the Association for Unmanned Vehicle Systems International (www.auvsi.org). On their website, you'll find information on industry events, trade publications, job boards, and more. Cyber Security is another good example. If this is your field in the service then start to attend association meetings and mixers long before your terminal leave begins.

Business 101

In many ways the military does in fact operate like a business. You have budgets, reporting, performance metrics, deadlines, management structures, staffing, logistics, and so on. The difference is the bottom line. In the military your bottom line is combat readiness/effectiveness, while in the private sector, the bottom line is profitability. Here's a list of additional basic business concepts and theories you should be familiar with:

- Six sigma
- Lean

- Break-even point
- Competitive advantage
- Economies of scale
- Viral (marketing, networking)
- Kaizen (continuous improvement)
- Porter's Five Forces
- SWOT analysis

Many of the concepts are extremely similar in both the military and business settings – they're just applied a little differently and with a radically different jargon. If you're serious about a job in the private sector, you're going to need to brush up on contemporary business lingo.

The good news? The military uses a lot of these same concepts. You may even already be certified in Lean or Six Sigma. Maybe you've had to write a SWOT analysis and brief your boss. All of these things will help you succeed in business.

Software
While Macs are gaining more and more market share in the business world each year, the de facto standard is still the Windows-based PC. That means you absolutely must be proficient with the big three MS Office programs: Word, Excel, and PowerPoint. Microsoft offers free online tutorials for all its programs. You must be familiar with software but do not put them on your résumé. These sound too much like entry-level clerical job skills when you are going for a much higher position. It's like saying I know how to email and how to use a cell phone. It's assumed you have these general skills, and can be very detrimental if they find out you don't.

Education and saving your GI Bill
As a veteran you may still have your GI Bill educational benefits to help fund training and education, plus some living expenses, after you separate from the military. This is a precious resource – you've earned it, so use it wisely! And if you're not going to use it, remember that there is a process that may allow you to transfer this benefit to

family members before you leave the service if you think they might really need it for their education.

Sadly, I can't tell you how many hundreds of times I've met veterans who have squandered their GI Bill benefits on education and training courses that did not help them reach their ultimate goals. There are manygreat schools in the US that cater to the military. They have special transition programs to ease you into getting back to studying and how to take tests. Many even have a Veterans Career Center that can be a safe haven if going back to school with students five to 15 years younger than you gets you down and school gets frustrating.

Then there are thousands of schools and universities out there (and believe me, the not-for-profit ones are just as guilty as the for-profit ones) who would love nothing more than to sell you some very expensive, and for them extremely profitable, education. And they aren't really concerned if that expensive education is something you really even need or want. Please do me a favor, and before signing up for any kind of GI Bill-funded courses, carefully evaluate the following:

1. Unless you are going into a skilled trade or technical skill, use your GI Bill benefits to fund your undergraduate (bachelor's degree). There are plenty of other programs out there to cover practical skills, including Army and Navy COOL.
2. Stay away from degrees with the terms global, security, and leadership. Schools know that veterans are naturally inclined toward topics in security, leadership, and global logistics. They would very much like to sell you one of their expensive degrees, but they aren't as concerned with helping you to secure a job in that field after graduation.
3. Look closely at employment rates. What percentage of the program's graduates is employed *specifically within that field of study* within 90 days of graduating? A university might advertise that it has a 94% job placement rate, but how many of their Global Leadership graduates are actually working for a company doing business all over the world, in a job that

actually relies on the knowledge they gained from that global degree? Ask to see a list of last year's graduates, detailing the companies they are currently working for, and their job titles. Ask if you can contact some of the graduates, to talk about if/how the degree was useful to them and worth the expense.

4. Opportunity cost – remember that the time you spend enrolling in school and taking classes is time that could have been spent on your job search and earning an income. *Education time is foregone employment time.* Also remember that if you do this while you're still in the service, you'll be able to spend more time on the job search and earning an income when you transition out.

5. Online is not the same as in the classroom. You are extremely busy – you've got a family to look after and a job search to manage. Completing your degree online will save you a ton of time, and might be less expensive. It could be the best option for you. If it is then take it. However, please know that sitting in front of the computer alone late at night is not the same as being in a classroom with a live professor and a team of classmates. The content might be the same, but the learning environment is dramatically different. The on-campus experience provides you with valuable networking opportunities with your professors and other students. Many schools (especially those who frequent the bases) offer hybrid classes. Try to get both.

6. Search before you decide. Trust the employment data the school's enrollment packet gives you, but verify – do a quick online search for jobs in your area that *require* the degree you are considering. I would bet that a quick search for "Pittsburg" and "master's degree in global security required" will turn up very little.

7. There are too many criminal justice graduates on the market. See item number 3 above. Veterans overwhelmingly want to go into law enforcement jobs, and although government agencies always advertise that they are hiring, very few veterans will actually land in these jobs. And even if you do get a job in law enforcement, a degree in criminal justice is

not required. Schools know that many folks join the military because they want to go after bad guys, and therefore they market their criminal justice programs to you, in order to fill their classes. Law enforcement agencies actually look for folks with degrees in finance/economics, history, and communications more than they do criminal justice degrees.

Looks *are* everything

As I've said before, I don't make the rules of the job market: my mission is to make you aware of the reality out there and this is another one that is unavoidable. Appearance and energy level are very important. We have images of military folks all looking like Navy SEALS. If they are not fit, we are harder on them because of our expectations. So please, eat right, exercise, get enough rest, respect yourself, and take pride in your appearance. Your career will thank you. A healthy body literally makes you feel more optimistic, thereby radiating positive energy. Being proud and confident makes it much easier to walk up to strangers and start a conversation. This will significantly increase your likeability factor, which will help draw people into your network who will, in turn, be helpful in your career search.

Job search

As we mentioned earlier, the job search game is all about numbers: the more calls and emails you make, the more contacts you gain. The more contacts you gain, the larger your network grows. The bigger your network, the more job leads you uncover. More job leads translates to more interviews, and from there, more offers. You can't control the number of interviews and offers you get, so focus on those things you do have direct influence over: the number of contacts you make. If you manage the small stuff, the big stuff will take care of itself.

So how many jobs do I have to apply for? Don't necessarily worry about the number of jobs you actually apply for; the key is to monitor and manage your job search activity levels. The more activities you have, the more leads you will uncover. I like to use the following scale:

- Email = 1 point
- Call = 3 points
- Online application = 3 points
- Face-to-face meeting = 5 points
- Interview = 10 points

Aim high: we advise candidates to shoot for 110 points per week. Some weeks will be much heavier on emails and calls, and other weeks will be skewed more toward meetings and interviews. That's OK, as long as your point levels stay high (or ideally increase week-over-week). You'll find that earlier in your search, your tally will be weighted more towards calls, emails, and online applications. However, these lighter early stage activities eventually generate meetings and interviews, so you should see the composition of your weekly points tally shift after several weeks on the hunt. And don't beat yourself up if you're not hitting 110 points per week right out of the gate – it takes a little while to get the hang of this job search thing. With a few weeks of practice, your proficiency should increase dramatically, which will eventually be reflected in higher and higher weekly points totals.

Activity tracker

While it's important to keep your activity level high, it's equally important to stay organized, which you can do with a simple spreadsheet. We call it the job search activity tracker, and we've included an example in the Appendix. Follow-up is how this game is won, and you can't follow up with the contacts you make if you don't have all your data in a user-friendly, centralized format. Feel free to modify the activity tracker as you see fit – it's important to devise a system that works for you. However, the most important part is that you have a system that keeps your activity levels on the rise.

If you can't measure it, you can't manage it. Without some kind of activity tracking system in place, you're just spinning your wheels. Here is another way of monitoring the activity that is used by the Honor Foundation.

50 cups of coffee

A good friend of mine, Joe Musselman, founded a wonderful organization called The Honor Foundation (THF). He saw a need for work readiness training for Navy SEALs to prepare them for reentry into the civilian workforce. Imagine an interview where you are asked what you've been working on for the last ten years. "Can't tell you." Well then where have you been assigned? "Can't tell you." What are your skills? "Can't tell you."

The great training at THF teaches former SEALs to sell the great talents they can talk about and how to down play the "can't tell you" parts. Joe says one of the clever ways to teach the SEALs to network is "50 Cups of Coffee."

The idea comes from an article by Peter Thompson via *Inc.com.* It explains that for every significant change in your life, you should have coffee with 50 people to get their views on your plans. By assigning our former SEALs to have coffee with 50 people, it forces them to be clear and realistic about their goals.

Starting with Phase I, and throughout the course, set out to have 50 cups of coffee with friends, existing acquaintances and connections to discuss their transition experiences.

Most of these meetings result in a new introduction, a new friendship, and in some cases, even a new job offer! It all circles back to our contacts talking about themselves, networking and getting comfortable with the new transition.

Structuring your time

You've heard me say: "If you don't have a job, your full-time job is finding a job." The point is well-taken, but that doesn't mean you need to be holed up in your workspace cranking out emails, calls, and applications for eight hours straight every day. Job searching takes a ton of energy, focus, and creativity…and it can be quite draining. Take frequent breaks to refresh yourself, and if you hit a particular milestone you've set for yourself, say two phone interviews before 3pm, reward yourself with a little something. I like to walk down to one of my local coffee spots for an espresso. Unless you connect with someone it doesn't count as a "50 cups." I know another very successful insurance executive who takes herself out for ice-cream on these mini-celebrations.

The human brain can only run at its optimum level for so long. After about two hours your comprehension, retention, and productivity inevitably start to fade. You may feel like you're still being productive, but trust me, everyone fades. That's why these little breaks are so important. Not only do they keep you performing at your peak, they also prevent you from burning out. If you push too hard, for too long, it will inevitably show in your mood and level of enthusiasm. If you're making calls or taking meetings in the afternoon, the other person needs to feel as if they're the first appointment of your day. You need to be fresh, enthusiastic, and on your game.

Get up and move. Sitting for long stretches of time in front of the computer is terrible on your body. Your circulation slows and muscles cramp. That's why I'm a big fan of the standing desk with a bar stool-height chair (IKEA has some very inexpensive options). It gives you the option to sit or stand and guarantees that you'll be on your feet, moving while you work. You might consider investing in a wearable fitness device such as a Fitbit. You can set the device to give you a gentle reminder to get up and move after a certain period of time. And the steps counter encourages you to be active throughout the day, and keep up with your physical fitness.

Getting inside a company

This next point is one of the most difficult for job seekers to get comfortable with: don't expect a response to your online job applications, emails, and voice mails. It's not that people are intentionally ignoring you; it's just that they are incredibly busy professionals and they get hit up by jobseekers all the time. In addition, hiring new employees is probably not their main area of responsibility – it's an ancillary function they have to perform only occasionally, when they need to replace or add a team member. They may even view the task as a pesky distraction from their real job.

That's OK, we're going to show you how to cut through this barrier. Once you have identified an individual you want to target, here's an easy plan of action you can follow. The key is that you don't get discouraged when your calls and emails go unanswered. You need to keep pursuing your target until you get to "No."

Unless your target contact person specifically tells you they can't help you, you should interpret their non-responsiveness as, "I'd like to help you, but now just isn't a good time for me. Please try me again later." This actually works to your advantage, as 99.9% of job seekers simply send one email, or leave one voicemail; when it's not returned, they give up and move on. Your persistence will immediately set you apart from your competition. And from the employer's perspective, their initial unresponsiveness is a way to quickly separate the wheat from the chaff. If you were in the employer's position, would you want to talk with the guy who is going to give up after just one shot, or the candidate who has shown his perseverance and tenacity?

I'm going to lay out an easy action plan for you to follow, starting with initial contact and escalating from there. However, I wouldn't expect you to follow this entire process for every company you come across. This is for those organizations you really, *really* want to work for, and for which you are comfortable investing some extra time and effort:

- Identify your target: must be a real live individual who either works at the company you are pursuing, or has strong contacts inside that company. Sending an email to a generic address such as hr@yourtargetcompany.com or calling the 800 number will rarely ever get you a response.
- Email #1: This is only the initial shot across the bow in a multi-step process. Email the individual to *briefly* introduce yourself, attach your résumé (customized to either the company or a particular position you've identified at the company), and ask if there is a convenient time to set up a quick phone call. Expect this email to go unanswered.
- Call #1: Follow up with a call 72 hours after sending email #1. This isn't actually a cold call, as you have already made

contact, so they know they are on your radar. Expect that you will have to leave a voicemail. Here's a solid voicemail script:

> *Hi Jim, Steve Whitman here. I'm calling to follow-up on my email the other day. I recently completed eight years of service in the Navy as an electrical engineer, and am looking to leverage that experience into a technical position here in San Diego. Your name popped up when I was doing my research on top companies in our area. When you have a few minutes, I'd appreciate an opportunity to get your feedback on potential opportunities at XYZ Company. My cell number is (619) 867 5309. Thanks, and I look forward to speaking with you.*

This script can also be used in the event you do actually get the person on the phone. The tone is light and casual, yet still very professional. Your strategy is to sound easy and conversational, so that your request (some of their valuable time and input) seems like no big deal, thereby increasing the likelihood they will agree. If you took a more formal approach, the request would sound more significant and time consuming, thereby decreasing their willingness to assist. If people think a request will only take a few minutes of their time to complete, and not require much follow up, they are much more likely to agree to it.

- Email #2: Now you're starting to build momentum, and hopefully your target is starting to feel guilty about not responding – this is to your advantage! 72 hours after call #1, you fire off your second email:

> *Hi Jim, Steve Whitman here again. I'm following up on my voicemail from Tuesday afternoon. I know your schedule is probably very tight, but when you have a minute, I would really appreciate an opportunity to connect. My cell number again is (619) 867 5309. Thanks, and I look forward to speaking with you.*

- Call #2: In the likely event that your first three contact attempts have gone unanswered, you are now in position to escalate your outreach. In the event you are sent to voicemail again for call #2, your message should now go something like this:

  Hi Jim, Steve Whitman again. Sorry I keep missing you. I'm actually going to be in the area on Monday afternoon around 3:00, so I might drop by to see if I can catch you for a few minutes. Thanks, and I hope to connect with you soon (the threat of someone showing up at their office often prompts a response).

- Show up: Steps 1 through 5 have been steadily building momentum – a sense of urgency. An email is a pretty light touch. Calling is more significant. Meeting someone in person is much more powerful still. And I promise you, this is definitely *not* something your competition is doing either. The thought of dropping by a company in-person and without an appointment is too much for most job seekers. They'd rather stay in their comfort zone, and just sit at home sending out emails all day. Taking this extra step puts you in another category altogether. And if it backfires, who cares? You never had anything to lose, as they weren't talking with you anyway!

Throw on your interview suit, grab your portfolio, and head on down to the company's headquarters, or location you wish to work at. Here's how to approach it:

Receptionist: Can I help you?

Job Seeker: Hi there, my name is Steve Whitman. I just transitioned out of the Navy, and am extremely interested in job opportunities at XYZ Company. I've been trying to reach out to Jim Hertzog for a few weeks, but I'm guessing he's extremely busy. I was in the area this afternoon, so I figured why not just stop by, and see if I happen to catch Jim at a good time. Is he available for a few minutes by any chance?

The conversation could go several directions from here, depending on company policy, and the receptionist's mood at that very moment. And remember, the receptionist is also the #1 gatekeeper, so be sure to treat this person with warmth and professionalism.

- Stone wall: Worst case scenario she advises that all job applicants have to go through their website, and there is nothing she can do for you. In which case you ask if you could please leave a copy of your résumé for Jim, and ask that she please let him know you stopped by. I'd also suggest handwriting a quick note on the top of your résumé:

   Jim, stopped by 06/25@3:15, sorry I missed you. Would appreciate a call when you have a moment." This not only makes it more personal, it also makes the receptionist's job easier, and reduces the chance of your résumé going into the recycle bin.

- Breakthrough: your competition isn't going to this extra effort, so the receptionist may not encounter this very often. There's a good chance she'll be impressed enough with your effort, honesty, charm and professionalism that she will actually pick up the phone and see if Jim is available.
- Rerouted: Jim might not be available, or for all you know, he might not even be the best person for you to speak with. Many large companies actually have a designated veterans outreach specialist. In which case the receptionist might steer you toward them instead, which is just fine…now you're inside!
- Dumb luck: your timing could actually be spot on. Jim could be available, and be so impressed with your extra effort (after your calls and emails, he should be familiar with your name by now), that he agrees to see you. Or as I've seen happen before, Jim might just happen to be standing there chatting with another colleague at reception when you walk in.

If at last none of these efforts succeed, take one last shot at connecting with Jim on LinkedIn. Just be sure to follow the strategies you'll find in the LinkedIn section of this book. If he doesn't respond to that last effort, then you can finally cross him off your list. That doesn't mean you have to give up on that company entirely, it just means crossing Jim off your list, and moving on to a new target person. And it's not really defeat – you should take consolation in the fact that you truly exhausted every avenue, with a level of effort that distinguishes you from the competition.

How to work a job fair

The first thing you should know about job fairs: recruiters and hiring managers dislike them even more than you do. Job fairs are the way hiring was done 10-15 years ago. It used to be that these events were one of the best vehicles for making meaningful contact with employers and potentially landing interviews. However, most employers now prefer online resources such as LinkedIn, job boards, and their own websites to attract and communicate with candidates. These channels enable them to target candidates with the skills and experience they need, instead of talking with whoever happens to walk through the door.

Other reasons we can't stand job fairs

- Inefficiency: as a job seeker, you'll often be provided with a list of companies that will be participating in the job fair, so you can see if it will be worth your time. Recruiters on the other hand have no such luxury – all we can do is sit at our booth and hope that the right candidates happen to show up. Hence, more and more employers are ditching job fairs in favor of online channels.
- Time: events usually last three to four hours, and many of the military-related job fairs require that employers show up long before the fair starts and stay through the *entire* thing; the total time commitment can easily surpass five hours. It's also extremely hard for me to spend a half day out of the office – I have clients and candidates I have to respond to – I can't be offline for half the day, sitting around hoping a unicorn candidate happens to show up at the job fair.

- Exhaustion: it will probably take you two hours max to successfully work a big job fair, and that will involve quite a bit of walking around. The recruiters have to be there for up to four-plus hours standing on their feet the whole time. (Recruiters who sit behind the booth/table instead of standing and talking with candidates need to go back to training.)
- Boredom: as a job seeker you will be talking with many different companies, listening to different pitches each time. We have to reuse the same pitch every time a new job seeker approaches our table. Imagine making the same pitch again and again for four-plus hours.
- Unprepared candidates: sadly, veterans are often the least prepared of any job fair attendees. From the confused facial expressions and sheepish body language, it's clearly a painful experience for them. The typical attendee will make one or two laps of the room, briskly moving up and down the center of the aisles, surveying the booths, but not daring to get close enough to engage in conversation. They often move in small groups of two or three, afraid to be caught out in the open on their own. Employer reps have to practically drag them over to the booth to get them to engage in conversation about their job search. And you can imagine how awkward that conversation is – the typical job seeker struggles to explain their background, and what position they are seeking after the military. It's a huge waste of their time, and ours.

If job fairs are so painful and inefficient, why do they still exist? To be honest, it's often times not about actually hiring anyone. It's about public relations and political correctness: the various military support commands and organizations want to be seen as proactive in assisting transitioning personnel with employment resources. Employer organizations want to be seen as pro-military, especially those that do business with the federal government. Firms therefore send their junior recruiters so that they can gain experience.

Fact: many of the organizations attending job fairs, particularly government agencies, don't actually have any immediate openings. A spot in the police academy that starts 12-18 months from now is not an open position; it's the *chance* that you *might* be a fit for position that *could* open up in 12-18 months. In my world, a job opening is one in which you will actually start work in 90 days or less – usually much less. When a search client places an order with Manpower, they are looking to sign an offer letter as soon as we get the right candidate in front of them. In some cases, it can happen in less than a week.

Now that we've spent several pages condemning job fairs, you still need to go to as many of these things as possible…and here's why: it's all practice. As a transitioning veteran, you need as much hands-on experience interacting with private sector business professionals as possible. You need to spend time out in the market, surveying the landscape: What employers are in my area? What careers do they offer? What industries could be a good fit for me? Does this region even have any jobs that interest me, or should I look to take a job in another part of the country?

Job fairs are a safe environment in which to practice and hone your networking and interviewing skills. Every interaction you have with an employer rep at the fair is like a mini-interview, except that you have nothing to lose at this stage. Your job fair strategy should therefore be as follows:

- Prepare: find out which companies are attending and spend some time researching them. Find out if they have any current openings on their website that excite you. If so, customize a version of your résumé accordingly.
- Suit up: dress for a job fair as you would an interview. And ladies, be sure to wear comfortable, yet professional shoes that you can easily walk in. Expect to be on your feet and moving for several hours.
- Arrive early: attendance at these things follows a bell curve – a dribble of attendees in the beginning, quickly rising to a plateau, and then tapering off toward the last hour of the fair. You want to get there early when the recruiters are fresh – before these poor folks have been on their feet for three hours and had the same conversation 214 times. You

also want to hit your priority employers first, when you are at your freshest and before lines start forming in front of those hot companies.

- Efficiency: you only have so much time and energy to spend at a job fair before you will hit the proverbial wall. Use your time wisely: on arrival, get a map of the room (most larger fairs should have this available) and circle the booth locations of companies you know interest you. Make sure you hit those first, moving methodically from one to the next. If there is a long line, skip to the next on your list and come back later.

- Résumés: the only piece of equipment you need at a job fair is your interview portfolio. Inside will be a notepad, pen, space for business cards, and many fresh copies of your résumé. Bring customized versions of your résumé for specific employers you know will be there. Also be sure to have plenty of copies of your utility résumé, the version detailing your skills and experience, but not tailored to a specific job or industry. Bring a USB drive with all the versions of your résumé as well, in case you run out. Many job fairs will allow you to print more copies for free on site.

- Be on your best behavior: remember, recruiters are all around you, and it may not be obvious who is a recruiter and who is a job seeker (dark suits all start to look alike after a while). Most recruiters will take a break at some point and go walk the aisles and stop by other employer booths for a chat. Treat every person at the fair like they are a recruiter, and wait patiently in line.

- Network with other jobseekers: you'd be amazed what kind of valuable intel you can gain from fellow jobseekers. Chat with other folks while you're waiting in line – it will help pass the time, and you never know – that person you thought was a fellow veteran in transition could actually be an HR Director at one of your target companies.

- Take breaks: if it happens to be a good job fair, you may be there for two or three hours, and you'll need to be on top of your game the whole time. Be sure to take a couple of breaks to recharge your batteries, and bring a healthy snack along (energy bars easily fit in a suit pocket or purse). You'll hit the wall hard if your blood sugar level drops. And of course, eat a good breakfast to power up before the event. Job fairs are endurance events.

- Schwag: job fairs are famous for free stuff. Most employers will have some sort of little trinket or doo-dad at their booth like pens, notepads, key chains, and the like. You may even be handed a shopping bag when you walk in the door, inviting you to load up. However, please remember that you are there to network, not shop. Before picking up that keychain, ask yourself: do I *really* need this? It might be free for you, but that keychain came out of somebody's marketing budget. Seasoned recruiters can spot a "shopper" from across the room. Shoppers greedily move from booth-to-booth, their eyes fixed not on the recruiters, but scanning the table tops, looking for more free stuff to shove in their bulging bags. It's almost like a drug for them, and definitely not professional behavior. Your hands should be free for carrying your portfolio and shaking hands, not loaded down with giveaways. If you simply must indulge, do so only after you've thoroughly worked the room and talked with all the employers present.
- Hit every booth: after you've spoken with a rep from each of the companies on your target list, use whatever time you have left for practice networking. Stop by each of the other employer booths, and just have a chat. It is great networking practice, and who knows, you may just uncover an awesome opportunity at an organization you totally overlooked.

Temporary staffing agencies

Frustratingly, we constantly hear candidates dismiss temporary staffing agencies, especially at job fairs. Too often we hear, "I'm only looking for a permanent position" or "a real job." That's an extremely short-sighted position that will cost you a lot of good job prospects. Here's why:

- Staffing firms don't just provide companies with temporary staffing – they offer lots of permanent jobs, too. In addition, a large number of positions are also long-term contracts as well.

- The fastest way into a permanent job is through a temporary job, especially in a slow job market. Remember the earlier section about HR Managers and risk avoidance? Starting a new employee on a temporary assignment is the best way to eliminate the risk associated with making a new hire. Would you buy a new car without first taking it for a test drive? Over the years, we here at Manpower have observed that approximately 40% of temp assignments eventually generate an offer of permanent employment. Think about it: if you work just three temp jobs, you have more than a 100% probability of landing a permanent job offer. I don't know about you, but I like those odds.

- Temporary staffing firms help reduce your risk as well. An employment relationship goes both ways: you need to carefully evaluate the company before committing to a permanent position. True, you can always quit, but that hurts your track record, and you'd also be surprised how many hiring managers at different companies know each other, especially in the same industry. Starting a new job on a temporary or contract basis gives you time to evaluate a new job, a new company, and a new industry. If it's not the right fit, then you only have to stick it out through the duration of the assignment. And learning what you *don't* want to do is extremely helpful in zeroing in on what you *do* actually want to do in your post-military career.

- Flesh out your résumé: if the military was your first job right out of school, it would be extremely helpful to get a few temp assignments under your belt. This not only provides some cash flow, but it also helps you to get your feet wet in the private sector workforce. Each temp assignment, even if it's just for a couple weeks, goes on your résumé, and should look exactly like your different military positions.

- Build your network: you will meet many different colleagues during the course of your various temp assignments. The more assignments you take, the more people you meet – many of who will be helpful in landing yourself a permanent job and throughout your career.

- Professional references: it's very helpful to have some private sector references to provide alongside your military references when applying for positions. The fact that you have private sector professionals who can vouch for your capabilities will help alleviate concerns a company might have in hiring someone who has spent most of their working life in the military.

Staffing companies should be a key part of your job search strategy – especially because they do a lot of the work for you. We only get paid when we get you a job that you like and want to stay in. Working with a staffing company is a very small investment of your time, which could have huge payoffs.

First, never pay for the services of a recruiter or staffing agency; our income comes from the employers who hire us to find them good people like you. Don't even pay for a résumé writing service. There are enough resources in this book, as well as available online, to get your résumé up to spec. A good recruiter should be able to see your potential, and help you with any final résumé massaging before submitting it to their client. And the recruiter should be willing to share a copy of that résumé they put together with you. You have every right to see what they are sending out about you.

Second, register with several different agencies at a time. Each staffing company has its own specialties and portfolio of clients. You may as well have several different agencies all working on your behalf. And know that each agency is only as good as the recruiter they assign you. If the two of you really click, and have a good working relationship, that recruiter is going to keep you at the top of his or her list. You'll be one of the first candidates they call when the plumb new job orders come in. If you like the agency, and they have a good portfolio of client companies but you're still not having a pleasant experience, see if you can be reassigned to another recruiter at the agency.

After you register, be sure to check in at regular intervals (every two weeks is adequate). You want the agency to keep you at the top of the "active and available" list. Here at Manpower we call it the MPC list: Most Placeable Candidates. These are the folks we are actively marketing to our clients, because we know they have great skills and are hungry for opportunities.

How should you go about engaging with staffing companies? Start with their websites. Most of the top agencies use an online application system to get you into their database. It should only take a few minutes to enter some key information and upload your résumé. It used to be that agencies welcomed walk-ins, as that was the only way to actually capture candidates. If you just pick up the phone and call, chances are you will be directed to their online system first.

Next, review the agency's online job board, provided they have one, to see which job opportunities they currently have available. You'll need to do this frequently, as new jobs come in constantly throughout the day. Each job opening is usually assigned to one particular recruiter. If you see something you like, make contact with that recruiter via the email, phone and in-person networking strategies we covered earlier. Although most agencies don't encourage walk-ins, it's still a great strategy to differentiate yourself.

My recommendation: start with several staffing agencies to get them working on some short-term job assignments for you. This will hopefully get some experience and cash flow coming in while you consider registering with a headhunter, who will be focused on more specific, long-term career opportunities. A Google search for "military job placement firm" and similar search terms, will turn up a list of agencies in your area. You will also find a number of firms that specialize in hiring transitioning veterans; for some, that's all they do. These agencies will definitely speak your language. Two firms I've come to know here in San Diego and respect are Amerit Consulting and The Lucas Group. Like Manpower, these two firms also have nationwide coverage.

Take some time to research a range of staffing agencies, and pick a few to meet with (hopefully Manpower will be on your list!) before deciding on who you'd like to start representing you. I'd also recommend taking a look at www.exfederal.com, which describes itself as "the job board and résumé database devoted to federal contractors." Federal contracting work may be another way to leverage your military skills as you continue evaluating and preparing for a career in the private sector.

Does no *always* mean no?

Decades of experience in this industry has taught me to never say never. Good recruiters and hiring managers always hang onto top candidates. Just because you ultimately were not selected for the role, doesn't mean you have no future with that company. Things change: the candidate they initially picked over you could turn out to be a dud, the department's budget could get an unforeseen bump (allowing them to hire a second), or a new role could become available in another part of the company.

If you enjoy Civil War era history, you might recall how Lincoln ultimately secured the nomination in the 1860 Republican primary – it was a hard race, and through multiple rounds of balloting, Lincoln never came out on top. However, he positioned himself to keep coming in second every time. Ultimately after enough rounds, all the leading candidates had knocked each other out and Lincoln ultimately came out on top of the ballot.

The lesson here: if you don't get an offer from your dream company the first time around, there is still much you can do to position yourself for future opportunities. And as I put the finishing touches on this book, I also happen to be working with just such a candidate.

Eighteen months ago I ran an executive search engagement for a large government agency here in San Diego. One of our candidates, Marco, did extremely well through the process, ultimately making it into the top five. He didn't have as much real estate operations experience as the other candidates, but his enthusiasm and sincerity almost closed the deficit.

Ultimately Marco was not selected, but we stayed in touch. He continued to check in with me on a regular basis (about once a month), and always returned my calls and emails immediately. Fast forward six months later. I'm catching up for coffee with the Senior VP of the real estate department at the same agency, and she mentions that her budget finally has some room to bring on a new Asset Manager position. Three weeks later, Marco signed his employment offer from the agency.

Email etiquette

Pay close attention to syntax and diction, i.e., your sentence structure and choice of words. Good writers (and hopefully the one whose work you are currently reading falls into this category) use sentences of varying length to add life to their text and help it flow more naturally. Proof read everything, and I mean *everything,* before you click send or drop it in the mail (more on handwritten thank you cards later). There is absolutely no excuse for typos, grammatical mistakes, and spelling errors. The more senior level the job you're applying for, the more critical this becomes. I can't tell you how many candidates I've passed over because they were too lazy to proof read an email or had a résumé riddled with errors. If I can't trust you to write a coherent email, then how could I trust you to run a piece of my business or impress my clients? Your writing is a direct reflection of you, so take pride in your work. Slow down, write thoughtfully, check, and then re-check your work.

Selecting your email address

Your email address may very well be the very first thing a potential career contact will see from you. Make sure you choose an email address that is as simple and professional as possible. It should be some derivative of your first and last name. That's it. No references to call signs, unit nicknames, or other military designators. I recently met a young Marine at MCAS Miramar who handed me a résumé with the email address devildog777@gmail.com listed at the top. Keep it simple – just use your name. You may have to use some creativity to find an address that's not already taken. For example, if your name was Robert Smith, here's some logical variations to try:

- Smith_robert@gmail.com

- R_smith@gmail.com
- Robert-smith@gmail.com
- Smith.robert@gmail.com

Once you've tried all the possible combinations and abbreviations of your first and last name, using periods, underscore, and hyphens, then you can look at incorporating a few numbers like Robert. smith1977@gmail.

Does it matter what email service provider you choose? As mentioned earlier, I don't make the rules of the hiring game and I don't necessarily agree with all of them, but my job is to make you aware of them. If you are using an email address that ends in @aol. com, @hotmail.com or @netscape.com, or any other 1990s/early 2000s ISP, you may be perceived as a technology neophyte and out of touch with the times. From my experience, I have yet to meet a master app developer or coder who is using an AOL account. Google provides free email accounts with free storage at gmail.com.

One last word of advice on email addresses: every person in your household needs to have their own private email account. Please know that when I see an email from an account such as thepearsonfamily@ aol.com drop in my inbox, I have already made the assumption that this candidate is most likely not the kind of person my client is looking for. This person probably still has a FAX machine too.

Subject headings

The first thing people look at when receiving an email is the sender's name. The subject heading is a distant second. However, it is also where I see the most typos. There is a setting in spell check that ensures it screens the subject line, as well as the body of the email. Make sure you activate this feature, but never rely on spell check as your final reviewer. Spell check can sometimes slip in a replacement word that will wreak havoc in your emails and documents. For instance, there was once a very senior executive in our company named Varina. You can imagine how many times I reread each message I wrote to her before finally clicking "send." Spell check is not, and never will be, bulletproof.

And one last suggestion on subject headings: invest a few seconds to make them targeted and relevant. Highly generic subject lines such as: "Hello," "Thank you," or "Good to meet you," are not only total throw-aways, they may also get your email dumped into the spam folder. A better subject heading would be: John Stevenson – Facilities Manager candidate.

Email content
It is never, *ever* appropriate to include any kind of phrase or image underneath your name at the bottom of the email. It's a total professional turnoff. Not a day goes by that I don't see a candidate include something unprofessional at the bottom of an email. The most common offenses we see are:

- Bible verses
- Parables
- Quotes from famous people
- Inspirational messages or quotes from famous people

This goes for your voicemail as well. I had to counsel one of my managers recently, as her voicemail message closed with "have a blessed day." That's fine on your personal voicemail, but definitely not for your work phone. Refrain from any and all religious references in business communication.

If you choose to include an auto-signature on your emails, which I would suggest, it should contain just three pieces of information: your name, cell number and email address. That's it. This allows the reader to quickly copy-paste your information into emails to their colleagues. And you definitely want to encourage that.

Cell phone voicemail
Never leave your home phone number as your contact phone. There is nothing worse than HRcalling you in for a phone interview or even just to set an appointment than for the phone to be answered by your three year old saying "Daddy's not here. Call back. Click!" We never call back unless we are desperate. Next bad practice is your

three year old making the recording for your voicemail. We feel like we called a children's nursery by mistake.

So use your own cell phone as your contact number. Keep the phone with you at all times.

Always answer it professionally as if each call is that job offer you've been waiting for. Be sure your phone message is very professional - I should be impressed, rather than concerned, if I made the right choice calling you in the first place.

If you are driving when we call, it is very appropriate to say I am driving now can I pull over at the next exit and call you back? We never want to hear the squeal of brakes or a crash during a phone interview. The same applies if you have your children with you. As parents ourselves, we are very understanding.

What's currently on your voicemail greeting? It should sound something like this:

> *"Hi, you've reached the voicemail of Phil Blair, I'm sorry I missed your call, but please leave a message."*

That's it: professional and to-the-point. No need to say and "I'll get back to you." We know that. That's why you have voicemail set up in the first place. Even worse are messages that say: "and I'll get back to you at my earliest convenience." That's essentially saying to the caller: if you're lucky enough to get a return call from me, it will only be when I feel like getting around to it.

Record your greeting, and then play it back to yourself numerous times. How do you sound? Do you sound like the kind of person you would be excited to speak with? Does your tone project enthusiasm, confidence, and professionalism (while at the same time actually sounding like the real you)? If not, erase and re-recording until it does.

Another faux pas: some candidates don't bother to even record a voicemail greeting. How is the caller supposed to know they've dialed the right number? "You have reached 123.456.7890. Please leave a message." A generic digitized voicemail greeting is impersonal, and makes you seem either lazy, or inept with technology. And one last suggestion: record your voicemail greeting in a quiet place. The caller shouldn't hear music, traffic noise, or a baby crying in the background when they listen to your voicemail greeting.

Social media

A word to the wise: be extremely cautious about your posts on social media. This includes LinkedIn, Facebook, Twitter, blog posts, and all other forms. Unflattering items have an amazing way of coming back to haunt you on social media. Most employers will do some kind of a background check on you before issuing a letter of offer. At the very least, it might be a cursory Google search, just to make sure you are as upstanding and professional as you led them to believe through the interviewing process. They will probably also take a look at your LinkedIn profile, and perhaps Facebook and Twitter. This is a very standard practice, and you need to prepare accordingly.

We won't go into too much detail on social media here, as there are entire books dedicated to online tools and building your personal brand. However, I will highlight some key concepts every job seeker should know about the online world:

- Facebook is personal – Generally speaking, Facebook is for keeping up with friends and family, where you can post pictures of that new puppy you just bought your daughter for her birthday. While many businesses run effective Facebook campaigns, and often use them for recruiting, it is still generally recognized as a non-work related social media site. Some Facebook suggestions:
  o Keep your page locked on private.
  o Keep it clean – even though your page is private, it's critical to avoid posts you wouldn't want your mother to see.
  o Some employers may ask for access to your page as part of the background checking process – refuse to comply with this at your own peril. The company just

wants to know what kind of person they're hiring – if you're a good person, what do you have to hide?

o   Facebook can still be used for networking purposes, particularly when you need to reach out to friends and family.

o   Post occasional updates about your transition – that way folks in your network can feed you leads or connect you with other friends who may be able to assist.

o   It's a huge time suck – be sure to limit yourself to just a few minutes on Facebook several times a day to check your page and respond to posts.

o   LinkedIn – This site is still the gold standard when it comes to recruiting. Invest the time to build a good profile, and watch the online tutorials to learn your way around the site and all its various search functions. You'll be amazed at the information you can get access to.

o   Photo – upload a professional picture (civilian business attire).

o   Messaging – proof read every message you write before sending.

o   Get a professional opinion – ask a recruiter to review your page and provide feedback.

o   Check it often – make it a habit to check your LinkedIn page as often as you check email.

- Negative content – Nobody is perfect. When was the last time you Googled yourself? Perhaps that wild night out with the guys while you were on shore leave in Singapore generated some less-than-flattering content on the internet. Unfortunately there's very little you can actually do to get that negative content taken down. It's probably up there to stay. You can however take actions to bury that content under a pile of good content. Get yourself mentioned in as many positive posts as possible. Blog frequently about topics on which you have expertise. Ask friends and colleagues to also mention or feature you in their content as well. If you've got enough good information out there, a hiring manager will have to spend quite a bit of time online sifting through all the posts about you. This not only decreases the likelihood that they'll even come across the bad information, it also means they'll be reading a ton of good news about you and come away even more impressed.

The 10/90% theory.

I spent much of my childhood living abroad. My father worked in the petroleum industry. In the 1960s, the quickest way to boost one's career was to volunteer for work overseas. Many of my father's colleagues were content to stick to the States, but not him. Folks thought he was crazy to leave the comforts of Oklahoma, to take his young family to foreign countries, but my father was ambitious. When a new oil field was discovered in, say, Venezuela, he would be sent there to open up offices. We, of course, went along. My father didn't love the job, but it paid well and he had a family to support. That's how it worked in those days.

For a kid it was an "interesting" life. We never stayed in a place more than a few years, much like Military families. I was shy. I started at a new school every few years, usually appearing in the middle of a semester. I attended elementary school in Caracas, Venezuela, and junior high in Tripoli, Libya. I was always the kid who walked into a classroom and was introduced by the teacher as "the new student." Everybody else knew each other. It took time to make friends, become part of the scene, and often, when that finally happened, it was time for my family to move again.

My mother was a big driver in my family. My parents were both of hearty Midwestern stock. They had strong, conservative values and an exceptional work ethic. Dad went off to work. Mom remained home, though she had too much energy to just clean and cook. As soon as my older brother and I reached high school, she got a job too, which was a pretty rare thing in the 1960s. My parents' work ethic rubbed off on my brother and me. Sitting around the house watching TV wasn't an option for either of us. If I wasn't going to keep busy with school and sports, then she figured I might as well be productive and do some odd jobs. So I mowed lawns, shoveled snow, sold pens and stationery, babysat. Mom always drove me wherever I needed to be. She was very empowering.

When you're a small business person (and I was, both in size of business and stature), you meet a lot of people. You learn how to carry on a conversation with adults — how to develop your business. I negotiated prices for weekly lawn services and snow shoveling after storms. The clients were several times my age, but I think I held my own. I became comfortable talking to, and negotiating with, people much older and more powerful than me.

I discovered, mostly unconsciously, that the more people I talked to, the richer I became. Not necessarily in money, but knowledge. Everybody has a story to tell. Everybody can teach you something. It might be practical information, like how to write a contract. Or it might be personal, like how to start up a conversation with a stranger. I've learned something from virtually everybody I've ever met. And the fun is, I'm still learning.

I am convinced that life is 10% what happens to you and 90% how you choose to react to what happens. Two people can see a troublesome situation so differently - one falls on their sword immediately, sees it as the worst thing to ever happen, gives up, and suffers the consequences. The other person takes the problem on as a challenge, works through it, and learns from it. Which kind of person are you and which kind of person do you want to be?

I have never understood the attraction of falling on the sword. I thrive on being around positive, upbeat people. People who see the cup half-full are, in fact, my favorite people. Have you met people who, for some reason, you just like being around? You feel better about yourself when you are in their presence? They are happy people. They find good things to say about other people. They laugh at themselves. They never take life too seriously. And they bring you out of yourself and make you an active part of their conversation or activity. They continually stretch and test themselves. They give you the confidence to do the same.

Equally important, upbeat people are rarely critical of other people. They understand other people's weaknesses and always try to help them through an issue. They even go out of their way to find the positive in everyone. Upbeat people rarely complain about anything.

These are the kind of people I want to have in my posse! This is the kind of person I want to be and that I want you to be as well.

I have a pet peeve: Sighing and moaning.

> *Sue, a salesperson who is no longer with Manpower, had a habit of coming into my office and letting out the longest, loudest sighs as she threw herself in a chair across from me. When she sat down, she moaned. When she stood up, she moaned—as if it was the hardest thing she had done all day. After the second time she did it, I told her she sucked all the energy out of the room! I realize selling is a hard and often frustrating job. But don't take it out on the rest of us. As a salesperson, Sue needed to bring energy into a room, not draw it out. She realized the negative vibes and body language she had unconsciously been portraying and quickly changed.*

I feel this way about loud yawns too. Yawns scream I am tired and/ or bored. For whatever metaphysical reason, we all find yawns to be contagious. Someone yawns and the rest of us unconsciously follow suit. Not a good thing. If you have to yawn, stifle it as much as humanly possible. And don't be one of those people who yawns without covering your mouth. I have no interest in looking down your throat.

Don't forget: people are your greatest resource. It's easy and natural in hard times to withdraw into your cubbyhole, to hunker down and wait out the storm. I know it can be depressing and even embarrassing to be out of work when it seems like everyone else has a job. This is when you most need to reach out and touch someone, anyone, and everyone. That's what this chapter is all about and it's easier than you think.

5.0   Networking 101

"But I don't know anyone!" is the first thing I hear when I start to talk about the importance of networking. I get it. You have left all of your "contacts" behind in the Army or Marines or some other branch of the military. They are still enlisted and so are of very little help to you on the outside.

So let's talk about your friends and acquaintances (friends to be) that have gone over to the dark side over the last few years. Hopefully you kept in touch and can talk to them about their experiences transitioning out: what they did right, wrong, and wish they had known then that they know now.

So your networking list has begun.

We moved often and I was always the new kid at school, arriving usually in the middle of the school year. The other kids had already made their connections with their friends that they had known for years and I felt like the odd man out. I was shy and breaking into the cliques took months of eating lunch alone.

But I also soon realized it was worth the effort to reach out to as many of the kids as I could and to respond quickly and with enthusiasm whenever they responded or reached out to include me. I realized many years later I was networking. I was making the effort to reach out to strangers and encourage them to accept me into their group. Much like an informational interview or job interview: meet me as a stranger and leave wanting to hire me and pay me money to join your group.

A simple exercise I recommend to clients who are shy or awkward starting conversations with strangers, exactly like I am going to recommend to you in this chapter, is standing in line at a grocery store. Think about it. A line of strangers waiting patiently with nothing to do. And they have racks of candies or magazines in front of them. The assignment is to start up a conversation with a stranger in front or behind you, or even better both, by asking them "If you could eat all you want of one of these candies and not gain any weight which one would you pick?" Pretty easy assignment, right? You will be surprised the size of the smile on their face because someone is talking to them.

Your challenge: meet as many of the above people as possible, while making each of those relationships seem genuine and meaningful. Most people are very good at identifying when they are being used – it can be very transparent when someone is networking merely to inflate their contact list. Although you want to build a large network, you also need to build an effective network. Quantity does not mean quality. It's much more helpful to have a network of 100 people with whom you have a genuine connection, stay in touch with regularly, and who are generally relevant to your career, than to have a giant network of 500 people who may or may not even remember your name.

How do you do this? Networking goes both directions: them to you and you to them. The best relationships are based not only on likeability, but on mutual assistance. Both parties want to stay in touch, as they recognize a mutual willingness and ability to assist each other in their endeavors. When meeting others, your goal is to listen as much as possible; get to know them, their projects, and how you might be of service to them. There's a classic saying: you have two ears and one mouth – use them in that order. People naturally like others who are good listeners. Most people love to hear themselves talk (it makes them feel intelligent and important). We are therefore naturally inclined to like other people we perceive as good listeners.

Let's say you're at a business networking event and engaged in a conversation. While you'll want to flex those listening skills, you also need to be careful not to waste your entire evening stuck with one windbag. At some point you'll need to tactfully extricate yourself from the conversation. One way you can politely signal that you are winding down the conversation is to ask something like:

> *Jim, I've really enjoyed talking with you and learning about your start in the aerospace industry. I'd definitely like to trade contact info with you (now is when you might extend a business card). Is there any way I might be of assistance to you in the future as well?*

They will most likely politely decline, but the key points are that you: 1) exchanged contact information; and 2) made the offer of assistance to seal the conversation on a strong note.

If you want to make a friend for life then when you go to a networking event and you see someone who is standing alone go over and start a conversation with them. They are probably miserable and want to flee the event as fast as they can. It can be as easy as, "Bet you don't know anyone here either?" You'll feel better for taking the initiative and have a new friend. It's then easy to draw in other stragglers into your group and you can move on. If it's an event where you know lots of people, then be kind and watch out for loners. Introduce them to your friends and they will never forget you!

Face-to-face: there is no substitute

Not all networking opportunities are created equal. No amount of emails, internet research, or even phone calls can substitute for an in-person, face-to-face, human-to-human conversation. Live meetings provide tremendously more information beyond what's simply stated verbally. Personal presentation, body language, and the overall energy or "vibe" a person gives off can't be communicated any other way. I'm not sure I would let a client of mine accept a staff job at the company he had never visited or met any of their current employees. Despite the fact that we live in a highly networked, digital world, most hiring is still done the old fashioned way – in person.

Your odds of landing a job in the city of your choice go up by a factor of at least 10, if you're actually living in that area, where you can interact face-to-face.

Here is a tough decision point. You are being discharged from the Army in Fort Bragg and think you want to move home to Memphis because that's where your roots and your family are. Do you move there and start your job search when you are actually a resident of the city, or start focusing your job search on Memphis and move there only after you nail a job? Do you only search Memphis and no other cities? What if I find the perfect job and it's not in Memphis but another exciting city?

Do it all. Put on a heavy press for jobs in Memphis; set up interviews and visit often. It's easy to convince interviewers you are serious about moving to Memphis when you talk about the effort you are putting into your Memphis job search. And keep an active search going nationwide for jobs in your chosen field. You may be very surprised what develops. Make the big move of your family only when factors are favorable; end of school year, lease is up, or house has sold, etc. You need to keep all these balls in the air until fate starts making decision for you.

If you have any doubt, consider this: depending on the position, we typically see about 200 applications for each job we post online. Which of those 200+ candidates do you think the hiring manager is going to remember? Résumé number 147 she's screened that morning or the candidate who actually dropped by her office in-person to introduce himself? That high level personal touch is something you can't easily do from the other side of the country.

Body language
Research has shown that when interacting with someone, we first notice their body language (good posture or slouching) then the tone of the words they say (energetic or monotonous), and then third, and last the actual words they are saying! Keep this top of mind when thinking about your interviewing skills. This is covered in depth in Chapter 8.

Using names

What's by far the favorite sound every person likes to hear? It's their own name. What's the best way to get an interviewer or business contact to warm up to you? Use their name. What's one of the easiest identifiers between management professionals and frontline staff? Executives remember and use people's names. This skill is not only an essential component of relationship building, it also signals intelligence and professionalism. I run this little test in our own company every morning and the results are always the same. People in decision-making roles always greet everyone by name, whereas the administrative staff just say "hi."

When, and how often should you use a person's name? The guidelines below apply to just about all forms of communication, especially face-to-face and phone.

- The first time you meet someone: Hi Phil, I'm Tony Katz. Very good to meet you.
- The first time you see them that day: Good morning, Phil!
- Perhaps once, maybe twice during an interview (anything more is overdoing it)
- At the close of an interview or conversation: Heather, it was great meeting you here at the Chamber of Commerce event this morning, and I appreciate your taking the time to speak with me about my job search".

Is it Phil, or Mr. Blair?

When meeting new people, especially for an interview, many people aren't sure when to use a person's first name or last name. This discomfort prevents them from using the person's name at all, which is the worst thing. While different standards apply in some situations, in general, the business world is moving away from formal titles and greetings. This can be difficult for those who have grown up inside the military hierarchy and might be more comfortable with formality. Here are some general guidelines:

- Generational differences: some older, very traditional types, still prefer the use of titles, not first names.

- Age gap: if there is clearly a huge age gap, go with Mr./Ms., until asked to do otherwise. If you are under age 25, default to Mr./Ms., until asked to do otherwise.
- Geography: the west coast tends to be more casual than the east.
- Setting: Mr. Blair for a conversation in the office sounds fine, but it would be odd to use the same formality if the interview was over coffee or an after work drink.
- Ms. vs. Mrs.: always default to Ms.; it will only be taken as complementary.
- Sir and Ma'am: you can strike these from your vocabulary altogether.

So which name should you go with? My advice is to call the interviewer's assistant or maybe the receptionist at the office. Here's your script:

> *"Hello, my name is Derrick Whitley, and I'm coming in next week to interview with Phil Blair. Could you please tell me if he prefers candidates to refer to him by Mr. Blair or Phil?"*

If you're still not feeling certain, simply err on the side of caution and go with Mr. Blair – it will be taken as a sign of respect and politeness. If he prefers to go by Phil, he'll let you know.

Also listen closely when you are meeting and they are introducing themselves. They will always introduce themselves by the name they want you to call them. But besides the Mr./Ms. Quandary, they have also use a formal name in writing but in person go by a nickname. I am a good example. On paper I am often Phillip but in person always Phil.

Business cards

Aren't business cards only for guys who already have a job or own a business? Absolutely not. Networking is a 24/7 365 full contact sport – you never know when and where you might run into a career-related contact. You can't fit a stack of résumés in your pocket, but unless you're swimming laps at the YMCA, you can always have a few business cards on you. "But can't I just give them my contact info to enter into their phone?" Trust me, it's much easier and smoother to just hand someone a professional looking business card. You can't assume they will have the time, patience, ability, or technical aptitude to enter your contact info into their phone. Besides, once a contact is saved in their phone, what's going to remind them to look you up? A physical business card is a much more potent reminder.

Hint: there is never a reason to put your home address on your business card or your résumé. I will not be driving by to see if you have mowed your lawn. In these days of too much information out on the web and social media, you don't need to advertise to the world where you live. If I need to mail you something to your home via snail mail then it will probably be your signed offer letter or benefits forms. There will be plenty of time to get your home address before then.

Keep your card simple and professional. It should be on plain white or off-white stock. The paper should not be glossy, as some pens can't write on glossy stock. You want people to be able to write notes on the back of your card as reminders. On the left-hand side of the card will be your name, branch of service, cell phone number, email address, and LinkedIn profile address. For a graphic on the opposite side of the card, you can use the seal from your branch of the military, although I didn't tell you that. Shawn thinks an image adds visual balance and looks nice. I feel like the candidate is holding on to their past military image and is not ready to let go. And to me that screams the candidate is not ready to make the transition to the private sector quite yet. Your call but you now have two different opinions.

Do not include a picture, otherwise you'll be confused for a real estate agent. Along the bottom of the card, include a concise statement like: Master Chief, US Navy, currently in career transition. If you have a specific career or industry objective, you could also use the back of the business card and include that information in the statement, in addition to specific skills you an offer. However, if you do choose to list skills, make sure they are specific capabilities like operations management, logistics, satellite navigation systems, etc.

As mentioned earlier, generic qualities like leadership, management and team building aren't actually that helpful.

Here are examples for the back of your business cards should you choose this option:

> "Navy veteran with 20 years' experience in procurement of hard goods, equipment, and services in Europe and the US. Seeking management position in international purchasing for large multinational firm"

Or the back could simply read:

> Human Resources
> Employee Benefits
> Marketing or Communications

How many times have we all left an event and when we emptied our pockets we had a stack of business cards that when we accepted them we were sure we would remember the person that gave them to us and what careers/positions they were interested in or what we had discussed. This solves that mystery.

Don't put any personal information on your business card that you would not put on your résumé. Nothing that EEOC (Equal Employment Opportunity Commission) would discourage. Nothing that refers to age, ethnicity, disabilities, gender, or sexual preference. Now having said that I can figure out your age by adding years of experience to your graduation dates, that you are a veteran from your assignments. Don't mention your race, gender, or preference, unless you want me to know because it may be to your advantage. I can deduce much by the organizations in which you are active. For example, it can be very telling if you volunteer for the Urban League, Black Youth Education Fund, the Junior League, Gay Pride Milwaukee, or were an Eagle Scout.

None of these organizations should be seen as a negative. It is a card you are entitled to play if you want to telegraph a message in a subtle way. If any of those organizations you are applying to are opposed to issues that are very important to you, such as Chick-fil-A or Hobby Lobby's very conservative thinking ownership, then as a proud and out gay person you wouldn't want to work there anyway.

Here's something that is helpful: you can get a box of very professional looking business cards shipped right to your home for free or very inexpensively. Almost sounds too good to be true, doesn't it! Check out sites like vistaprint.com or moo.com. You'll find a number of similar options online, all of which feature user-friendly templates for designing your card.

Make volunteering part of your transition plan

The reality of today's career paradigm is that work is not a rigid social structure and activity. The time, location, and relationships defining what we call "work" are becoming more and more fluid: sometimes you'll work full-time, sometimes part-time, sometimes you'll be paid, and sometimes not. The most valuable work opportunities are sometimes the ones that pay the least (or even don't pay at all). Depending on your financial situation, the idea of taking an unpaid "job" may sound ludicrous. However, maybe you should reconsider volunteering or taking an unpaid or paid internship. Both can open a wealth of career opportunities you would never otherwise have come across. It just requires you to rethink your definition of compensation. With a good volunteer experience or internship, you're actually getting "paid" in other highly valuable ways.

Selecting the right volunteer opportunities

Volunteering for the sake of providing a valuable service to the community is highly commendable. You will definitely add value to the organization as a result of your military service. But there is more to it. The volunteer opportunities on your radar need to be stepping stones or door openers as part of your career transition. Your time, whether paid or unpaid, is valuable. And every minute you spend volunteering, is another minute you could be researching companies or networking. The opportunity cost is very real, so make your selections carefully. While you do need to believe in the organization and enjoy the people around you, the work itself must be worthy of your experience and talents. Chances are that's not ladling soup or stuffing envelopes. Board seats sound impressive, and they can provide amazing networking opportunities, but keep in mind that many require both a long term and financial commitment. If that's not for you, try to identify roles in the organization that will give you exposure and connections in your field of expertise. If a finance or accounting position is what you want to transition into then volunteer in the Finance Department of a large nonprofit. You very well may care less about what the cause is and much more about who will be your working peers and what projects you can work on that will broaden your knowledge and private sector experience. Work to tee up a well-respected senior person in the nonprofit organization to be a reference for you. It will be a reference from a very current connection and from a private sector employer; for example, person in accounting who has seen your work first hand. As you meet management and board members you will make such an amazing impression on them that they will gladly make lots of networking referrals for you. It's their way of thanking you for giving your valuable time to their organization. Start volunteering whatever time you can while still in the service, maybe use your terminal leave to really dig in, because of the nature of volunteering the organization will be very flexible when it comes time to schedule interviews or networking opportunities. Really it's a win/win all the way around.

Our Business Development people at Manpower told me they always volunteer at the check in desk at major events, especially SHRM (Society of Human Resource Management) events. They see all the name tags, where everyone works, and maybe even their title. They can be overly helpful and friendly to attendees they want to meet and follow up with. Think how this might work for you, too.

Staying in the game

As we've mentioned before, the longer you are out of work, the more difficult it is to find work again. Skills become outdated, professional networks go cold, and in effect you lose your "edge." However, you can arrest this slide, and even reverse it, by finding challenging, meaningful volunteer work. Volunteering can keep your career moving forward while you're undergoing transition – you're meeting new people, acquiring training, learning new skills, and continuing to develop yourself, personally, and professionally.

In some manner, the interviewer will get around to asking, or you will find a way to interject into the conversation, what you've been doing while you had lots of free time. It sounds so desperate to say "looking for work full time." We as interviewers are hearing: why, for six months is no one else hiring this person, what am I missing here? Remember our "stale" conversation? Or worse is: "Been working on my golf game and have my handicap down four strokes." I hear unmotivated goof off and I sure am not going to let him or her learn to get back in the habit of working on my payroll.

Your answer will be, "While actively working on my job search I was able to volunteer for the American Red Cross 20 hours a week in their Finance Department. I am really proud of the project they assigned me, which was to reorganize their Accounts Payable Department. I was able to use my finance experience in the Navy and introduce new accounting technology software to save the Red Cross $100,000 a year.

That's pretty dang impressive and sounds like someone I would want in my accounting department. A couple of other points here: one, volunteering can be much like temp to perm. Hopefully you did such a good job on your Red Cross project that you tee yourself up for a permanent job with them. If you save them that much money on one project, I am sure there are many more, and the money you saved them will pay your first year's salary. And two, think about veteran friendly organizations like the Red Cross. Their charter demands that they focus on supporting military men and women in uniform and their work is as similar to military efforts as almost any other corporation.

It doesn't have to be full time...nor should it

One of the best things about volunteering is that you can list the experience on your résumé just as you would any paid position, but rarely will the interviewer ask exactly how many hours per week you spent there. It's like getting credit for working full-time, when the actual volunteering may have only amounted to just a few hours a week. (Nota bene: always answer truthfully if asked your actual number of hours.) And just how many hours per week should you allocate to your unpaid volunteer/internship efforts? Enough that you take advantage of all the learning and networking opportunities they afford, yet not at the expense of your job search activities. Unless you have virtually zero outside commitments (family, health, etc.) and only sleep two hours a night, I would suggest no more than 20 hours per week for volunteering. Remember, your career transition is still your first priority!

Free training

While most nonprofits can't afford to send their volunteers on expensive training courses, you will no doubt require some instruction as you come into the organization and your new volunteer role. Chances are this will come through what we call on-the-job training and mentoring. These informal training opportunities can in fact be more impactful than formal courses, as you're learning directly from a civilian colleague and the instruction is catered to you. Most important, you can ask all the questions you want. Soak it up! Learn as many new skills as you can. Gain exposure to all areas of the organization – remember, running a nonprofit is in many ways just like running a business. And be sure to find a mentor – someone with skills and experience in an area important to your career. Sit down with that individual at the outset and explain not only what you can offer the organization, but also what you hope to gain, and how they can assist in your career transition. This is the future reference person I mentioned earlier. Volunteering should be a two-way, mutually beneficial relationship between you and the organization.

Safe environment in which to take some risks

Although you're a volunteer, you still need to give your role 110%. Establish clear expectations with your managers as to your weekly time commitment, and then pour your best into every hour you're "on the job." This is also a safe environment in which to take some risks you might not otherwise take in a paid position (especially when you're the new kid on the block). Now let's be clear about what we mean by risk: never ever do anything that would compromise the organization or your professional integrity in any way. We define risk as an opportunity to step outside your comfort zone. If you've never had any experience in HR, volunteer to assist on the employee benefits committee. Do you need some sales or marketing experience? Ask if you can work with the nonprofit's Business Development Director. Ask if you can make the report to the Board on the project you have worked on. Bingo: exposure to 30 business and community leaders. You have much to learn and your enthusiasm and inquisitiveness will be appreciated.

Volunteering as an experience accelerator

Since nonprofit organizations have to run very lean on staffing, you may have opportunities to assume higher level duties than you would otherwise normally be assigned if you were working in a larger, private sector entity. Less structure and management hierarchy may also afford you the opportunity to move around the business more easily than if you were working in a big firm with formal procedures. Experience as much as you can – get a copy of the org chart and network your way across every division. You may discover you have interests and talents in areas you had never even considered. As you select the one or two organizations that you volunteer for, keeping in mind the 20 hours per week limit. There are big differences between large and very small organizations. A large one will have a very active and sophisticated Finance Department where you can learn new skills but a very small organization will give you a much larger variety of experiences from the necessity of four people doing everything.

Leveraging your volunteer experience into a nonprofit career

As you probably noticed very early on in this book, I'm making a huge push for veterans to seek out rewarding careers in the private sector (i.e., for-profit businesses). Statistically this is where the vast majority of the jobs are, and they also tend to pay better. However, many veterans I meet with express a strong desire to continue serving their community after they take off the uniform. If this truly is your heart's desire, then you should seriously take a look at a career in the nonprofit sector, particularly in social services (or human services as it's also often referred to) like the Red Cross that I mentioned earlier. While the nonprofit sector can't usually match private sector salaries, there are a number of other non-financial benefits to a nonprofit career, particularly if your primary driver is mission, purpose, and giving back to society. Manpower has placed dozens of San Diego veterans into nonprofit careers, the majority in counseling and other direct services roles. And starting as an unpaid volunteer is hands-down the best way to get your foot in the door and test drive this potential career path, before making a commitment. How sweet to be offered a job for pay that you cared enough about to do as a volunteer.

Toastmasters (or any other public speaking training group/class)

Of all the pieces of career and networking advice I give, this one is one of the most critical. And sadly, I am concerned only a small percentage of job seekers see the value of it and ever follow-through... to the detriment of their careers. Toastmasters is an international society of clubs dedicated to the art and science of public speaking and discourse. There are clubs in just about every city and town. It's easy, convenient, almost free, effective, and fun (yes, public speaking can actually be fun once you master it!). Furthermore, it's a great way to meet new people and expand your network. Public speaking skills will make you much more confident in networking and during interviews. Once you land a job, these skills will also help position you for advancement. All management-level staff must be able to articulate and sell an idea or concept, and win over an audience. Toastmasters is where you can begin developing these skills. Even if you think you've already mastered the art of public speaking, attending your local club for some brush-up sessions will only help (www.toastmasters.org).

If you have children at home, I encourage you to have them check out Speech classes, the Debate Team at their school, or Young Toastmasters groups. Just like brushing their teeth, they will thank you later.

phil-osophy 101   6

"Résumés: The process by which we market ourselves to others."

Before I get into the details of developing your résumés (yes plural) it is important that you understand the purpose behind résumés. Your résumé represents you as your calling card, for any and every job you are the least bit interested in pursuing. It is also a living, breathing project that needs to be massaged and changed for every use. Yes, you will have a generic version that lightly covers all of your skill sets and talents. That version you will use for occasions when you didn't have warning to produce a customized version. It lightly covers your talents because you don't know what to emphasize and what to down play.

When I read someone's résumé, whether they are applying for a specific job or just want to make me aware of their availability, I want to know that they took the time to highlight the information that I am interested in and have not wasted my time reading about skills and jobs that are not pertinent to my search. If you won't spend fifteen minutes rewriting a résumé that will interest me, then why should I spend my time reading your generic résumé?

You will notice I call it customizing your résumé. I am not suggesting starting over with a blank piece of paper each time. Highlight the part you want me to see and down play the irrelevant parts. If you are a technical writer and 20 years ago you sold real estate for three different companies, then lump it together in one line as: "sold residential real estate for local and national brokers." Down play it by combining the jobs into the 20 year bracket. This way you have not left a gap in time on your résumé that could raise suspicions.

You will also soon be reading about ways to turn a simple business card, essential for your successful job search, into mini résumés. Often it is not convenient to carry a full résumé with you and have it be in a condition to be proud to hand out. Not so with business cards; most athletic shorts even have a small key — and business card — pocket!

And pay special attention to the section titled Key Word Searches. If you have always wondered if your resume goes into a big black data base hole, be assured it does. So how do you get your resume to come to the top when a recruiter begins searching resumes? Read on.

6.0   Résumés

You've identified a company or a specific position in which you're interested. Next comes the résumé. Although it's not rocket science, for some reason the résumé seems to trip up countless veteran candidates we meet with. We won't go into pages and pages on résumés here, as there are a number of great resources out there on this topic which provide good templates you can use to craft your military-to-civilian résumé. Although not written specifically for veterans, one of my favorites is Tony Beshara's *Unbeatable Résumés*. I thought it would be fun, and enlightening, for you to see a veteran résumé in transition. The modified version that was handed to us. The changes and the final version of a typical veteran to private sector transition can be found at the end of this chapter.

Here we'll spend some time to give you an overview of the résumé process and insights we've gained from screening thousands upon thousands of résumés every year.

Many paths to success

This first point is really more of a disclaimer about résumé advice. During the course of the year, I sit on a lot of career coaching panels, comprised of staffing and recruiting experts from just about every industry imaginable. For the most part, the experts sitting on these panels generally agree on most career topics and the advice we give to participants at these events is usually pretty consistent. However, the one area that exposes differences of opinion is résumés. Each hiring manager has a particular style, format, and length they find most effective. And in many cases, there is no single right answer. Just know that you don't please all the recruiters all the time and that everyone, and I mean everyone, will have suggestions for changes. The most important thing is that you are proud of the résumé you submit and feel that it represents you very well. Next most important is that you have the skills needed to customize your résumé for every opening. More about that later.

The suggestions I provide below are from the vantage point of a private sector hiring manager and recruiter. As I mentioned earlier, my staff and I interview approximately 15,000 candidates every year, so you can imagine just how many résumés we have to screen before we even get to those interviews. Needless to say, when it comes to résumés, we have a pretty good idea as to what works, and what doesn't. Whichever format you use, please keep in mind that in many situations, the résumé will be the very first contact point a recruiter has with you, so its strategic importance cannot be underestimated. That document might be your only chance at making a first impression, so it's worth spending the time and effort upfront to get the job done right. Hit me with your best shot!

Getting started on your résumé

Before you start writing, you have to assemble all your building blocks – a list of all your positions and accomplishments in each of those positions. I have put a copy of this form on the *Job Won!* website (job-won.com) where you can work with it online or download it. You will see it asks about all the key information you will need to begin developing your résumé. The reason for leaving column is there not because the information should be on your résumé but it will come up in interviews and you need to have a concise answer. If you are interviewing for your first job out of the military most reasons will be "new orders."

As I said, I have also included an actual résumé rewrite in the back of this chapter. We changed the name of the veteran for confidentiality sake, but you will see the transformation from the original he handed in to us for our Jobs4Veterans classes, the written changes, and the final product. What a difference!

Dates	Job Title	Location	Duties/AOR	Accomplishments	Reason for Leaving

The accomplishments column is the most important one. This is where you list assignments you did that went above and beyond your job description, such as: outstanding performance, additional responsibilities you took on, and records you set. Think about things you did that had impact on your unit, team or organization. These are the things that employers really care about, and that will set you apart from the competition. The "Reason for Leaving" column might seem an odd category to include, especially since you never really left any position in the military – you simply went where your orders told you to go next. However, this will definitely come up for any jobs you had before or after your time in uniform. A good recruiter's job is to get a complete picture of you as a professional, and how you've moved and developed throughout your career. To that end, we need to know if your changing positions was due to positive factors such as promotions, educational opportunities or reassignments to get more experience.

If you were actually terminated, or left a position under less than ideal conditions, that reason needs to be logical and well-thought out – actually rehearsed. You can read about this in much more details in the interview training chapter.

Let's say you were in fact terminated or quit. Here's a few ways you could handle that situation:

- Although the job gave me some great exposure to a new industry, I realized it just wasn't a good fit for me.

- I was promoted into a new position that was not a good use of my skill sets.
- After five years on the job, I felt I had accomplished about all I could in that role, there was no upward mobility, and I was ready to move on.
- My manager and I talked it through and we both agreed it just wasn't working out. My strengths are in operations and the company really needed someone who could manage facilities. We parted on very good terms and I'm still in touch with my boss and lots of my colleagues at the company.

The last example above is particularly powerful, as it accomplishes a number of different things for you, and very nearly turns a negative situation into a positive:

1. Makes a termination sound more like it was your choice to resign.
2. Alleviates any concerns the interviewer might have had about personality conflict on the job.
3. Reinforces that by pointing out you maintain good relations with other employees still at the company.
4. Reiterates for the interviewer that you have a strong operations-based skill set, which is new position that you are discussing.

Objective statements

This is a real pitfall for most job seekers, and one of the most common errors we see. I so often see an objective like:

> *"Objective: a challenging position where I can use my military based skills as a leader and team player to grow and advance my career in a company that will appreciate my focus and hard work."*

The glaring problem here is you are telling me as the recruiter exactly what you are looking for in a job…and I could really care less. Never lose sight of the fact that I am considering hiring you not to make you happy and to fulfill your ambitions, but to do a job that I need done. This is all about me as the business owner or employer and my needs, not you and your goals. When I am reviewing hundreds of résumés, I am looking for the best candidates to do the work I need done. I do not care to read what are you looking for and I certainly am not considering how I can help you meet your goals. Also know that you are being hired to perform a job that will make me, the business owner and the firm's CEO, more money. I will hire the applicant that will make me the most net profit. If you are at all uncomfortable with this, then seriously consider working for a nonprofit. So instead, if the job description for the position you are applying for sounds like this:

> *"We are looking to hire a senior facilities manager for a very large warehouse system with a minimum 10 years' experience in worldwide facilities management in the defense industry……etc."*

And I come across a résumé with an objective that says:

> *"Objective: to use my 20 years of international Naval facilities management and facilities operations degree and MBA to help continue the dynamic growth of a large defense oriented firm."*

Which résumé will not only catch my attention but will jump off the page at me? Wow, this applicant is looking for the exact job that we are looking to fill. I will clearly read on and make sure the résumé validates all the points that the applicant made in his or her objective statements and odds are really good you will make the short list. You also make my job easier by the criteria I was looking for in a candidate jumped right off your résumé in the first sentence.

You just made my job much easier and I like you already!

Know that when you choose a résumé with an objective you are committing to rewriting and customizing your objective and your résumé for every job that you apply for. Thank heavens for computers today that will allow you to easily make minor changes and customize the objective statement on your résumé and match it as close as you can to your skill sets for every position. Put your résumé and the job description side-by-side, and see how many of the key criteria listed in the description are reflected on your résumé. Make the necessary adjustments and updates such that your résumé instantly tells the reader you have most of what that job description calls for.

> *Joan is someone I will always remember. She wrote to me after one of my TV segments, very angry that she had submitted her exact same résumé to, according to her, 2,000 job postings. Some of the jobs were clerical, some retail, and some marketing. Do you think her number one mistake might have been not focusing her résumé and the one version she used had missed all of them?*

If you are serious about a position that you are applying for, then commit to writing a customized résumé for each and every position or don't bother applying. If not, stop and ask yourself why you are applying in the first place.

But there is a place for a generic résumé. Unless you are writing a highly targeted résumé for a very specific job, you're better off not including any kind of objective statement at all since it may be misleading. It may be a casual encounter from someone at a networking event saying their company is doing a lot of hiring and they are happy to walk your résumé down to the HR Department. So there is no specific job to write an objective statement for and this company could hire you for several different career paths you are exploring. There will be time later to develop your specific position oriented objective statement and résumé. The amount of damage caused by a misguided or weak objective statement is worse and simply not worth the risk. In all my years of recruiting, I've never dinged a candidate because they didn't have an objective statement at the top of their résumé. When I'm reading a résumé, I'm going to make a decision about the candidate's fit for the job based on their accomplishments, skills, and experience, not based on someone telling me what they think I want to hear through an objective statement. The proof is in your work history, not your objective statement. Either your objective highlights your skills for the position or don't use one.

Availability date

If you're still on active duty, it's critical that you make it very clear to prospective employers when you will be available to start a new position. This doesn't mean you have to have your DD214 in hand before your first day on the job. Many veterans are actually able to start their new private sector jobs while still on terminal leave. Bottom line: the hiring manager doesn't care about the difference between your ETS date and the date you actually separate from the military. They only care about when you are actually able to start a new job without any additional military encumbrances or obligations. So include your availability date in your cover letter: March 16, 2017.

Learn to sell yourself

One of the most common concerns we hear from hiring managers is that veterans fail to adequately sell themselves, both in the interview, and on the résumé. Earlier we covered this concern. E.g., when a veteran writes and speaks in terms of "we" not "I." In the military you're trained from day one that your unit and the mission come first. Period. Understandably, any kind of bragging or self-promotion is highly frowned upon, and with good reason. In a conflict zone showboating can literally get you killed. And since this "we" has been drilled into your head for 20 or more years you will need to consciously avoid it.

Given that the military's entire ethos and culture is based around teamwork and unit cohesion, it's oftentimes extremely difficult for transitioning veterans to focus on themselves as an individual. However, that interviewer is looking to hire you, not your entire unit, not your entire platoon, and certainly not the entire Navy. You need to get comfortable using "I" and ditch the "we," at least for the time being.

Rich was a highly trained Navy SEAL that I was career coaching. He and his wife were ready to settle down and start a family and for him to transition into the private sector.

He was very sharp, professional, and confident but I had the hardest time getting him to talk about his specific skills and accomplishments. He answered every question with "we" or "our unit" or "my commander." I refused to give up and stopped him every time he should have said "I" and did not. Rich actually had to leave with a homework assignment, practice on his own, and come back. I had him write down on paper his personal skills and accomplishments that he could talk about (but that's another book specifically for Special Operations veterans) and then practice saying them starting with "I." This has worked for lots of veterans so you may consider the same exercise.

On the résumé this means highlighting the contributions and achievements directly attributable to you as an individual, not your unit. Go ahead and brag! Tell us how you were selected for special assignments. Highlight that you were in the top 10% of your graduating class. Make special mention of the fact that due to your initiative, readiness levels increased from 80% to over 95%, and that it was the highest ever achieved in your squadron. Recruiters aren't impressed by accolades your unit received, the fancy hardware you were entrusted with, or the details of each mission: we care about the contributions you as an individual made during your time in the military. The skills demonstrated by your contributions and achievements are what we want.

Once the job offer is signed and you're integrating into your new organization, it will be time to bring out those teamwork skills and camaraderie. And you will want to revert to the "we" or be very unpopular.

Quantify, quantify, quantify

Don't just tell the reader you're good, prove it! Nothing reflects confidence and professionalism more than data. Put a number on anything you can quantify – nothing jumps off the page like the $ and % symbols. And don't just slap a number on it; provide some context for the reader to understand the significance of that number. For example, don't just state that you increased your unit's readiness to

98%. Also mention that this is 5% above the standard for comparable units performing at even the highest level. You might also be able to extrapolate further, adding that this higher readiness level resulted in annual operating savings of approximately $300,000 due to reduced maintenance costs.

It is very important that you can quantify those accomplishments with actual facts and figures: percentages and/or dollar amounts. This data becomes more powerful on paper, as well as in the mind of the interviewer. "I saved money on personnel costs" is much less impressive than "My department came in 12% under budget on staffing costs, which saved the unit $189,000." Saving that kind of money is impressive!

Military and private sector companies have more in common than you might think. Both entities are focused on doing more with less. In the military, you create real value by increasing efficiency (which can include lower defect rates, process improvements, cost reductions, fewer man-hours required), increasing readiness, decreasing costs, etc. Those things all add real value to the bottom line. Know that you are being hired by a company to do one of two things: sell more of my product or cut my costs. Both lead directly to profit on the bottom line.

Living document

Your résumé is never done. Sorry, this is one project you will continue to revisit for the rest of your career. You will constantly update this document for the different positions and industries you are targeting. You will probably also walk away from each interview with new ideas to incorporate into the résumé – skills you had overlooked, accomplishments you hadn't mentioned, or stronger verbiage to better highlight and clarify your individual contributions. You'll have numerous different versions of your résumé. The first, and most important, is your "utility or generic résumé." As I said earlier, this version isn't targeted towards a specific industry or occupation; rather, it provides the most comprehensive overview of all your skills and experience. This is the version you always have in your portfolio, and that you could leave with any company, in case you don't have a version tailored specifically to their industry or open jobs. However, once you identify a particular job you'd like to pursue, you'll take that generic résumé and customize it to that job.

Key word searches

When a recruiter begins searching for candidates for positions he or she is filling, where do they start? With the job description. They identify the most important traits, trainings, education and/ or experiences that the ideal candidate will represent on their résumé. These become the (typically) five or six key words that they are searching for on all the résumés. Hence the "key word search." By using Applicant Tracking System (ATS) software, they can enter those five or six key words into their database and then search thousands of résumés in seconds, looking for those specific words. What happens next is that the résumés in the database that have all six words included pop up first, those with five of the words next, and so on. The recruiters of course first review the first group and then work their way down.

So you need to get as many of these key words into your résumé as you possibly can. The software even highlights the words on the résumé to make it really easy. It's always a guessing game, but you become as proficient at anticipating the key words as if you were the recruiter.

> *Jamie, a senior HR Manager, told me about a trick she thought was funny, yet effective. At the bottom of the résumé she has seen candidates key in (using a white font) words that may be used for key word searches that the candidate could not get into the résumé. Since they are white they do not show up on the résumé, but the software does read them. And if there might be geographical differences in describing job titles, try to use both version - call center and customer call center is an example.*

Proof reading

Obviously you are going to proof read carefully and use spell check. Also ask other people to proofread your résumé for spelling, grammatical, and typing errors. However, there's another critical step: print the résumé and proof read the hard copy again. Slight irregularities in font style, size, spacing, and other subtle formatting are often only visible on the hard copy. I can't tell you how often I see typos that slipped past the proofreader because they were only looking at the online version.

While you are having other people read your résumé, I suggest you also ask some people that you don't know all that well. Ask after they read it does it sound like the résumé describes someone that is accomplished, educated, and interesting? Would they like to meet this person if they could? It's a big plus if you can write your résumé in a way that recruiters want to call you in and meet with you.

Keep it simple

The résumé is not the place to demonstrate your creativity. It should be on quality plain white paper, normal photocopier stock (thickness), with a one-inch margin all around. It should be no more than two pages. I can mostly chart the last 10 years. Anything beyond 10 years is pretty much old and stale. If space becomes a problem, condense your work history as:

> *Various Administrative Positions in the Foreign Affair Department   1995-2005*

My font of choice is Calibri in 11 point size. This font is highly professional and classic, yet it also has a fresh, contemporary look. It's also a much more space-efficient font than both Arial and Times New Roman. And please don't put the résumé in any kind of binder, folder, or cover. I guarantee you, these do nothing but annoy the recruiter who has to pull them apart to get at the résumé. That fancy folder is going right in the trash. A nice, clean, professional résumé doesn't need any kind of gussying up.

Other key details

I recommend a two-page résumé unless there are extenuating circumstances like important articles you have written or relevant accomplishments that need more explanation. I don't want to read a book about you. If you're good at what you do, and very accomplished,

I'm going to want to read on to learn more. The exception of course is Federal/GovJOBS.gov, which will entail a much longer résumé.

Just the résumé please; do not include transcripts or letters of recommendation. If the hiring manager needs them, they'll ask for copies at the appropriate time. Do not add "References provided upon request" on the bottom of your résumé. You don't need to remind me. Much more on references later.

Education: the highest degree attained should be listed on top. Your MA would be listed first, with your BS/BA following underneath. Do not list an AA degree if you have a BS/BA – we only care where you finished college. Do not list your high school, even if you don't have any college experience. Listing a high school diploma will only draw more attention to the fact that you don't have a college degree. If you graduated fairly recently, be sure to also list any scholarships, awards, varsity sports, and student government positions you may have held.

Tell your story through your accomplishments, don't just regurgitate your job description or MOS. Hiring managers don't care so much about the responsibilities you were given, as they do about what you actually did with those responsibilities.

Hiring managers are impressed by students who worked during college to put themselves through school. It shows self-reliance, determination, and gives the impression of a down-to-earth hard worker. If you worked while you were in school, be sure to add a bullet point under the degree earned. It might look something like this:

Michigan State University
BS, Mechanical Engineering
Phi Beta Kappa honor society
Worked 20 hours per week throughout college to help fund my education

Plugging the gaps

The following is one of the most awkward (and deadly) conversations in an interview:

> *Recruiter: I see you have a one year gap here on your résumé. What have you been doing since you left your last position?*

> *Job seeker: Oh, nothing really. I've been looking for work the whole time.*

Result: You just shot yourself in the foot. You are damaged goods. And I don't mean the fact that you've been out of work for a year. It's a tough job market out there. For highly specialized occupations and senior management roles, the gap between paid positions can be significant. Good recruiters know this, so don't hold that against yourself. In this example, the fact that this person has been unemployed for a year wasn't a deal breaker. After all, they did make it to the interview stage. The red flag went up when it became obvious this person didn't take the initiative to use that time for personal development, like obtaining a quality volunteer job in your field (our Red Cross example earlier), an internship opportunity, or going back to school, or ideally, some combination of the two. Show that recruiter you're proactive, determined, and like to be kept busy. You have a high energy level as represented by all the additional skills and experience you've been accumulating since your last job.

Awards and recognition

You may have received a number of awards and recognition during your time in the military. We all know that some of these are a bit of fluff – they're handed out to just about everyone in the unit for showing up and completing the mission. However, others are very hard-won and extremely prestigious. Make sure you list these honors and give a brief (one line) explanation of what you did to deserve the award. You could also mention how few are given out each year, or what percentage of service members even qualify. Remember, anything you can attach a number to becomes much more powerful.

I understand there is a correlation between people who earn their Eagle Scout for Boy Scouts or Golden Arrow Award for Girl Scouts and those who serve their country in the military. If you are one of these then play it up like crazy on your résumé. Why you ask? Doing all the work, and excelling to earn the highest award in a well-known organization during the most awkward teenage years of any one's life is very commendable. If you can accomplish that, I think you can pretty much accomplish anything you set your mind to as an adult.

Cover letters

As with résumés, opinions also differ when it comes to cover letters. Some recruiters tell me they read the cover letter and if of interest go on to the résumé and as many others tell me they read the résumé and if of interest go back to the cover letter. I am in the latter camp As someone who screens hundreds of résumés every year, I have some pretty strong opinions about cover letters and it seems most applicants don't understand the reason for them. With regards to cover letters, please know that cover letters are suggested for good reasons and they have a purpose. Remember earlier when I said you should try to use your résumé to make yourself interesting? A good cover letter can help do that. It has three parts and they are the three paragraphs:

1. The first paragraph tells me what job you are applying for and how you heard about it. Don't just say the Marketing opening. I may have 20 marketing jobs open. Tell me the specific job number if is there one, the job description, Senior Marketing Manager for the Latin Market, or at least tell me the marketing job advertised in the *Wall Street Journal* on August 14. Now I know where to start. Hopefully you have networked well, as we discuss later and you can add "John Jones, Senior Marketing Manager in the Atlanta regional office is my uncle and he suggested that my skills were a great match for this new opening." You just got behind the fire wall by mentioning a relative that works there!

2. The second paragraph is why you feel you are a great match and interested in the position. You are doing the recruiter's work and we like you for that. Here you can use the same

thought process on writing an objective on your résumé. Briefly discus how your skill sets and experience match up with the key job requirements in the job description. Hmmm, got my attention.

3. The third paragraph tells me how I can most directly contact you via cell phone or email and even that, if you have my contact information (which is rare these days), you will give me call on Tuesday at 10:00 if that is convenient for me. I might ignore that or wait for the call but it does show initiative and confidence.

Know that I've never hired a candidate on the strength of a cover letter – the résumé is the real workhorse in the hiring process. The key reason for a cover letter is to let me see if you can communicate clearly and briefly make your key points. Do you write well? Just like in a phone interview, I am testing your verbal communications skills this is the written test. Do you stick to the subject or ramble? Is your writing boringly professional or does some of your personality come through?

Again, make sure there are no typos or grammatical or formatting errors. This speaks volumes regarding your attention to detail.

There are numerous cover letter templates available online. If the application specifically requests a cover letter, do not skip this step. Follow the instructions carefully and provide them everything they ask for. If they don't ask for one, do it anyway. It shows you have put more effort into applying for the job then others who just forwarded a résumé.

Résumé pitfalls

How do you make your résumé stand out? First, take extreme care not to use the same tired, vague, and over-played pseudo-business language other candidates often employ. Remember, recruiters and HR professionals have to screen hundreds of résumés each week – please do them the courtesy of not submitting another "me too" résumé. Here are the worst offending trite terms to avoid according to a survey from Harris Poll and CareerBuilder:

1. Best of breed
2. Go-getter
3. Think outside of the box
4. Synergy
5. Go-to person
6. Thought leadership
7. Value added
8. Results-driven
9. Team player
10. Bottom line
11. Hard worker
12. Strategic thinker
13. Dynamic
14. Self-motivated
15. Detail-oriented
16. Proactive
17. Track record

Candidates are particularly tempted to overload an already watery objective statement or candidate summary at the top of their résumé with these terms. Using language like this tells the recruiter you are either unimaginative or trying to mitigate a lack of real content and accomplishments on your résumé.

According to the same study, here are some of the most effective terms used on résumés today. You will see they are mostly active verbs which add energy to your communications, especially your résumé:

1. Achieved
2. Improved
3. Trained/mentored
4. Managed
5. Created
6. Resolved
7. Volunteered
8. Influenced
9. Increased/decreased

10. Ideas
11. Negotiated
12. Launched
13. Revenue/profits
14. Under budget
15. Won

The difference is stark: the first group of phrases are vague and "hollow," or what I would call "fluff." They lack specificity and can't really be verified. The second group is much more concrete, direct, and could probably be backed up by data, if required.

Trevor's top 10 résumé slip-ups

My son Trevor was, until recently, Director of our Executive Search Division. He reviews résumés from very high level applicants and has made his own list of slip-ups:

1. Mismatched fonts
2. Block text instead of bullet points
3. "Creative" formats
4. Functional or hybrid résumés
5. Bland, generic or "brown-noser" objective statements
6. "Fluff" skills instead of hard skills
7. Laundry list work experience descriptions
8. Use of weak verbs
9. References included
10. High school and AA degree listings

phil-osophy 101 7

This is the place to stop and talk about paying it forward. We recently had the honor of dedicating the Manpower Lobby at San Diego Hospice in honor of a dear friend of the Katz and Blair families who passed away after receiving great care from the hospice. When we were touring the hospice building, we were struck by how all of the naming opportunities were family names. There were no corporate sponsors. Hospice has always been generously supported with gifts from families in honor of their loved ones. As a big believer in cause marketing—the use of marketing dollars to support nonprofits rather than just philanthropic dollars (which are drying up quickly), we decided to name the lobby under our corporate name. In my comments at the luncheon, I told the crowd that as corporate leaders, we need to think about paying it forward by supporting services that our employees need now rather than after their need of service.

In fact, within one month, a Manpower staff person was sitting in the hospice lobby, checking in on her very ill mother, when she looked up and realized that the company she worked for was a tangible hospice supporter. She couldn't find the words to describe how proud she was of the company where she worked.

This is a long way to get to the importance of "paying it forward" in our personal life and in our job searches. The friend who called his father on my behalf when I was looking for work was doing me a big favor with no expected payback. You can be assured I will forever go out of my way to share any contacts I have and to support him in any way I can when he asks or needs assistance.

During your job search, go out of your way to help others, just as you would like them to help you. If you hear of an opportunity that's not right for you, stop and think about whom it might be right for and contact them immediately. That's paying it forward.

Phil

7.0   It's Time to Apply

Inside the HR Manager's mind

It's important to understand the HR Manager's or business owner's role in this process. In theory, this is the person who will make or break your chances of landing a job at their company, right? In a large organization, their role is purely administrative. Chances are they are squirreled away in an office far from the shop floor and away from the heart of the company's operations. In the military, you may have served with this person at a previous command but that is likely not the case here.

Unfortunately this also means the person responsible for your application, the HR Manager, or a junior HR Generalist or Assistant, probably knows very little about the actual job for which they are screening you. Even though you may be the ideal candidate for the job, the HR Manager's lack of direct experience in your field could cause them to overlook your résumé. And it's not their fault. Most HR Managers are trying the best they can, working underneath a pile of other responsibilities. The vast majority of most HR Managers' time is not spent on the fun sexy stuff like recruiting and talent management. That's only about 25% of their job. Most of their time is spent on tedious administrative and legal duties. The hiring process is often just another deadline that gets inserted into their already overloaded schedules.

I realize I'm making some huge assumptions here, but I've met enough HR Managers in my time to see some very clear trends. By helping you get inside the mindset of the typical overworked HR Manager, you'll be better positioned to leverage the recruitment process to your advantage. I'm probably not making myself any HR Manager friends here, but I feel these are some important things you need to know about the mindset of the typical HR gatekeeper. Here's a peek inside their world:

1. Many HR Managers did not intend for a career in HR; it was something they ended up in. Unlike Finance, Accounting, Engineering, or IT, most professionals working in the HR field did not go to college or graduate school for a career in human resources. Apart from some industry credentials, such as the PHR and SPHR certificates they might have picked up later in life, most HR professionals don't have an undergraduate or graduate degree specifically in HR.

2. Most HR Managers are overworked. They are trying to do the best job they can, but they probably don't have enough resources (i.e., staff) in their department to get everything done that is asked of them within a 40-hour work week.

3. Some companies see the HR department as a cost center not a profit center. Human Resources is an administrative function; it costs money to run the HR department, but HR does not generate any revenue. Therefore companies try to pare it down as much as possible. But many more innovative organizations see HR as a strategic function that can help drive the company forward. These are the companies you want to work for.

4. The HR Manager's job is one with many major responsibilities, most of which if not done exactly right, can cost the company a ton of money in lawsuits and fines.

5. Most HR work is not fun. Much of the work that goes on in a large HR department is painful, tedious paperwork. Their days are consumed with the administrative burdens of employment law, compliance, audits, benefits administration, workers compensation issues, and the like. It is actually very important work; one small mistake on a filing form can literally cost a company millions. It can be extremely stressful!

Now that we have an appreciation for the challenges under which many HR Managers toil inside large companies, here's how it affects the HR mindset:

1. You are not their priority: they have a million other things on their desk, many of which are much more important than responding to your email.
2. Candidates are constantly hounding them: we see an average of 250 candidates responding to just a single job opening. If an HR Manager for a large firm has 10 open jobs at any given time, you can imagine the amount of phone and email traffic they get swamped with.
3. As much as they would like to, they may know nothing about the job they are hiring for: as mentioned earlier, they may not be able to answer your technical questions about the role, because they are just the ones who posted the job description, as approved by the Line Manager, to whom this role actually reports.
4. They too are frustrated with delays in the process. Here's a scenario to illustrate: a good HR Manager may have screened 50 candidates and forwarded a solid crop of semifinalists to the Line Manger (note that applicants 51-200 probably don't even get a look). The Line Manager is supposed to review the résumés and advise the HR Manager whom he would like to meet. However, the Line Manager has since experienced equipment failure on one of the production lines, and hasn't had time to check email to review those résumés. This leads to the communications back-up, and why candidates say they never hear back from HR. And this is an example of a fairly straightforward hiring process; each additional person involved adds another potential for delays.
5. HR Managers are extremely risk averse: if I worked under these conditions, I would be too. Their jobs are surrounded by more legal requirements and penalty threats than just about any other executive. This means they are forced to move slowly and cautiously in everything they do.
6. Risk aversion naturally encourages HR Managers to protect the status quo. Change is scary.

7. Hiring a new employee means breaking the status quo: it is bringing an unknown entity, inside the company they are charged with protecting. They can't be sure how you'll turn out. What if you're a disastrous employee who gets the company into a big lawsuit? Yes, even HR Managers can get fired if they recommend weak candidates for positions.

8. HR Managers are preprogrammed to screen candidates out, not in. As a result of all these factors, the HR mindset is, "the answer is always going to be no, until you can convince me otherwise, or until my boss says yes."

Networking your way around HR

I know this is a pretty bleak picture, and I sincerely apologize to all the hardworking, underpaid and underappreciated HR Managers out there. However, this stereotype is very real, and it's highly likely you will encounter it during the course of your job search. So how do you overcome it? You network your way around it, by connecting with other individuals inside the organization who can go to bat for you. If you can build relationships with other people of influence who work at the company, they can dramatically increase your chances of getting an interview.

Here's a list of job titles for people who may be able to assist you getting inside:

- Sales Manager
- Business Development Manager
- Recruiter
- Regional Director
- Talent Acquisition
- Talent Management
- Community Relations
- Government Relations
- Veterans Outreach Specialist

The people in these positions are much better to network with than HR. Their jobs depend upon their ability to be visible in the local business community, build relationships, and get the company's name out there. As such, the people who apply for and excel in these jobs tend to be high-energy extroverts, not risk-averse introverts. Their job revolves around talking with people outside the company, so they are much more likely to give you a warm reception. Besides, their job probably requires them to make dozens of similar cold calls every day. They get paid to reach out to strangers, just as you are doing. Similarly, they also have to deal with rejection a lot, so they are more likely to lend a sympathetic ear to your request. The people in these roles can provide valuable information about the company, and may be able to connect you with the actual hiring manager, not just the HR contact.

Seven times the chance

When another employee at the firm approaches the HR Manager and says: here's the résumé of someone I think is a really good candidate for this job opening, you've increased by a factor of 7 your chances of getting hired. You've effectively just unblocked a number of logjams in the hiring process. You are now a known entity to the HR Manager through your association with that employee. Furthermore, they have just been saved a ton of résumé sourcing and screening work. Since you've come recommended, the HR Manager also knows there's a good chance you will do well through the rest of the hiring process, thereby making them look good. Through your networking efforts you have effectively mitigated a huge amount of risk for the HR Manager, and that will undoubtedly make them very happy.

Job descriptions. 75% is close enough

Great candidates are often discouraged from applying for a position, because they see that they don't already have 100% of the skills and qualifications listed in the job description. My suggestion here: if you identify a job opportunity that you are *really* excited about and you have *at least* 75% of the job requirements, go ahead and apply. What have you got to lose? And your military experience is going to be a huge bonus to any company, so it will stand out.

Most employers write job descriptions using what I call the "kitchen sink" approach: they dump everything in there, whether it's essential or not. Sure, it would be nice if your IT Support Manager could also speak four languages and cover for the Accounting guy when he's on leave. But are foreign language and accounting skills *really* required to get the IT Support job done? Of course not! This example is extreme, but it highlights my point: many of the items employers put in their job descriptions aren't actually core to the position. If they find someone with a great personality and a positive attitude who has most of the skills and experience they require, they're going to hire him/her.

Your attitude just might win you the job!

A great personality and soft skills can compensate for other skills and experience, which according to the job description, you might be lacking. I can't tell you how many times I've seen the guy with the weaker résumé get the job because he was able to project energy and enthusiasm in the interview. Managers hire people they are excited about working with; use your personality to your advantage. We all get much more pragmatic when we meet a candidate we are excited about and rationalize that they can quickly learn whatever skill it is that they don't currently have.

The hiring process flow

In many organizations, particularly larger ones, the hiring process is coordinated by HR. This isn't completely dissimilar to how the military works in the orders process, except civilians aren't usually dealing with project rotation dates or the end of active obligated service. Here's how a company might go from identifying that they need to hire someone, to actually bringing that person on board:

1. Line manager (say Engineering Supervisor) realizes he needs to add one more person to his team in order to meet an increase in customer orders.
2. Line manager's supervisor approves request and sends authorization to the HR department to commence the recruiting and hiring process.

3. HR department contacts the Line Manager and takes down list of the job requirements, which HR will then craft into a job description.

4. Once approved by the Line Manager, HR then posts the position description to the company's website and waits a couple of weeks for the applications to come in, then reviews the résumé, and contact the top 10 candidates for a phone screen.

5. The top five from the phone screen will be invited in to interview with the HR Manager. The process continues until the supervisor selects his choice.

The scenario above is very typical for a medium to large-sized company that elects to manage the recruitment process in-house instead of hiring a professional staffing or search firm. The larger the company, the longer this process can take. Big organizations have more controls, procedures, paperwork, and people involved in the process, all of which decrease the company's responsiveness to your application. You will need to have patience, especially with large, public sector (government) organizations. You can expect many positions in law enforcement or with federal agencies to take over 18 months from your initial application to signing your offer letter.

Online applications

As mentioned earlier, the internet doesn't hire people...people hire people. Chances are you will not land your next career through an online job application, but through a connection you make through a real live human being. However, the online application process is still a key component we need to address here.

We counsel job seekers that the internet is great for researching companies and networking with individuals, but rarely ever does the internet alone get you hired. And that includes online applications. They are simply a box to check in the hiring process, particularly for large companies or any government agency. Quite frequently, the job is already filled before it's even posted. As I write this, we're working with a government agency on a senior real estate position. We proactively submitted a candidate before the hiring requisition was even approved. The hiring company had several meetings with our candidate, and made a decision to hire before the HR department was posting the position online. However, the agency's policy mandates all positions be posted online for at least seven days, so a number of unfortunate candidates wasted their time completing an online application that went straight into a black hole: our guy already had the job. In many cases such as this, the organization is only posting the job online due to internal policy requirements, public relations purposes, or government Equal Employment Opportunity Commission (EEOC) requirements.

Does this mean you should ignore online applications altogether? Definitely not. Your job search is really only starting after you click submit on the online application. As in the case above, you can't control when or even if your application will ever get read by a human. I suspect millions each year are never viewed, despite the fact that they can take hours upon hours to complete. So why bother at all?

Job boards and online applications are not the end point; they are actually the opening salvo. Now that you've seen a position posted, you know who is hiring, what the position was, where it was, what it pays, and what skills and experience the employer is looking for. Now you know exactly what organizations to target: if they hired for that position once, there's an extremely good chance they will hire for something similar in the future. Networking activities position you to be "that guy" with the inside track in my example above. Next time, you will be a known entity already in position before they even know they need to hire.

You need to eliminate every possibility for the hiring manager to say "no" to your advancements. Usually when you make contact with a recruiter at a large company, they will try to turn you away by saying all job applications are taken online. To which you will politely respond: "that sounds good. I've already completed the online application and uploaded a résumé. I was hoping to speak with someone about next steps in the process. Who would you recommend I speak with?

Here are some key things to remember when completing online job applications:

1. Proof reading: before clicking the "submit" button on any online application or document, print and proofread it in hard copy. If there is no "print" button easily identifiable onscreen, simply take a screen shot, paste it into your word processing software, and print the image from there. As mentioned in the résumé section, you'll be amazed how small errors that are nearly invisible on screen suddenly become obvious in hard copy.

2. Text boxes: I advise opening your word processing software, typing all your answers there, and then copying and pasting them into the text boxes of the online application. The word processing software will give you much more control over formatting, grammar, and spellchecking. It also allows you to save a soft copy for your records from which you can copy/paste for future applications.

3. Sentence structure: always write in complete sentences, and use all the necessary punctuation.

4. Never leave any box blank: it's much safer to write N/A, should that question not apply to you. And never write "see résumé" for any question either. That response looks lazy. Take the time to fully answer each question.

5. Salary: many online applications will ask you for either your minimum salary requirements to take a new job or for salary figures from each of your prior positions. Conventional wisdom is to put "open" or "negotiable" in this box. Instead, let's not waste anyone's time: the hiring manager knows exactly how much he or she has budgeted for the position and you probably know the bare minimum salary you need to live comfortably enough. With a little research, you can probably find some good compensation data out there for that occupation in that region of the country. If you're confident that you have an excellent track record and will hit the ground

running, then you can probably go up to 20% above the top salary quartile for that job. Any higher than that and you may price yourself out. Answering with a low-ball figure will only create an anchor point and weaken your position when it comes to actual salary negotiations. A bargain basement salary figure also signals to the recruiter that you either don't have strong skills or lack confidence in your abilities. You are not contractually held to any salary figure you put on the application unless it's a government agency, there probably will be some negotiation.

6. Location: conventional advice also says that in order to maximize your chances, answer this question with "open." Again, don't waste anyone's time: if you know you need stay in the area where you now live because that's where all your family lives, then fill in the box with the city. Don't write "Southern California region" unless you really are okay commuting within the region every day, because that could very well be what you get. The recruiter is smart enough to know the area. However, if you are unattached and truly are open to relocating just about anywhere in the country, then by all means, go ahead and answer "open." The more flexibility you have, the better your odds of getting hired.

7. Full disclosure: always be 100% honest. If you have some kind of felony conviction on your record, even from way back when, you need to declare it on the online application. You don't want something like this coming back to bite you later in the process. Make sure you read up on the laws in your state for having criminal records expunged. In some states, anything older than seven years can be sealed. It's not the same as having the record erased, but it certainly helps. There's a wealth of advice online and some very good books with strategies for working around a criminal record in your job hunt. After listing the type and date of the conviction, you can also add "would like to discuss further at interview." This shows you've got nothing to hide, and it will give you an opportunity to shed some positive light on the situation, with a quick explanation of what the experience taught you. Don't let it hold you back from pursuing your dream career! Also

know that convictions in a military court will not necessarily show up if the company runs a civilian background check. If you have any concerns about what an employer might see if they run a background check on you, go ahead and run one on yourself first. You can pull a DMV report quite easily, and a background check on yourself can be done online for as little as $15. However, more extensive checks that go back farther in time and cover more states and counties will probably be more expensive. If you've moved around a lot, it's worth investing in the more comprehensive check.

Once your application is spotless and you've clicked "submit," what's next? This is where your ground game commences. The online application is sent off into the cyber ether, and you begin networking to build relationships with influential people inside the organization.

Small to medium size businesses approach

Small to medium size businesses have very similar processes but may be a bit less intense. You may be meeting with the actual business owner. They are adding employee number two to a company of 25 and every hire is very important. A bad hire can literally derail their entire company. Here, personal connections are very important. "This veteran has all the skills I need but is he someone I want to be with 60 hours a week?" If you feel you are right for the job then your assignment is to make you the best choice. Smaller companies are very much like families – be the favorite son or daughter, not the hated brother in law.

A few other key features of smaller businesses
- The company may be owned by Veterans.
- You will be expected to multi-task and jump in and help every department when needed.
- The firm may be cash strapped at some time and you may need to be "understanding."
- A small business is where you can learn new skills.

- The personality and leadership style of a business owner drives the corporate culture of the company.
- You may have an opportunity to get options in the business and the possibility of striking it rich.

There are advantages and negatives to both large firms and small ones. Only you know which is right for you at this time in your career.

phil-osophy 101   8

When you get called in for a job interview, you deserve a pat on the back. Just getting the interview means you've successfully overcome significant hurdles to reach the BIG moment. Now let's make sure you shine!

Job seekers make the common assumption that an interview is an opportunity for the employer to grill the applicant, try to catch them off guard with trick questions, or ask subliminal questions intended to probe their inner soul. The candidate assumes that since the interviewer called the meeting, the candidate has to sit there, "take it," and hopefully survive the inquisition.

Not true.

I want you to take control of every interview as if you called the meeting.

Think of it this way. You've worked really hard to get this interview. You've crafted a world-class résumé. You've networked like crazy. You've followed up on leads until your own mother thinks you're verging on being a pest. Now, the big job interview arrives and you, and most others, think you should take all the cues from the interviewer. It's their office. They called you and set the meeting time. They have the job you want.

That makes perfect sense, but I want you to think about the interview from a different perspective. Think of it from the interviewer's perspective: "I need to fill this position. My superiors are judging me on how fast I find the right candidate to hire. I want the person I am interviewing to come in here prepared to sell me on why they are the best person for this job. Don't make me pull it out of you. Hit me over the head. Wow me with your talents, energy and experience and how they apply to this exact position. Show me you are someone I would enjoy working with and that you understand the culture of our company. And most of all, tell me that you want the job!"

If you ever walk out of an interview thinking, "I never got to mention my experience at ABC or how my volunteer work at the YWCA was pertinent to the job," or anything else that would have shown you are a better candidate for the job, then shame on you. Don't come out of an interview with, "But she never asked me about..." Yes, it is okay to bring with you a list of points you want to make in the interview. In fact, it shows you are very prepared. I want you to walk out of the meeting thinking, "Dang, I made all my points, I hit on all cylinders, and if they don't select me, there was nothing else I could have done." This is true whether you have a professional HR person conducting the interview (they will appreciate your initiative) or a small business owner or department supervisor who is perhaps less prepared and more nervous than you. Unless you're ready to seize the day, the interview will be a disaster, with failed expectations and disappointment on both sides of the desk.

Regardless of how experienced or deft a job interviewer is, it's important, maybe critically so, for you to take charge of the meeting. But make sure you do it in a nice, polite, respectful way. Walk into the room and begin the conversation with pleasantries: how nice it is to meet the interviewer, what a beautiful view they have from their office, how excited you are to discuss the open position.

When the interviewer asks you, in one form or another, "Tell me about yourself," I want you to hear, "Why should I hire you? Why are you the perfect candidate and for this job?" Do not say, "What do you want to know?" Be ready to share your elevator pitch – or some germane version of it. Be confident. Be concise. Smile.

Think of an interview as the ultimate sales presentation and you are the product you are selling. This is your moment. It is time to sell yourself, your experience, your education, your qualifications. Dig deep into the responsibilities of the job, and more than anything else, reach out and grab the job by making it clear that you're absolutely the best possible candidate. You want to be proactive, engaging, dynamic, self-assured, and deeply interested in the job.

Yes, you need to pace yourself. The interviewer needs to think they are in control. They probably think they should lead the interview since in their mind they invited you to the meeting. Let them think they are guiding the meeting and be respectful. I want you to be able to highlight your strengths and make sure you get your points across. Hear and react to what the interviewer asks you, showing that you are a good listener, but make sure you ask questions as well. You know what aspects about you the interviewer needs to know. Make sure you weave them throughout the conversation.

And at the end of the perfect interview, you want the interviewer to think there is no other candidate for the job. You want to set the bar so impossibly high that potential employers think they'd be fools not to hire you. And, of course, they would be.

8.0   Interviewing

"It's okay to fail, but never okay to give up."
    ANONYMOUS

"During job interviews, when they ask, 'What is your worst quality,' I always say, 'Flatulence.' That way I get my own office."
    DAN THOMPSON

"So many people out there have no idea what they want to do for a living, but they think that by going on job interviews they'll magically figure it out. If you're not sure, that message comes out loud and clear in the interview."
    TODD BERMONT

Nobody likes interviewing
Katherine Hepburn once opined that death would be a great relief. Why? "No more interviews," she replied.

Hepburn, of course, was referring to the agony and tedium of being endlessly queried as a movie star and celebrity. Still, most of us can relate — at least a little bit. We tend to feel the same way about job interviews.

For you, as someone who has likely never had to interview for a position because someone in the military told you where to go and what your next job would be, it may seem even more imposing. The good news? No one will be screaming in your face. The bad news, they may talk behind your back. But that's great! Your military experience has prepared you for this.

It may come as a surprise to some that HR professionals and business owners often dislike conducting interviews almost as much as job candidates. Imagine spending entire days speaking with tense job candidates, trying to be warm and witty, open and friendly, while at the same time probing for information or clues the candidate may not be willing to provide. It can feel a bit like an inquisition — on both sides — but until someone comes up with a better way of doing things, this is HR's best and only option.

An interview of some type is necessary for every job before someone can be hired. This is where the pedal hits the metal. It's the only direct way for employers to assess job candidates, up close and personal. Do they truly live up to the reputation and image presented in their cover letter, résumé, and references? How do they handle themselves? What do they look like? Are they likeable in person? Would I want to work with them? Would I want to have lunch with them? Are they right for the job?

That's why job interviews are so dreaded. There's a lot riding on what happens during a job interview; a career can be made or sunk, depending on the outcome. Candidates all tend to sweat bullets, some literally when they are interviewed. Mostly because they don't feel prepared and have no idea what is going to be thrown at them.

Of course, there are a few nifty tricks to faring well in a job interview and I'll cover some of them with you in this chapter, along with a few caveats and cautionary tales. But more important, I'll show you how to prepare so that you know generally what to expect in any civilian interview—and how to have the right responses firmly in mind. Maybe even go so far as to be comfortable and enjoy the experience.

Job interviews come in many shapes and sizes. I'm going to focus on the two most important types: the informational interview and the job interview. Let's start with the informational interview, which necessarily comes first, often long before a job interview. Do the first well and the second follows much more easily.

Informational interviews

Throughout this book, I have talked about the value of networking — the process that never ends, even when you have the perfect job. Again, it should begin before you get out of the military. The informational interview is the fundamental core of networking. Simply put, it means sitting down with someone to discuss one of three things: your interest in the company where that person works, their industry, or their own career path. You can do this years before you leave military service, or anytime really. You should start this part of your search now.

You may or may not know this person. Effective use of networking will get you in front of lots of people you don't know, but who you think can help you learn more about those three key categories. We're talking here about seeking "career option advice," which sounds a lot less desperate than "help me find a job." You are meeting with people as equals with no rank involved, discussing each other's past, current, and future jobs. Typical topics are about how the industry is going, why they chose their career path, and about the company they work for. Remember, you are not interviewing for a job, but if the possibility pops up, jump on it. You may have suggestions for them from your experiences. It is very appropriate to wind up the discussion asking who else in the company, or the industry, do they think you should speak with. It's "who do you know that they know" in its best form.

These referrals are the quickest, least threatening way to get in front of a potential decision maker at their company or another company. The person you are meeting with for an informational interview probably is not hiring at the time you meet. However he or she can still make a huge difference in your career search and ultimate success.

Some people balk at this notion. They ask why they should waste their time meeting with people who have no jobs to offer and may not influence the hiring decisions where they work. That's a bad presumption. Here's why:

First and foremost, anyone and everyone can make a difference in your job search. You might not know who will be instrumental, how, or when, but you can be sure that sitting in front of a computer perusing classifieds and employment boards will never get you where you want to be. You want to be in front of people, discussing your career interests, and gathering information, advice, leads, and actionable tips from them and playing your veteran card while it still works. You are asking for a chunk of their time to learn from them about their industry, their company, and/or their own career.

There's an amusing line I sometimes hear quoted by business people: "I know that half of all my advertising dollars are a waste. I just don't know which half until I spend them."

The same holds true for informational interviews. Probably half, if not more, of informational interviews are in fact a waste of your time and the time of the person who has graciously agreed to meet with you. Which informational interview will help and which will not? Like the trenchant quote, it's an enduring conundrum. You don't know the answer, so let's learn and prepare together.

Phil Kendro, who has been a great help to me with advice for this book, swears that more than 90% of the people he reached out to via LinkedIn, cold emails, mutual connections, etc. have accepted his invite to meet. Use your veteran's card: you earned it!

When someone asks for five minutes of my time, I snicker inside. Nothing happens in any meeting that is five minutes long. How naïve do they think I am? I am often tempted to say yes to the "five minutes," confirm the five minutes, and then hold them to it when they arrive. Bet they would never use that five minutes phrase again!

A more reasonable time to request is 30 minutes. It's not asking for a lot of time but some very meaningful dialogue can happen in half an hour. So why not ask for it upfront? If the meeting seems to be going well, meaning they are enjoying the conversation, learning from it or feeling like they are being helpful, they may be comfortable extending the time.

I am always impressed when someone I am meeting with stops the conversation to acknowledge our time is up and ask if it is alright to continue. If they ask, I usually give them more time. If they don't ask then they are assuming they can stay as long as they would like and I find that disrespectful. They asked for the meeting, they should manage the time.

Preparation

Everything starts with preparation. Over the years, I've often been asked, "What is the number one mistake most job seekers make when they meet with you for an informational interview?" My answer is quick and easy: "it's lack of preparation!"

Here is a typical scenario. It should give you some insight not just into what you need to do and say in an interview, but also what's going through the mind of the HR person.

I limit myself to one informational interview per day, otherwise it would be a full-time job. The person, whom I typically don't know, is looking for advice and guidance on finding a job, a little more direct than "career option advice." Since our company does nothing but put people in jobs, I am a great candidate with whom to meet. My assistant now has them go to the Job-Won.com website and download and read *Strategies for Success,* which outlines the basics of the job search. She does this because she wants them to have a fair chance with me, and being prepared is the most important piece of the puzzle.

Make sure to preface any request with the fact that you are a veteran looking to transition into a civilian industry. Remember how I mentioned that at least 50% of informational interviews are likely to be a waste of your time. The percentage is a whole lot higher for the interviewer. That's an important point to bear in mind. The interviewer is committing time in their busy day to participate in what will likely be, from their point of view, a non-productive use of time. It is incumbent upon you to try to make it as productive a meeting as possible.

Your military experience may both help and hinder you in the informational interview. You may be used to very direct interactions but that's not always the case in the civilian sector. These things often start with small-talk or a "getting to know you" phase where family, education, etc., are discussed before getting into the meat of the interview.

Someone like me would be the ultimate informational interview. We specialize in hiring people, we work with HR representatives of major companies and small businesses throughout the community, and we hear about job openings long before they are posted.

You don't want to blow such an opportunity. If someone uses a chit, or pulls a string to get an informational interview with me, they should be prepared for both their presentation to me and for my honest feedback. I do not balk at telling someone what they did wrong or need to do better. On the plus side, my observations are meant as friendly advice intended to help someone avoid the same mistake during a real job interview.

> *Roger, the son of a good friend who had just graduated from college, was having a devil of a time finding a job. My assistant escorted him in to my office and I did a double take—he was chewing gum. I asked him about it and he was very embarrassed and quickly said he had meant to "spit it out," (interesting choice of words in an interview) but had forgotten. As we talked more, I stopped him mid-sentence and asked him if he realized how many times he had cracked his knuckles in the short time we had been meeting. Right as he was saying he doesn't crack his knuckles, unconsciously he cracked them. Now he was embarrassed a second time. I sternly told him if he had been an applicant for a job with my company, I would have thrown him out the second I realized he was chewing gum. Likewise he would have been escorted*

out because of an unconscious irritating habit of cracking his knuckles.

These are two habits I would not expect from someone with a military background, but watch out for your version of this behavior which may be, standing at attention or generally being very uncomfortable. Ask friends, wives or husbands —they will tell you?

Better he learn the error of his ways from me, a neutral observer, than to screw up an interview for the job of his dreams. I never knew what happened to that kid because, surprise, I never heard from him again. If you have nervous habits, get them under control before the interview. No matter what your education, experience, or skill, they will most likely kill your job opportunity. The only exception I can think of are engineers who have very specific, hard-to-find skills.

Another thing to avoid is wearing your uniform to an informational interview. You'll want to dress for the job you want, not the job you have. Be very cognizant what folks who work in the industry regularly wear to work and match them.

Just like in a job interview, the job seeker should take immediate charge of the informational interview. After all, you asked for the meeting, so you should assume control of it. And don't be afraid to open with your current military status and when you separated or plan to separate.

Usually, the conversation begins with pleasantries like, "Thanks so much for taking the time to meet with me. Jane has told me so much about you and Manpower." Blah, blah, blah. We've all heard and said such things. They're conversational lubricant, necessary to get things going and should be quickly followed by an explanation of why the person has asked to meet me, what they want to talk about, and how I can help.

All too often, however, I've found job seekers to be alarmingly reticent, as if I'm supposed to know what we're going to talk about or the goals for the meeting. A rough beginning can be a case of nerves or uncertainty on the part of the job seeker, both completely natural and understandable, but it's still not acceptable. Now is not the time to appear confused and flustered; now is the time to be confident and forceful (in a nice way). You know why you're there. Let the other person (me) know too.

When a job seeker doesn't grab initial hold of a meeting, after an awkward silence, I tend to take charge. And I usually start with the same question: "What can I do for you?"

When I meet with someone as a favor, I don't want to intimidate them or put them on the spot. On the other hand, I don't go out of my way to make them feel comfortable and at home. This is an opportunity for them to rehearse their interview skills, not learn them. It's like a two-person play. I know my lines. I expect the other actor to know theirs.

I always seat the other person across from my desk. And yes, I have a large "I-am-the-boss" kind of desk. It's actually a piece of art, nice to look at, but it also serves a couple of important functions in meetings like this. It is a physical barrier between me and the job seeker, a visual power play that establishes the hierarchy in the room. I also have a couch and chairs in my office. They're nearby and quite comfortable. But during informational interviews (not to mention actual job interviews), they are strictly off-limits.

The reasoning should be obvious: I want visitors to experience a typical informational job interview. I won't be too tough or too easy. If I am either, it's not a true interview scenario and they can't do their best to impress me. I expect job seekers to be a little nervous, but not shaking in their boots. If they are, it means they're not really ready to conduct a successful informational interview, let alone a make-or-break job interview.

Once we're seated and pleasantries have been exchanged is the time for you to kick off the conversation with why you actually asked for the informational interview. Remember the three reasons are:

- To learn more about his/her career path (CFO, Sales, etc.) and maybe apply it to the military construct.
- To learn more about his/her industry (telecommunications, manufacturing, etc.)
- To learn more about their employer (Qualcomm, Nokia, etc.)

Always remember: You requested the informational interview. Much like dating, if you asked for the date, you are the de facto host. You take control of starting the conversation and interview them about one or more of the three reasons above. This is your chance to wow them with your knowledge because you have done your homework and prepared for this meeting. You can also wow them with ideas on how you might fit into the company.

I like concluding an informational interview with job seekers asking me, "Is there anything I can do for you?" Recently, I saw that the person I was meeting with had worked for a company that Manpower really wanted to turn into a customer, but so far had no contact. I mentioned this and he replied that someone in Purchasing was a good friend. Within 24 hours, he had set up a meeting for our salesperson. The meeting was beneficial for both of us.

Actual job interview

Now you are ready for an interview for a specific job opening.

Your résumé has convinced the hiring manager that you can actually perform the job. Otherwise the company would have never bothered to set up an interview. Now that you've made it to the next stage, the focus will shift. The interview is much squishier – it's less about facts and figures, and more about intangibles like "fit" and "likeability". The purpose of the interview is to give the hiring manager an opportunity to imagine you working in that position inside their organization. They are thinking: I know he can do the job, but can I see him fitting in around here? Will my other staff members like him, and will our customers like him?

Dispelling the rigid soldier myth

In short, your job is to make everyone like you as much as possible. Show that you are not only capable, but also flexible – you are able to "roll with the punches," and adapt your work style as the situation requires. The number one stereotype I hear about veterans (and not coincidentally, the number one reason veterans get passed over for the job) is that they come across as too rigid, unable to think creatively, and act independently.

To be fair, the United States military is still a very hierarchical structure, based on a top-down command structure. It's a system that has worked well for over 240 years, and has proven its effectiveness time and again through the strains of war. However, there is also a perception that this focus on structure creates people who are very good at following orders, but not necessarily good at thinking creatively and taking initiative. I had an experience recently that made me cringe. I had an email from the HR Manager at one of our client companies, who relayed the story of a highly qualified young marine she interviewed the week before. On paper he was stellar and in person, his presentation was impeccable.

However, things fell apart towards the end of the interview, when the questions turned to his experience innovating and problem solving. The HR Manager said she ended up cutting the interview 15 minutes short. Her overall impression: he was a really sharp guy, and an extremely hard worker, but he also came across as the type of person who just waits around to be told what to do. As she said, "Although our firm has moved far beyond its startup days, we're still a rapidly growing small business. We don't have the luxury of waiting around for our CEO to draw up formal orders and instructions for everyone. Our team members have to be able to anticipate what our customers need and then jump in there and just do it. And if it hasn't been done before, we just have to create a new way to get it done." Hiring managers really like candidates who can think creatively and take initiative. If you can demonstrate these character traits, you'll blow that rigid stereotype out the water.

Interviews formats

So your résumé is dialed in and it's starting to get some hits. You know an interview is the next step in the process, but what exactly will that meeting look like? First, try not to think about the interview as a grilling, 20 Questions, or something from the Spanish Inquisition. We advise candidates to look at the interview as a two-way conversation, between individuals, who are each evaluating whether there might be a potential working relationship together in the future.

Think of it this way: an interview is a conversation that *you* initiated. It occurs because *you* took the initiative to reach out to an organization and effectively said, "I'd like to learn more about your company, and I'd like you to get to know *me* and what *I* can bring to your company." Reframing the interview in these terms will empower you. Since you are the one who initiated a potential relationship with this company, you are actually the one on the front foot. Don't look at the interview as a lopsided power dynamic in which you are cowering on the other side of the desk, trying to survive the interviewer's barrage of questions. Like I said above, a good interview should look and feel like an easy, but professional, conversation between colleagues.

What will the interview look like? Organizations use a variety of formats, although all are essentially designed to accomplish the same objective: enable the interviewers to get to know you better and envisage how you will fit in at their company. Some common formats include:

- 1:1 interviews (one meeting with one person on one date)
- Panel (multiple interviewers meeting with a single candidate at one time)
- Group interview (multiple candidates and multiple interviewers)
- Revolving door (several back-to-back 1:1 interviews, whereby the candidate either moves from office to office for each interview, or the candidate may be asked to stay in one meeting room, while different interviewers come and go at set times)

Of all of the above, the group interview is the least common, but in many ways the most interesting. It's a very time efficient way for multiple interviewers to meet multiple candidates in a single meeting. I used to have several large clients (all financial institutions) that preferred this format. Here's how it works: the candidates all meet in the lobby, and are led into a large conference room. Everyone is provided a nametag, and the hiring managers are seated at one end of the table. As an icebreaker exercise, everyone goes around the room and introduces themselves (there is usually one interviewer designated as the facilitator to lead the process). The candidates may all be vying for one job or the company may have several openings to fill.

In a group interview situation, I coach candidates to assume it's the latter case, to help them approach the whole exercise with a collaborative mindset. Here's why: the group interview format is designed to see how you function in a diverse, team-based environment. The facilitator will assign some kind of a group activity, which may involve everyone at once, or you could be split into smaller groups. Usually you will be asked to solve some kind of problem together, and then present your results to the panel of interviewers. The interviewers aren't really concerned with your team's product. They are observing how each of the candidates performs in a team environment. Who is a natural leader? Who tends to fall back or maybe not contribute? Does anyone tend to be domineering and not solicit input from others? Which candidates seem to really listen to one another and give constructive suggestions?

You would be absolutely amazed at some of the behaviors that come out in these group exercises, particularly if there is a strict time limit or a prize on the line. Your goal is show the interviewers that you "play well with others." You participate actively, work well with different personalities, are able to step forward and show leadership and initiative when required, but also know when to listen and let others step forward. It's a delicate balance!

Back to the most common interview format, the classic 1:1. The actual flow of the conversation is highly dependent upon the style and personality of the interviewer. Some hiring managers will come with a list of prepared questions they will ask all candidates in exactly the same manner. Other interviewers prefer a much more folksy "getting to know you" style, whereby the interview will feel like 60 minutes of easy chit-chat. While this may seem like a dream, don't let your guard down! Of course you want to be easy-going and friendly, but make sure you keep it professional. This is after all, still a job interview. And behind the interviewer's breezy dialogue there is probably some intense analysis going on.

Your interview checklist

- Prepare: treat each interview as if it's the very first one. This means you take each one extremely seriously and approach it with the same level of rigor and professionalism. Most companies will put you through a series of up to five or more interviews before issuing an offer. Candidates sometimes start to get cocky by round four or five, thinking, "I have this one in the bag," As a result, they will sometimes let their guard down and make rookie mistakes.
- Who will you be meeting? Get the names of all the interviewers you'll be meeting with and be sure to Google them and read their LinkedIn profiles as part of your pre-interview research. The more you know about the people you'll be meeting, the more comfortable you will naturally feel: knowledge really is power. However, don't request to connect on LinkedIn until after you've already had a chance to meet them or talk over the phone. You will otherwise be seen as overeager.
- Know the format: ask how long you should expect to be at the company and what will be the format of the interview(s). For example, will you be meeting each player individually, or will there be a panel interview?
- Special instructions: ask if there is a particular place they would like you to park and if there are any security or check-in procedures upon arrival. If so, ask if you should allow some extra time to complete these before meeting your interviewer. If you'll be parking on the street, will you need quarters to feed a meter?

- Do a fly-by: if you live in the area, drive to the interview location and take a good look around. How long did it take you to get there? Are there any potential delays that could arise on interview day? Traffic patterns, road work, etc.? Feeling familiar with the route and the destination will help you relax on the big day.
- Research: read the company's profile on Wikipedia, LinkedIn, and Facebook (yes, organizations have Facebook pages too), as well as those for some of the company's competitors. Also search YouTube thoroughly for content about the organization, especially video interviews with key executives.
- Early arrival: arrive at the interviewer's office no less than five, but no more than 10 minutes ahead of your scheduled interview time. You don't want to cut it so close that you are stressed, but hanging around in the lobby for 15 plus minutes is kind of creepy and you also don't want to give the impression that you have nothing better to do. My suggestion: arrive at the building 20 minutes early so that you have plenty of time to relax and collect yourself before going inside. If you drive, then use this time to sit in the car and listen to some music or meditate. If you have to walk from a bus or train stop, you might want to use this time to cool down or warm up inside, depending on the time of year.

For example, if you have an interview in Washington DC in the middle of August and you have a 15 minute walk from the nearest metro stop, you're *definitely* going to want a few minutes inside to mop your brow and cool down. Walking into an interview with sweat trickling down your face is not a good way to make a first impression. And if you do have a walk to the interview location, then arriving more than 10 minutes is perfectly acceptable. Use this line when checking in:

> *"Hi, my name is Trevor Blair, I'm meeting with Kara Hertzog at 11:00, but I figured it would be smart to arrive early and have some time to cool down – that summer humidity is brutal!"*

This friendly, light-hearted approach is a great icebreaker – it will help the receptionist warm up to you and will help you relax by turning your early arrival into a demonstration of your excellent planning skills.

- Everyone is the CEO: extend the same level of warmth and professionalism to everyone you see and meet, from the security guard in the parking lot to the actual CEO. A good hiring manager will always ask for feedback from the receptionist or whoever had first contact with the candidate on arrival. If our receptionist ever tells me the candidate was a jerk while he was waiting in the lobby, I immediately drop him from the list. Why? This tells me he lacks sincerity: he's the kind of guy who sucks up to authority and doesn't care how he treats those he perceives to be below him. That's not the kind of guy I want on my team, and definitely not the kind of guy I would put in front of our clients.
- Eat: this is not the time to skip breakfast even if nerves have sapped your appetite. Eat an ample, healthy meal before your interview. Your brain must be fully fueled to run at peak performance. You may also want to have an energy bar stashed in your suit pocket or purse in case you will be staying to meet with multiple interviewers. Although be sure not to over-fuel, as you don't want to be nodding off in the interview due to a food coma. Avoid heavy foods.
- Allow for extra time: however long your interview is scheduled to go, give yourself at least an extra hour on the back end in case the conversation runs long or they have some paperwork for you to complete. You don't want to feel rushed, if the interview goes long. It's usually a good sign if the company asks you to stay longer than originally scheduled: they wouldn't be wasting their time with you if they didn't see a potential fit.
- Business portfolio: don't show up empty-handed. Bring a professional business portfolio. It should be a leather or canvas folder, containing a pen, pad of paper, fresh copies of your résumé, and business cards. One of my biggest pet peeves is when a candidate comes in for an interview and

sits down at the table with nothing to write with. It makes them look painfully amateurish. It's highly likely the interviewer will share important details about the job, and you may also want to write down questions to ask later in the interview. How will you capture this information if you didn't bring anything to write with?

- If you drive to the interview: take the time to get the car washed and make sure the interior looks clean from the outside. Why? Your car is actually part of your first impression. I don't care what you drive, but I am interested to see if you are the kind of person who is diligent enough to take care of your car. This is particularly true if you are interviewing for a sales or management level position, where you might be driving to client locations or even transporting clients to and from meetings, the airport, etc.

- Upcoming availability: do you have any upcoming travel, medical leave, or other periods when you will be unavailable? If so, advise the interviewer at the end of your meeting. Add that if these dates conflict with the recruitment process, you will do everything possible to try to reschedule them.

- Practice, practice, practice: go online and download a list of common interview questions for your targeted industry/ occupation, suit up, have a friend or family member question you, and use your phone to record your responses. How do you look? Do you come across as alert and professional yet also relaxed and confident? I hope so. How does your voice sound? Do you project energy and enthusiasm or is your delivery flat and monotone? Is the cadence appropriate or do your nerves get the best of you? We all tend to ramble quickly when we're nervous. In sum, do you look and sound on video like someone you yourself would get excited about working with? If not, keep practicing until you do, and be sure to review the film with others to get their opinions too.

- Be yourself: attempting to be someone or something you are not will only end in disaster.

Identify your golden nuggets

You should have a battle plan for each interview situation. This ensures that you not only go in prepared, but that you also deliver your key messages to the interviewer.

1. Do your homework: research the company, their industry, the person(s) you are interviewing with, and at least 3 key things the company is looking for in this position.
2. Craft your value proposition: simply put, why are you the right choice for this position? You may be able to sum it up in just one sentence, or maybe it's a few bullet points. Your value proposition will probably have a lot of similarities to your elevator pitch.
3. Breakdown your value proposition into three to five nuggets: key messages you want to leave behind with the interviewer as to why you are the right person for the job. Examples would be: 1) demonstrated team building experience; 2) strong IT skills; and 3) excellent communicator.
4. Crafting your responses: these nuggets serve as your roadmap for answering each question. You don't need to worry about structuring each response perfectly, just answer the question and try to relate it to one of your three to five nuggets.
5. Reinforcement: make sure you hit each nugget at least twice during the course of the conversation.

Interview questions you should be ready for

As you've probably already gathered, not all interviewers are created equal. Some hiring managers are good at it and some quite frankly shouldn't be interviewing. It's clear when someone either doesn't have the skills or just hates doing the job of interviewing. One way you can tell, is that they will ask incredibly generic questions that don't speak to either your background or the position. To begin with, you will find below a list of what I consider to be some of those unimaginative questions. You need to be prepared for these as you will definitely come across them at some point:

1. *Tell me about yourself.* This is a trap! The interviewer is looking to see if you will start with, "Well, I was born in Great Bend, Kansas, not far from my grandfather's farm..." They really don't care about anything prior to the last 10 years, so don't take the bait and go rambling on about your life's story from day one. They want to see if you can keep your answers relevant and concise. You should instead interpret this question as: I'd like to hear about your professional background (briefly) and why that makes you a fit for this role. Stay out of the personal stuff, unless they specifically ask where you are from, etc. Give them a 35,000 foot overview of your professional self in no more than three minutes, and then let them ask a follow-up question to drill down into areas of specific relevance to the interviewer. And if you've had numerous jobs in the military, you will not have time to list each one; just mention two or three of the most significant – those that are either most relevant to the job you're applying for or those that encompass a broad category under which several of your jobs have fallen, such as IT, logistics, or administration.

2. *What do you consider your main weakness?* Another classic trap! They are probing to see if you will volunteer some kind of deal breaker shortcoming that would compromise your ability to succeed in the role, thereby eliminating yourself from contention. Alternatively, they are also probing to see if you are so full of yourself that you either a) can't identify a fault or b) consider yourself so perfect that your only imperfection is you work too hard. Those strategies of trying to identify a fault that is actually a strength, such as working too hard or putting too much pressure on yourself have all been used and abused for decades.

Be honest. Be human. We all have faults – pick something that is real and that you can actually speak to with specific examples. For example, you could say that you need to do a better job managing up. In the past it came to your attention that you got so involved in a project that you forgot to send daily updates to your commanding officer, to keep him appraised of your progress. So to address the situation, you scheduled regular update reminders in your calendar, to prompt yourself to put in a weekly call or email status update and ask for input and feedback. In this example you have cited a believable shortcoming, but also shown how you immediately took action to implement a solution.

The key here is to choose a subjective weakness that can be easily corrected, such as better communication, instead of an objective weakness that you cannot easily remedy at the present moment, such as lack of a college degree, or no relevant experience in the field.

Question 1: *What is your biggest asset?* This is another instance in which the interviewer is giving you a lot of rope, but answering smartly will prevent you from hanging yourself. The two obvious mistakes to make in this situation are to either undersell yourself and fail to demonstrate your capabilities, or to err in the opposite direction and project yourself as a self-absorbed jerk. Our suggested strategy: carefully chose a skill or unique kind of experience you will bring to the position that directly speaks to one or more of every organization's three goals:

- Make us money
- Save us money
- Fit in

Note that these are also ranked in order of importance from the vantage point of most hiring managers. All three are good, but number one is clearly the best. For example, if you were interviewing for a logistics position, you would discuss how your 15 years of experience in supply chain management will enable you to quickly get up to speed (saving the company training expenses), and help the company optimize its warehouse operations to get the same amount of product out to customer sites in less time (making the company more money).

1. Question 2: *What is your biggest failure?* Very similar to question 2 above, the interviewer is providing you with an

excellent opportunity to deep six yourself. Your strategy here should be to choose a failure that is real and meaningful, but also something that is not detrimental to your ability to perform the job you are applying for. The interviewer is looking for two key ingredients here:

2. Humility, honesty, and the ability to accept that we are all human
3. Your ability to learn from your mistakes and take direction (coachability)

Here's a good example:

"When I first took over as commander, I had my sight set on winning the battle readiness pin for our unit. I knew the competition would be tough, so I built an extra hour of skills training into our daily schedule. However, after three months, we weren't seeing any major improvements in our ratings. Turns out that extra hour was scheduled at the end of the day was when my sailors were already tired and approaching burnout. So I sat down with one young ensign, who explained to me that the best time to add something new into our daily routine was first thing in the morning, when they were fresh and could better absorb the additional training. We failed to win the pin in that rotation, but I learned a valuable lesson as a new manager (note use of civilian term here, not commander): first introduce a new concept to the team and then solicit their feedback before actually implementing it. I also learned that many times it's the folks on the very front line who actually have the best ideas."

This last part is key: you have to show how you learned from this experience in a meaningful way and improved your professional capabilities as a result. Never, *ever* say that you can't think of a significant failure in your career. This immediately signals to the interviewer that you are:

- Lazy, and have always set low objectives for yourself
- Too risk-averse, and lack a backbone

- Completely full of yourself
- An outright liar

More common interview questions

Although these questions are still somewhat generic in that they could be asked by any interviewer to any veteran applying for any position, I feel they are important to highlight. These questions do actually help the interviewer understand you, your motivations, and the path that has shaped you.

1. *Why did you leave the military?* This one is actually a fair question, and one for which you must definitely be prepared. First and foremost, don't say anything negative about the military, your commanders, or the government. Only focus on the positive in terms the skills and experience you gained through serving (more about this in the next section). Examples of solid, honest answers might be:

   - "The Navy was very good to me. I really enjoyed serving my country, I got to see the world, and my education was covered. I felt that after 12 years, I accomplished all that I had set out for myself when I signed up, and now I'm ready to start the next chapter of my career."
   - "My years in the Marine Corps were some of the best times of my life, and I'd gladly do it all over again. However, I'm now at a point in life where my family and I want to settle down and be closer to my wife's parents."
   - "The Air Force really kick-started my career and gave me a strong technical skill set. It was a great lifestyle when I was in my 20s and early 30s, but the deployments do take their toll. That's why this IT Analyst position would be a great fit for me. I would use a lot of the training I gained in the Air Force, with the possibility of some regional travel around the southeastern US, instead of six- to nine-month global deployments."

2. *What did you gain from your time in uniform?* We touched on some material you could use above. Here are some additional good responses:

   - Ability to work under pressure: after surviving my first fire fight when our patrol was ambushed, I realized how well the Army had prepared me to think clearly and perform in high pressure situations.
   - Teamwork: it all starts with boot camp. By the time I graduated from basic training, I really knew what it meant be a team player and work with different personalities and skill sets. That's the key is to identify everyone's strengths and work together as a cohesive group to get the job done.
   - Flexibility: I know the military has a reputation for hierarchy and rigidity. However, it also requires a huge degree of flexibility, as you have to be ready at a moment's notice to pick up and move. We do whatever it takes to accomplish the mission. And in a combat situation, that mission can change dozens of times. The battlefield is an extremely fluid environment, not unlike the business environment. The military taught me how to think on my feet and adapt.
   - Professionalism: the Marine Corps has zero tolerance for slack. As a 19 year old kid, I was taught what professionalism really meant: being on time, fully prepared, and ready to do whatever it took to get the job done. And it also taught me respect for my team, for my commanders, for the civilians we served, and for myself.

3. *Tell me about a time you had to build a team.* This is one of my all-time favorites. Although I'm not asking the question because I want to hear you blab on about your management style and theory of leadership. I'm also going to have my antennae up to make sure you don't talk about using your rank, chain of command, and military protocol to get the job done: that's the kiss of death in the private sector. We want to make sure we're hiring team members who understand people, not rigid authoritarians who bark orders.

How do you answer this multifaceted question successfully? You need to convince the interviewer you understand that team building and leadership is all about the human side of the equation, and not solely dependent on superior strategy, resources, and training. We need to be convinced you can:

- Relate to individuals at all levels: superiors, colleagues, and those reporting to you
- Understand people from a wide range of backgrounds
- Motivate individuals around a shared goal
- Teach, coach, and mentor others to boost their morale and performance
- Listen to input from others at all levels, especially those reporting to you
- Show humility and admit when you're wrong

I'm not saying your response to the team building question has to touch on every single one of these areas, but make sure at least a couple of these themes come through loud and clear. Use specific examples of actual situations you've encountered. You may want to read up on the management philosophy of *servant leadership* as well. To summarize, this is a very effective leadership strategy based on supporting your team and recognizing that the organization's success has to come from them, not from a high profile macho CEO who throws down bold, daring new strategies and commands.

Keep your answers brief

Human nature, especially when we are nervous, is to pack in as much information into our answers as possible. Veterans in particular have an affinity for data and technical specifications, which leads them to give extremely long answers infused with far too much detail. When it comes to interviewing, less really can be more. No response should be more than two or three minutes long. With each answer you provide, you want your listener to hear one key message. But if you cram in a ton of other details, that message gets diluted or even covered up altogether. You might be thinking: but if I only have two or three minutes per answer, how will I be sure I hit the target? The solution is to provide a thorough, but concise, answer. If you are worried that you may have had to leave out key details, simply check back with your interviewer with phrases such as:

- Is there anything you'd like me to elaborate on?
- Did I fully answer your question?
- Can I provide any additional detail?

Never badmouth in an interview

The military is an amazing institution, but we all know it also has more than its fair share of bureaucracy and nonsensicalness. Keep these thoughts and frustrations to yourself, and never speak disparagingly of a former boss, colleague, or employer. Every good interviewer should ask your reason for leaving each position (for those roles you've held after separating from the military). We need to know if you left of your own accord (ideally because you were hired away by another company that recognized your amazing skills) or if you were terminated for underperformance. When I interview, I take lots of notes on the résumé as we talk. I write RFL next to each organization you've worked for (Reason for Leaving) and the reason you left. This question very often triggers candidates into badmouthing their last company or the incompetent boss they used to work for. Although this may be true, keep in mind that there are always two sides to every story. Negative comments are going to send up a major red flag in the interviewer's mind. The automatic assumption the interviewer is going to make is that there is more to the story than you're providing and a big part of the problem may have been you.

Ask good questions

We mentioned earlier that a good interview should feel like an easy conversation between two professionals. This can't happen if only one person is asking questions. Otherwise it looks and feels more like a verbal firing squad. One of your most important functions in the interview is to ask good questions. Be sure to have them written down in your portfolio, which you'll have with you in the interview. Obviously you want the interviewer to lead the conversation, but you need to have a number of well-thought-out questions at the ready to either insert into the dialogue at the appropriate time or to close with. Many interviewers will use the first half of the allotted time to ask a set of standardized questions and then use the second half to answer questions from the candidate.

Here's why you need to come prepared with good questions:

- Demonstrates that you've done your research about the company and industry
- Shows you actually care about the company and getting this job
- Provides evidence of your professionalism and level of preparedness
- Indicates that you can carry on a conversation, and not just respond to orders

How do you formulate good questions? Make sure you do all your research on the front end, as we discussed earlier. Again, key informational sources include internet searches, company website, press releases, annual reports (not available unfortunately for smaller privately-held companies), LinkedIn, Wikipedia, talking with every person you know in that industry, etc.

Here are examples of some really bad questions I often get in interviews:

- What are the company's main goals or objectives?
- How did you get your position here?
- What's a typical day like in this division?
- How would you describe the company's culture?

Hopefully you're noticing a theme here: these questions are all incredibly generic, indicating that the candidate has not done their homework. They could be asked of any hiring manager, in any interview situation, for any position. Furthermore, these broad, unimaginative questions would all require a pretty lengthy response from the interviewer, who would have to regurgitate information that is most likely readily available on the company's website or information the candidate could have found on their own with just 20 minutes of internet research. We hate these questions!

And here's one that's so bad it deserves a paragraph of its own. Candidates usually lob this one out there towards the end of a call or meeting: what do you see on my résumé that you feel makes me a good fit for this role? (Other variations would be: how did I do?) This question is trying to play the reverse psychology game – and I know some career guides actually advocate this tactic. Trust me; it's only a surefire way to shoot yourself in the foot. Here's why: that question essentially tries to corner the interviewer into one of two responses:

1. They feel forced to tell you how great you are for the role.
2. They have to tell you to your face what you are lacking and why you are not a fit.

This question is trying to use reverse psychology to get the interviewer to convince herself that you are the candidate they need. Since it's uncomfortable for most people to provide criticism to another person's face (option 2 above), especially without time to prepare, the question is trying to make the interviewer default to option 1. It's a highly transparent and tired strategy that is only going to make both of you uncomfortable, thereby damaging your prospects.

I kid you not, this very scenario happened in an interview last week (as I write this):

> *I had a candidate interviewing for a CFO position with one of our clients. He made it through to the third round, which was a 1:1 interview with the CEO. The meeting went well enough, until they were wrapping up the session, and the candidate asked, "So now that we've had some time together to discuss the position and my background, what convinces you that I am the right fit for the position?" The CEO ended the conversation right there and promptly called my cell phone to relate the story. He asked that this guy be eliminated immediately from consideration. Needless to say, he was*

pretty annoyed the candidate played the reverse psychology card. Don't be that guy.

Here are some examples of good questions:

1. How would my performance in this position be evaluated?
2. Which department or team members does this position interact with most frequently?
3. How does the rest of the recruitment process proceed from here?
4. I read that ABC Company was expanding into a new product category. Is that project still on track and would the position we are discussing have a role to play with that?

I also need to point out that timing matters when it comes to questions. Your first or second interview is not the time to start talking about anything related to salary or benefits. That's too presumptuous. It would be like asking how many children the other person would like to have on just the first or second date. Although questions about compensation, relocation, and healthcare benefits are definitely relevant, they should be saved for later in the process, once it's pretty clear the company is considering making you an offer.

Using your volunteer experience in an interview

There are two ways to list your volunteer experience on your résumé. If you haven't been out of work very long, then you may want to include a separate section at the back, immediately following your last paid position. Title this section something along the lines of "Volunteer Positions", or "Community Involvement". Alternatively, if you've had some time since your last position, list it right at the top of your paid positions. Since these will be listed chronologically anyway, it makes sense for it to be the first on the list. (Nota bene: *don't ever* use a functional résumé …*please!* That format is incredibly tedious for a recruiter to tease apart, and won't score you any points. We need to see what you were doing, when you were doing it, and with which employer. A functional résumé also covers up gaps in employment.

When I see a functional résumé, I can't help but think the applicant has something to hide. Whichever format you choose, treat the volunteer roles exactly as you do all the other paid positions on your résumé. It should give a very brief description of the organization, and list responsibilities and accomplishments you had during your time there. I encourage every job seeker to list their volunteer experience on their résumé: it shows you're compassionate, you're engaged in your community, and you have much to offer. In addition, managers viewing your résumé may have been impacted by the work that organization does. Imagine what a powerful ice breaker you would have if you volunteered for The American Cancer Society, which happened to fund a study that led to a breakthrough that led to a new treatment that saved the life of the mother of the recruiter you're about to interview with. You two now have lots of great stuff to talk about.

Virtual interviewing

If you don't live in the same city as the interviewer, your first and second round interviews may very well be conducted via Skype, FaceTime, or some other video conferencing platform. You need to get comfortable with this kind of interview, as it is becoming extremely common.

- Treat a virtual interview *exactly* as you would an in-person interview.
- Dress and act as if you were sitting right there in the interviewer's office.
- Do several practice runs with a friend or family member on another computer to make sure you have a good internet connection and your computer's camera, speakers, and microphone are working properly.
- Make sure you have a plain, professional looking background behind you, as the interviewer will be able to see everything in your home. The more you can make the room look like an office (within reason), the better.
- Set a time when you know you will not be disturbed.
- Make sure your computer's camera is level with your forehead, so the person on the other end isn't looking up your

nose or down at you. If using Skype, make sure you have the picture-in-picture function turned on, so that you can also see yourself in the bottom right hand corner of your screen. This enables you to make any corrections, should you not feel comfortable with the image the interviewer is seeing.

- Make sure you are making good eye contact on-screen the whole time and not looking down at yourself too frequently in the picture-in-picture.
- Ask for the interviewer's username/Skype handle ahead of time. Look them up in Skype, so that you are ready to go at the designated interview time. For example, if you are supposed to Skype me for an 11:00 interview, and you log on at 10:55 to search Phil Blair (39 options, as of this writing, will pop up, more than half of which are located in the United States). You would never be able to identify the correct Phil Blair in just five minutes, making you late for our interview.

Body language

The way you look and the image you project to the interviewer virtually has to be consistent with the words coming from your mouth. Humans are visual creatures: no matter how brilliantly you answer each question, if your body language and personal presentation isn't backing that up, the interviewer isn't going to hear a word you say. So what exactly should a good interview look like? Go back to YouTube and pull up interviews with top corporate executives. You'll notice some trends. Most of them exhibit the following:

- Good eye contact with the interviewer (but make sure you blink with normal frequency)
- Sitting up straight, but still looking relaxed and comfortable
- Air of confidence, yet likeability
- Usually dressed in a suit, or something equivalent

The strong close

It's important to end any interview, again in-person or via phone, on a strong note. You want to leave the interviewer with a strong final impression of you and your interest in the position. Toward the end of the conversation, or as your final statement, use something along these lines:

> *"Tom, it was great speaking with you this afternoon, and I appreciate you answering my questions in such detail. I'm even more excited about this opportunity, and I look forward to the next step in the process."*

> *"Sharon, it was very good to meet you this morning, and I appreciate being considered for this opportunity. Could you please give me a quick overview of the next steps in the interview process, and when I should expect to hear back?"*

Tips for acing the phone Interview

It's highly likely that your path to an interview invitation will start with a phone interview/screen. And most of the same rules of engagement apply over the phone:

1. Preparation: Make sure you've done your homework. Print out your notes and have them in front of you when you take the call. The research you should have done by now includes:
    * Who will be calling you? Have you Googled them? Have you looked at their LinkedIn page? As we mentioned before, the more you know about the person interviewing you, the more comfortable and confident you will be.
    * What do you know about the position? Make sure you have a good understanding about the job for which you are interviewing. Print out the job description and have it ready with your other materials for the call.
    * Have your questions ready. Most phone interviewers will either start or finish the call by asking if you have any questions for them. Personally, I like to start interviews with questions from the candidate – it tells me a lot about their communication skills and level of preparation. This is your opportunity to not only get answers to any burning questions you might have, it is also your chance to show the interviewer that

you are prepared, thoughtful, curious, and serious about the job and the company. Have at least two or three good questions at the ready. You don't want the interviewer to feel you are wasting their time with a question about something that is readily available on the company's website.

- Some phone interviews are just a few minutes, but others can go for an hour or more. Make sure you have eaten an adequate breakfast or lunch, and avoid heavy or sugary foods that might put you in a food coma or sugar crash during the call. You want to maintain your energy and enthusiasm throughout the entire duration of the call. It's also a good idea to have some water on hand in case your throat goes dry from talking; just make sure you mute or cover the phone when sipping.

2. Schedule a set time: Most jobseekers want to show the interviewer they are eager and flexible, and hence, make the mistake of taking the phone interview on the spot. BIG mistake. Schedule the phone interview far enough in advance such that you have all the items listed above at the ready. And if possible, pick a day and time when you know you will be relaxed and at your best. If you're not a morning person for example, see if you can schedule an afternoon call.

3. Batteries and Bluetooth: Make sure your phone has adequate battery life for a long conversation (some phone interviews are only a matter of minutes, but others can easily go over 90 minutes, and you may not have any indication as to which the case may be). You may want to have your phone charger at the ready, just in case. A headset will free up both hands for taking or reviewing notes during the call. If you plan on using a Bluetooth headset, make sure its battery is also fully charged, it is paired with your device, and provides excellent sound quality for both you and the caller. The phone interview is not a time to start experimenting with new technology. Only use a headset if you have been using it for a while, fully understand its functionality, and trust its performance.

4. Leverage technology: You may want to use your phone to bookmark websites with key information for your phone interview. Just make sure you know how to easily access them without dropping the call.

5. Use a landline: This applies only if you have a landline (which I don't). Most cell phone coverage is good enough these days that land lines are superfluous. However, if you have any doubt about cell phone connectivity in your area, make alternative arrangements to use someone else's landline. You don't need any additional stress during the interview, such as a bad phone connection.

6. Silence is OK: Don't be afraid of a pause in the conversation. It may mean the caller is taking notes on your responses, or formulating their next question. Resist the temptation to fill gaps in the conversation with chatter. Your comfort with pauses and silence actually demonstrates confidence and a relaxed demeanor.

7. Location matters: This one is pretty obvious, but is still worth repeating: take the call when you have quiet and privacy and you know there will not be any disturbances. This becomes even more critical for interviews via Skype.

8. Watch your body language: Even when we are alone, the tone and energy in our voice is a reflection of our body language. Behave as if you were actually in a live face-to-face interview. Have a mirror in front of you if possible, so you can keep an eye on your posture and presentation. Make sure you smile as much as possible – it really does come through your voice. And finally, try taking the call standing up, and maybe even walk around the room a bit as you talk. It will naturally help you breathe more smoothly and project your voice, ensuring that you sound calm and confident.

9. Project energy through the phone: The interviewer should feel the smile and enthusiasm in your voice. A dull mumble will almost always kill your chances. Since we can't express ourselves with our body language over the phone, your voice and tone become even more critical. Speak clearly, express enthusiasm and don't chew gum. You may think it's not discernible on the other end, but it *definitely* is.

10. Be professional: A phone interview is every bit as formal and official as a face-to-face interview. Be sure you treat it as such. Avoid overly casual language.

11. Finish on a high note: Thank the interviewer for his time, and reiterate your interest in the position. An abrupt end to the call isn't necessarily a bad thing – the interviewer may simply have to move on to another task. And remember, there is no set duration for a phone interview: some are simple five minute administrative formalities, and others are a central part of the hiring process. Every company is different.

Dressing for success in the private sector

Unless you are interviewing in a factory or some other kind of production environment, you can never go wrong in a business suit. While you might not enjoy getting dressed up, the upside is that it takes all the guesswork out of getting ready for your interview. Always err on the side of formality, and go with a conservative suit (solids are easiest, but a subtle stripe is fine) in blue or gray. And you don't have to spend a small fortune to look sharp. Great business attire for both men and women can be found at stores like Macy's, Banana Republic, and Brooks Brothers (although you'll find much better deals at the outlets for the last two). The general "look" these stores carry is professional and contemporary – exactly the image you want to project. Another option is custom tailoring. You'll be amazed how easy, quickly and inexpensively you can get a custom made suit from overseas. Take a look at options like **iTailor.com**. Through all of these sources, you should be able to get a great suit at around $300 or less. Macy's often has amazing sales, where you can buy two or more suits, which drives the price down even further. And I would definitely suggest getting two complete suits, in case you have back-to-back interviews and your first-string outfit encounters a catastrophic coffee spill.

Dry cleaning is expensive, but if you take care of you suits, you should only have to dry clean them a couple of times per year. And when you do, be sure to dry clean both the jacket and trousers at the same time, otherwise the colors and fabric will wear differently and may not match perfectly. I'm also a big fan of non-iron shirts

(Brooks Brothers and Nordstrom's make some good, inexpensive options). They look sharp, travel well, and will dramatically reduce your dry cleaning bill. Styles change so make sure you are current.

A few additional tips on professional dress and presentation:

- Moderation is key: the only jewelry men should wear is a wedding ring, watch and maybe a class ring if you have one. Even cuff links can be perceived as a bit stuffy these days.
- Tie tacks, tie chains, collar bars and other ornamentation are a definite no-go.
- Women should carry a small to medium sized handbag at most, not a mega-bag you can fit a poodle into, even if they are in style these days.
- Shoes: although less comfortable, leather soled shoes are more professional than rubber, even if the uppers are identical. Go for leather, and make sure they're polished and clean.
- Heels: ladies, higher is not necessarily better. Go with two, maybe three inches, maximum, and don't wear a shoe with any kind of a platform sole. And they should be closed toe.
- Tattoos: should not be showing.
- Nose rings: remove them.
- Ear rings: none for men, no more than two per ear for women.
- Clothing fit: make sure your clothes are well-tailored. This means pants are hemmed, but allow a good break, sleeves are appropriate lengths (should extend past your wrist to barely touch your palm), and your shirt collar when buttoned barely allows you to insert a finger between the collar and your neck.
- Socks: over-the-calf business socks for men will not fall down under any conditions. Black (but not your patent leathers from your uniform) is always the safest bet, no matter what suit you are wearing.
- Wristwatches: huge chunky diver-style watches are very in right now, but not appropriate with a suit. Wear something

slimmer and more modest that will actually fit under your shirt cuff.

- Phones: should be shut off, not just on vibrate, and stowed away. And never, *ever* wear one of those Bluetooth ear pieces. Nobody is that important that they need to be contactable every instant of every day. Have you ever seen a successful executive, and I mean a real executive, not someone who just thinks they are, wearing one of those? I really doubt it. Bluetooth earpieces worn anywhere but in the car signal the user is pretending to be way more important than they really are.
- Tablet devices: do not bring to an interview. Unless the interview involves something specific to be presented on the tablet, it is simply distracting.

The job interview

There are three primary steps to preparing for and doing well in an interview:

1. Fully understand your career history and professional strengths. You should be able to tell your story forwards and backwards, ably and persuasively. If you cannot, no one else can. Make sure you don't give details about violent or secret things that you did while in the military, but figure out how to civilianize your military story. Talk about any awards you may have received on active duty for excellence at your job.

2. Practice your job interview skills until you've mastered them, until they become second nature. Study the interview do's and don'ts that I describe throughout this chapter. Remain calm and confident throughout your interview. It's not as if you're being stood up before a firing squad. If you've followed the advice of earlier chapters, done your homework, and practiced, go in smiling. You'll really impress them.

3. Develop CAR stories—short for Challenges, Actions, and Results. These are brief narratives in which you are the star. Relate an experience to an interviewer in which you confronted a **C**hallenge, took **A**ction, and got **R**esults. You should have several of them, each reflecting a different sort of

accomplishment. CAR stories enhance the interview process and can be hugely helpful with open-ended questions that require you to illustrate your strengths and abilities. The open-ended questions used by an interviewer usually begin with, "Tell me about a time when…" These are called "behavioral interview" questions and are all the rage right now.

An example of a behavioral interviewing question might be, "Tell me about a time when you were not meeting a goal and what you did about it." Using the CAR approach detailed below, the abbreviated version of your answer would be: "Last year, we were 30% behind on our recruiting goal six months into the year. I sent our recruiters to a training seminar for one week and, due to new techniques and re-energized motivation, within four months we were exceeding our sales goals."

How to build a CAR

CAR stories can be surprisingly effective. They make a strong, positive impression upon employers because they illustrate specific Challenges, Actions and Results that you met, took, and achieved.

Employers often ask leading questions designed to assess whether you fit their company's culture and plans. CAR stories are an effective way to turn a simple question into one that helps answer those concerns. They're also particularly well-suited to the military.

Just as we are all individuals with unique work histories and experiences, so too are our CAR stories. However, here are a series of questions you can ask yourself as you construct and then tune your CAR story:

C: Challenges you faced or encountered

- What needed to be accomplished to overcome the challenge?
- How and why did the obstacle arise and how did you discover it?
- How did you initiate action to remedy the situation?

- What were your specific assignments, responsibilities, or duties related to carrying out the solution?

A: Actions you took to resolve the problem or situation

- What skills did you use (interpersonal, technological, multitasking, etc.) to achieve a solution?
- What was your solution and how was it successful?
- How did you execute your goals, plans, and procedures?
- How were your actions creative or innovative?
- What did members of your team achieve under your supervision and guidance?

R: Results achieved

- What did you accomplish?
- Who benefitted and how?
- Can you quantify or measure the results?

The actual job interview

Much of what you learn and perfect to conduct a successful informational interview applies naturally and directly to conducting a successful job interview. Remember the informational interview is much more about data-gathering and does not involve a job opening. A job interview is directly related to a specific job opening. That shouldn't be surprising. If you learn to present an impressive case for yourself during an informational interview, you certainly can do so during the real thing.

By now, you know a lot about what goes into a successful interview. You know how to dress and communicate. You know what you're looking for in a job and career. You know yourself.

At its most fundamental, a job interview is all about questions—theirs and yours. It's the whole point of the meeting, after all. What makes it so harrowing is what Donald Rumsfeld, two-time U.S. Secretary of Defense, once famously—albeit confusingly—referred to as the knowns and the unknowns:

> *"There are known knowns. These are things we know that we know. There are known unknowns. That is to say, there are things that we know we don't know. But there are also unknown unknowns. There are things we don't know we don't know."*

Rumsfeld wasn't talking about job interviews, of course. To be honest, I don't know exactly what he was talking about, a case of a known unknown, I guess. But Rumsfeld's point seems to neatly apply to job interviews. To wit: applicants go into job interviews knowing they will be questioned. They know, or think they know, what some of the questions will be. They also know they will be asked questions they cannot know in advance or anticipate.

Much of the rest of this chapter deals with questions. In some cases, I'll talk about possible responses, but mostly it will be up to you to come up with answers. Using stories from your time in the military is a good thing, but do not talk about anything that wouldn't be suitable to tell a classroom full of fourth graders. No blood and guts. Generally speaking, interviewers ask three kinds of questions: positive, neutral, and negative. You have to be prepared to capably and seamlessly respond to all three—often in the same interview. Here are some basic examples:

Positive
- What are your strengths?
- Why should we hire you?
- What can you contribute to our organization?
- Why do you feel you are qualified for this position?
- How have you been successful in your career and why?
- Tell me about job responsibilities you enjoy.
- Describe your ideal job.
- Tell me about a situation when you felt very effective in your job.

Neutral
- What will your references, including former supervisors and co-workers, say about you?
- How would you describe your communication style with supervisors, peers and assistants?
- How do you handle working under pressure?
- What are your salary requirements and expectations?
- Why are you interested in this position?
- What is important for me to know about you?
- What are the key lessons you have learned in your career?
- How do you set priorities?
- How do you feel about relocation?

Negative
- Tell me about a work situation when you felt ineffective?
- What did you not like about your last position, supervisor or company?
- What is the biggest mistake you've made in your career?
- Tell me how you've handled a difficult co-worker, supervisor or junior peer?
- What have supervisors criticized about your work style?
- What type of business environment do you find most challenging?

Before you go into any interview, review these questions and have answers in mind. More specifically, imagine questions the HR person is likely to ask about the particular job you're seeking or about your particular situation. Take time to work through your answers. Write them down. Rehearse them. In the interview, you don't want to sound like you're reading from a script, but you do want to know the answers well enough to deliver a response directly and without effort.

Learn about the employer

A job interview isn't just an opportunity for a potential employer to learn more about a job candidate. It's also an opportunity for the candidate to learn more about the employer, a company's philosophy, the different aspects of the job you're applying for and what the company requires of its employees. The questions you ask are as important to you as the questions asked of you. HR professionals really do want the interview to be a two-way discussion.

On a different note: I don't want you to walk out of an interview thinking, "What just happened here?" You chatted with the interviewer for an hour and know nothing more about the job than you did going in. In fact, you and the interviewer didn't have a professional conversation about the position, the company or the industry. This is most common with department managers who are not trained well by HR to conduct interviews for their departments. They are not professional HR staff, but rather company employees who may be conducting the interview because the position falls in their department or they're familiar with the work than needs to be done. That might sound like sufficient qualifications to interview clients—and sometimes it is—but often you wind up with a person who thinks the right job candidate boils down to, "Who do I like best?"

If you are serious about wanting the job, even when facing a potentially flaky interviewer, then you need to take control, just as we discussed in the introduction to this chapter. The interviewer will thank you later.

As you saw above, when you step into a room for an interview, the person on the other side of the desk isn't always experienced—or even very good at what they do. Perhaps the most common example of this is what I call a "Chatty Cathy." Beware. Such people tend to talk about anything and everything, most of which has nothing to do with the actual job or its requirements. They'll pontificate about the weather or local sports team. They'll ask you personal questions that may actually be inappropriate and perhaps illegal. It's often a result of their being very nervous. So what do you do?

Take charge of the meeting. Subtly and gracefully, bring the conversation back to discussing the job, your excitement about it, and the interviewer's expectations. If they persistently wander off topic, persist in equal measure.

At the end of the meeting, you want to have achieved three things:

1. Fully described why you're the right person for the job.
2. Had all your questions about the job answered.
3. Performed in such a delightful way that the interviewer thinks he or she has just conducted the perfect interview.

You should have several questions already in mind going into the interview and an expectation that others might arise during the interview itself. Don't be afraid to write your questions down and bring them with you. Doing so will help you remember them, articulate them during the interview, and improve your performance. It also shows that you prepared for the interview. Be sure to ask your questions respectfully and from an informed perspective. You don't want to ask, "So does ACME have a good future?" Your questions should expand upon what you already know about the company from your earlier research.

Years ago I was hiring additional salespeople and a sharp, young articulate lady came in for an interview. We started talking about Manpower and she stopped me and said, "By the way, what does Manpower do?" I was flabbergasted. A salesperson of all people coming to an interview with zero knowledge of the company she was interviewing with to be a salesperson. After that comment, I can assure you it was a very short interview.

Here are some sample questions, which you can tweak to meet your particular circumstances:

About the company
- What future plans does the company have for this position?
- What are some of the company's short- and long-term goals?
- What are the key points in the company's corporate culture?
- What are the company's values?
- I am fascinated by the ABC new product. Can you tell me more about it?

About the job

- Is this a new or existing position? (If new, why was it created?)
- With the areas of responsibility, what are the two or three most significant goals you would expect me to accomplish?
- Where does this position fit within the company's structure? What level is this position (entry, advanced, supervisory, etc.)? What are the position's main responsibilities?
- Which job duties/activities would I split my time between and how?
- Are there opportunities for growth and advancement? If so, what additional career opportunities might be open to me?
- What are the goals for the department I would work with? How do they support the company's overall mission/goals?
- What are the major challenges in this position (and for this organization)?
- What would you see as great outcomes in my review at the end of my first year on the job?

I strongly suggest that you take notes during the interview. And yes, it is very appropriate. A lot of issues may be discussed that you will want to remember later, maybe even to include in your thank you note and for polite follow-up collateral. Your notes might include such things as objectives of the department, key functions of the job, and potential growth opportunities. Also, we, including HR folks, are impressed when someone feels what we said was important enough to write it down. You may be making your grocery list for your stop on the way home, but I don't know that. All I know is I said something and you wrote it down.

Answering questions in an interview is as much about how you say it as it is about what you say. No answer should be shorter than fifteen seconds or longer than two minutes. Too short and it seems abrupt and rude. "Have you ever had bottom line responsibility?" If your answer is "No." it catches me off guard because I am not ready with the next question and it appears to me that you are dismissing my inquiry as unimportant to you. Instead, you might answer, "I have not had actual bottom line responsibility, but in our department at ABC Company, we were all very aware of sales and costs of products and the manager reviewed the monthly P&L with the entire office. I am very aware of the importance of cost controls and hitting sales goals." Wow: a whole lot better than "No."

In your longer answer, you reinforced your knowledge, awareness and appreciation of the importance of hitting goals, especially sales and controlling costs. Without me asking directly, you just hit two of the hot buttons of every manager. High five to you!

Conversely, I don't want you to be that Chatty Cathy I referred to earlier. Anything longer than two minutes and I have lost interest in whatever you are saying and may even have forgotten the question. I will spare you an example, but a rambling unfocused answer to my question is not the way to impress me. We all have a tendency to ramble when we get nervous. An interview can be a nerve-wracking situation, but with practice and a timer you will become aware of how long you are speaking and get it under control.

If you feel it's an involved question that deserves extra time and detail, I suggest a "check-in," as in, "Am I going into too much detail? Am I answering your question? Would you like me to continue?" These are appropriate check-in questions. You may get a pleasant, "Oh no, please continue, this is very helpful." Or you may get a "Thank you, I've heard enough." If you get the latter, thank heavens you did a check in. If you get the former, you know you are hitting the bull's-eye!

Interview questions

In his excellent book *201 Best Questions to Ask on Your Interview*, author John Kador offers 15 rules for framing and asking effective questions:

1. Ask open-ended questions that can't be answered with a "yes" or "no."
2. Keep the question brief.
3. Don't interrupt the answer.
4. Construct questions so that the answers emphasize the positive.

5. Use inclusive language, like "we" instead of "you."
6. Ask questions the interviewer can answer.
7. Avoid questions you can easily find the answer to.
8. Avoid "why" questions.
9. Avoid questions calling for a superlative, such as "What's the absolute best thing about this company?"
10. Avoid leading or loaded questions, such as "Don't you think employees who go above and beyond should get bonuses?"
11. Avoid questions that might be construed as threatening.
12. Avoid questions that sound desperate.
13. Avoid "what about me" questions. Frame them in terms of what you can do for the company.
14. Don't ask irrelevant questions.
15. Go ahead and ask the person if you're right for the job.

There are, of course, questions you shouldn't ask. Avoid asking your interviewer personal questions about their job experience. Such questions include asking how they got their job or what their opinion is of their company. These might seem important to you, but a first interview is not the time to ask them. It is also inappropriate during a first interview to directly inquire about salary, retirement plans, vacations, bonuses and holidays. It sounds very presumptive and cocky. These are subjects to be discussed when you are negotiating a job offer or have received one.

There are some questions you should never ask. Don't ask if they have ever served. First, if they have they will proudly let you know immediately. If they haven't, they may feel uncomfortable about it. Do not discuss personal topics or subjects like politics and religion. Also, be careful about voicing support for specific military action that you may have been involved in, you never know where the interviewer lands. These are employment minefields that are bound to blow up in your face. You're walking blind here. You don't know your interviewer well enough to venture into these areas and, even if you think you do, a job interview is not the forum for such discussions.

Don't ask your interviewer's opinion of a former employee; for example, the person that had the job for which you are interviewing.

It's inappropriate for the interviewer to talk about this kind of personnel matter and it's really none of your business. Stay focused on why you're there and why you're the right person for the job.

Thought-provoking questions for all applicants

In the course of most interviews (especially those for serious and much coveted jobs), a tough or tricky question will come up, probably several in fact. The interviewer's intent isn't malicious. He genuinely wants to hear your answer. He also, if he is doing his job right, wants to see how you think on your feet.

The interviewer has two reasons for asking penetrating questions. First, he wants to see if you have expertise in the area in which you are applying for work. You should be able to discuss in-depth topics about this field. Second, if you are hired, you may very well be standing in front of your company's largest customer someday. If he asks you an off-the-wall question, the HR interviewer wants some idea of how you will handle yourself.

Below are some sample questions and recommended responses. Before you get into an interview situation, ask yourself these questions, devise your answers and then practice them until they can be delivered quickly and smoothly, as if you never practiced at all.

- You seem to switch jobs a lot. Why?

    If you're just leaving the military, you won't have to deal with this. These days being a trailing spouse (the spouse who gives up their job to follow their spouse's job change) is acceptable as long as you can convince the HR person you (and your spouse) are here to stay. This will be particularly easy if you are transitioning from the military and having that discussion. If this will be your second job out of the military then this becomes an issue. Unfortunately, the recent transitioning veteran often finds their first job out is not what they want to do long term and therefore have some explaining to do when they interview for their second private sector job. The wrong answer, of course, is simply to say you're always on the lookout for a better job with better pay. Nobody's going to hire a candidate who so clearly sees every position as a stepping stone to the next. It is reasonable to change employers after three years or so because a new opportunity has arisen that is not possible with your current firm. Anything less than three years requires a convincing explanation. Acceptable reasons for switching employment are downsizing, job situation, career advancement, back to school, or a temporary personal situation.

- What would you change about your former job?

Never speak negatively about your former position, co-workers, or commanding officer. If your former job was in the private sector, use the opportunity to express how you wished you could have had more responsibilities or that you wanted to become a more valuable member of the team. Seeking additional opportunities to rise to the occasion on a job demonstrates admirable initiative, something employers like and seek. If you have an idea that is positive and would change the military, share that!

- Where would you like to be in your career five years from now?

This is difficult because no one can foretell the future, but if you consider the promotions you might earn if you work hard for the company you're applying to, it's conceivable that you might be able to broadly sketch new duties or status. The important thing here is to emphasize that you plan to be at the company for years to come. Do not answer with "I want your job." With few exceptions, such as retiring, no one is anxious to hire someone who is gunning to take their position, even kiddingly. A better answer might be something like, "I would like to work toward a job similar to yours." It sounds much less threatening, but says the same thing and sounds respectful to the interviewer.

- What's an example of a major problem you faced and overcame?

Here's a terrific moment for a CAR story, one that relates to an event in your military service, at school or civic activity. Remember to deliver the story in a thorough, compelling manner. Provide important details. Avoid anything that would confuse the central theme of your tale, which is how you conquered a problem. Be very careful about sharing a combat story here. This kind of question is asked by interviewers who want to observe how you define a problem, identify options, decide on a solution, manage obstacles, and solve predicaments. Do your best to relate your example to a private sector company. For example, an issue of cutting expenses is important in both military and private sectors. Do not include any examples that involve war, death or sadness. It is always nice to end a tale with what you learned from the experience and why you are now a better potential employee for the company.

- What has been your greatest accomplishment? What did you learn from it?

Here is where a personal anecdote might actually serve well. While recounting how you saved the Army $1 million in costs might be quite an achievement, it will ring false in terms of personal accomplishment. Better to mention your marriage, the birth of a child, or how you helped someone in need. One anecdote that I encourage job seekers to emphasize is if you worked full-time to put yourself through college. Talk about an example of hard work and perseverance. The details in your answer can be used to reveal attractive elements of you the person and what traits you will bring to the job. On the other hand, this is not the time to talk about overcoming drug abuse, alcoholism, or failed marriages. Way too personal and alarming. That's a whole different book.

- What was your greatest failure? What did you learn?

Fessing up to failure shows maturity. Everybody fails. It's human nature. Of course, don't cite a failure that is so breathtaking that the interviewer forgets everything else about you. Avoid examples that might reflect upon your ability to do the job or could potentially reflect poorly upon your character. A good example might be a fear of speaking in public that prompted you to join Toastmasters. As a result, you're now quite comfortable giving presentations. Such an example illustrates not just that you're human (we all have flaws) but that you've successfully acted to fix a shortcoming.

- What is your greatest weakness?

Again focus on work, not your personal life or character. Turn this question from a negative to a positive by showing how your commitment to work sometimes translates into working long hours, sacrificing free time to get the job done. You might note, for example, that you've become much more organized and now prioritize better so that essential projects are always completed on time.

- What motivates you to do a good job?

Don't say "money." While we all work for a paycheck, no employer wants to hear it, especially from someone who doesn't even have the job yet. A better answer might be that for the same reason you joined the Navy you're motivated to tackle challenges and overcome them, that you draw deep satisfaction from doing every job well. A second reply might be that you like new challenges. The better you do on current projects, the more likely you will be given new opportunities to learn new skills.

- Have you ever been fired from a job? If so, why?

Be honest. It's difficult to hide one's work history for long, and doing so will always come back to bite you. Remember that being laid off or a force reduction doesn't necessarily reflect poorly upon you. Between downsizing, outsourcing, and new technologies, lots of good military people are being allowed the opportunity to find challenges elsewhere. If you were fired from a civilian job for reasons related to personality differences, it is okay to say so, but be ready to explain why and what you learned from it. Often the personalities don't mesh and there may be no way to resolve the conflict in-house. So someone has to go. If it was you, it's only fair that you explain the situation to an inquiring potential employer who would want to make sure such a situation would not be repeated. That's to your benefit as well.

- Have you ever been convicted of a crime?

In some states it's legal to ask this question if it has a bearing on the job you're seeking. A bank, for example, would not want to hire a convicted robber or embezzler to work in the vault. If you have a court martial, it's best to admit it, explain what happened, and any mitigating circumstances. It is essential that you discuss how the experience has made you a better person and what you've done to make amends. For example, if you were convicted of using drugs as a teen, explain how you went to a rehab facility, got clean, and learned how to make better friends and choices. Basically you acknowledged the weakness, conquered it, and learned from it.

Real (and really dumb) questions
Actually asked during interviews:

- What is it that you people do at this company?
- Why aren't you in a more interesting business?
- What are the zodiac signs of all the board members?
- Why do you want references?
- Do I have to dress for the next interview?
- I know this is off the subject, but will you marry me?
- Will the company move my rock collection from California to Maryland?
- Will the company pay to relocate my horse?
- Does your health insurance cover pets?
- Would it be a problem if I'm angry most of the time?
- Does your company have a policy regarding concealed weapons?
- Do you think the company would be willing to lower my pay?
- Why am I here?

Checklist

Every job interview is unique. There are basic themes and experiences central to all, of course, but the details vary in every situation. The one thing common to them all is you, though even you are changing and adapting as needed.

No one has yet concocted an absolute, foolproof guide to conducting the perfect job interview. What follows is my checklist of things to do and think about before, during and after an interview. Follow them. Add to the list. It will serve you well:

- Strive to be the last interview for an open position. This can be tricky. But if you know a company is interviewing several candidates, it's better to be interviewed later than sooner. You will be fresher in mind when the hiring decision is made. How do you do this? If they say they are interviewing Wednesday and Thursday, ask for Thursday afternoon.
- Do your homework before the interview. Know what questions are likely to be asked and what your answers will be. Have questions of your own. Research the company and be able to discuss its product mix and goals.

- Look and behave with respect, seriousness and a positive attitude.
- Listen more than you speak, but stay engaged in the conversation.
- Take notes, if possible. It's a good way to remember names and details for later correspondence and follow-up.
- Use humor smartly. Poke fun only at yourself. Never be sarcastic. Don't force it. If the interviewer is being deadly serious, follow their lead. When in doubt, play it straight.
- Why would I want to join this company?
- How much longer will this process take?

I want the job!

A final bit of advice, which might seem obvious but is often not followed by civilians, but especially veterans: as your job interview winds down or comes to an end, there will be a moment for you to make a statement. That statement should be something to this effect:

> *"Thank you for this opportunity. I'm excited about the prospect of working here. I really think I am a good match for this job because of my culture match, experience in logistics, knowledge of cybersecurity, and the potential to apply my military and civilian experiences to help the team succeed!"*

Telling a would-be employer that you want the job would seem to be a "no-duh!" suggestion, but I can tell you that I've been in hundreds of interviews where that sentiment was never expressed. I've met scores of candidates who have worked hard to get a job interview. They've smartly conducted that interview, impressed HR with their skill set, their work experience, and what they could bring to the position and company. But they never say they want the job. It's not a small point or minor oversight. Employers want to be convinced that the person they're hiring wants the job, that getting it is Job #1 for them.

The best, fastest way to persuade a prospective employer is to express that priority in clear, concise, compelling terms.

Of course, you have to mean it. If you don't think a job is right for you, if you're no longer interested, you should say so. Not at the job interview; be gracious. Thank them for their time and consideration, then withdraw your candidacy the next day.

But if you want the job, tell the person!

The learning points here are about preparation. Expect the unexpected. Prepare for the worst. Take charge if you can. Schedule your interviews with plenty of time for unforeseen events like a request by an interviewer for you to stick around to talk with others in the company about the job. Keep relevant materials handy. And if you do get caught in your car or another less-than-conducive place for an interview, say so. Ask the interviewer if you can call them back when you're not driving or when you've found a quieter location. It shows you value the interview and want to ensure it is productive and free of distractions for everyone involved.

References

I know it's seems like every page talks about an issue that can make or break your career search. Well, add one more. This time it is references.

Let's start with what not to do. In the old days you had two choices: "see references below" or "references available upon request." Forget both! As you read on you will learn how references need to be fine-tuned to help you make a particular point to support, reinforce, or cover for a weakness. So you don't know which references to list until you know the exact job opening that you are asking them to be a reference for, and most important, why you are asking specifically them. The second statement, "upon request," is just foolish.

Let's say you have made it through the interviewing process and are a final candidate. You nailed it on financial management (got your MBA after separation), did really well on leadership and team work (military experience) but feel a bit week on your market development experience.

References to the rescue.

How about if you listed a Finance professor from one of your MBA classes to reinforce your finance savvy, and your Commander in the Navy for your leadership and team work talents, and President of the Red Cross where you volunteered after separation and developed a fund raising campaign to market their new services. When I call them as references, I know they are people who know you and your work habits well, can speak to your strengths, and, most important, make me comfortable that your one weak skill set is really not a weakness it has just not been utilized in the actual jobs you have held, but you do have the innate skills to oversee a marketing campaign.

But how did these individuals know what was going to be asked of them and how they should answer? Because you contacted them well beforehand, told them the exact position you were applying for and were now a finalist for, who would be calling, and what company they were with. And most important, you told them where you felt you were strong. Reinforce that information with examples of term papers, projects, campaigns, etc. that you ran well. Explain, equally, where you felt you are weak in experience or education and how, if they were comfortable, they could bring up examples of where you demonstrated those strengths. Don't hesitate to remind your references of specific experiences. Don't expect them to remember specific details about you without you reminding them and even re sending examples as reminders of your work.

Don't ever offer a reference without first getting their permission. What a disaster if you think they will remember you and they don't, or are lukewarm about you because they were not all that impressed with you, or they got you confused with someone else.

Also check for the best contact information for them, do they prefer phone or email? Some may request references in writing. Some may just say no, either they are not comfortable or their company/school does not allow them to be references for students or ex-employees. Better to know it now than have the potential employer inform you of the fact.

You will see that you will need different references for different positions. References have to know you well (you reminded them they know you) and feel comfortable answering a variety of questions about you (which hopefully you tee'd them up for). Flash back to networking skills. They are equally important to develop a list of potential references. Check in with past bosses and co-workers, professors, and community leaders so they know you are in the job search and, if needed and relevant they would be willing to be a reference for specific skills they saw you demonstrate. Think of a list of ten or so references that you can pick from as needed.

Interviews from Hell

As serious as interviewing for a job can be, we also have to keep our sense of humor.

The Internet can be fantastically useful—and amusing. Vice Presidents and Personnel Directors from 100 of the nation's largest corporations were asked to recount their most unusual experiences interviewing prospective employees. I can't really vouch for the absolute authenticity of their comments, but after decades of doing interviews, I can believe anything. Needless to say, I don't recommend any of the following:

- A job applicant challenged the interviewer to arm wrestle.
- The interviewee wore a Walkman, explaining that she could listen to the interviewer and music at the same time.
- The candidate fell and broke an arm during the interview.
- The candidate announced she hadn't eaten lunch and proceeded to eat a hamburger and French fries in the interviewer's office.
- The candidate explained that her long-term goal was to replace the interviewer.
- The candidate said he never finished high school because he was kidnapped and kept in a closet in Mexico.
- The balding candidate excused himself during the interview and returned a few minutes later wearing a toupee.

- The applicant said that if he were hired, he would demonstrate his loyalty by having the corporate logo tattooed on his forearm.
- The applicant interrupted the interview to phone her therapist for advice on how to answer specific interview questions.
- The candidate brought a large dog to the interview.
- The applicant refused to sit down, insisting on being interviewed while standing.
- The candidate dozed off during the interview.

Real and really weird things said during an interview

- I have no difficulty in starting or holding my bowel movement.
- At times, I have the strong urge to do something harmful or shocking.
- I feel uneasy indoors.
- Sometimes I feel like smashing things.
- Women should not be allowed to drink in cocktail bars.
- I think that Lincoln was greater than Washington.
- I get excited very easily.
- Once a week, I usually feel hot all over.
- I am fascinated by fire.
- I like tall women.
- People are always watching me.
- Almost everyone is guilty of bad sexual conduct.
- I must admit that I am a pretty fair talker.
- I never get hungry.
- I know who is responsible for most of my troubles.
- If the pay were right, I'd travel with the carnival.
- I would have been more successful if nobody had snitched on me.
- My legs are really hairy.
- I think I'm going to throw up.

And my personal all-time favorite

I still cannot believe this happened. Meet dear old Sam:

Sam was an applicant for a senior engineering job and had gotten far enough in the process to merit a meeting with

John. When he arrived for the meeting, John immediately noticed that Sam had a Bluetooth wireless headset stuck in his ear. John thought this a bit off-putting, but chose not to mention it. The candidate was, after all, an engineer. The two men soon launched into a productive, interactive discussion, with John keeping the focus on the candidate's engineering talents and experiences.

Suddenly, Sam's expression changes without obvious explanation. He touches his ear. His eyes dart back and forth.

He becomes stony-faced, then completely quiet and still, almost as if under a sudden, unseen spell.

After a few silent, awkward moments with John just staring at him, the candidate whispers very quietly, "I'll call you back."

phil-osophy 101   9

The other big black hole.

The first black hole is the place your résumé goes after you send it to the hiring firm's database—apparently never to be heard or seen again. Then, miracle of miracles, you're summoned for an interview, the interview you labored so hard and long to get. You meet the hiring manager and have a fantastic session. You hit every talking point and believe you made a great impression. Heck, the manager even said so, promising to get back to you very, very soon. Wink, wink.

Enter the black hole.

A question I hear repeatedly from job candidates is how long should they wait after an interview before pressing the hiring manager for a decision or just an update. If you haven't heard back from a company within two weeks of a final interview, there's a good chance one or more of the following is happening:

- *You're not the only candidate being considered. The company is talking to others, and it may be taking a while for all of these interviews to be scheduled and conducted.*
- *The decision-makers at the company are having difficulty coming to an actual decision. It might be as simple as the fact that it's a committee choice and the committee is having trouble getting everybody together. It may also be that the decision-makers are traveling and can't get together to make the decision.*

- *Maybe it's just a tough choice. Maybe you're not the company's first choice, but your application is strong enough that HR doesn't want to cut you loose just yet. If choice #1 doesn't work out, HR wants to keep you close by and available.*
- *Or perhaps the job situation has changed. After conducting several interviews, it's possible the hiring manager's view of the open position has changed. He or she thinks the job specifications need to be altered, upgraded, or shifted. While that's going on, everything's been put on hold. Now, with all of the interviews done, the decision-makers are reconsidering the job description, the compensation package (up or down), or the experience/education requirements. You and your peers gave them feedback that made them wonder about their current criteria for the job.*

These are all viable reasons for a company to step back and not rush a hiring decision, which isn't much consolation to you, left hanging there. In this chapter, we'll talk about what you can do during this excruciating period in the hiring process. This is the time to show your professional patience, rather than reveal any frustrations or, heaven forbid, lose your temper. Display your understanding of this wrinkle in the HR process and you may further impress those HR folks and the people you hope to work with. Let other candidates flail and fume; your job is to remain patient and focused on getting the job.

9.0 Polite Persistence to Job Offer

The big job interview is over; your job is not.

Take a deep breath. This is not a sigh of relief. This is preparation for the next step.

You've come a long way, prepping before you left active duty and working hard on those early self-assessments, established networks, written résumés, made phone calls, pounded the pavement. It has been a labor that would exhaust Hercules. Your reward was the job interview you wanted and needed.

Now it's time to seal the deal.

The period after a job interview can be maddening. In the military, your job interview is often meeting with your classifier, detailer, monitor, or other person whose job is to place you at your next gig. In the civilian world, you must actively interview and that can be challenging but you've passed the first hurdle. Job candidates often feel ignored, abandoned, left to wander in a desert of doubt and disquiet. (Is that piece of paper that's drifting on the wind your application?)

Unless HR or the person doing the hiring has clearly and explicitly laid out a timetable for the decision-making process (something that's rarely done, and even less often accurate), it's likely you'll be left to wonder what's happening until something actually happens.

And, unlike the military, folks in the HR field rarely move with purpose or swiftly to accomplish the mission.

This might seem like a time of relative powerlessness. The decision to hire you or not is now in the hands of others. While that's indisputably true, you can still do a lot to influence the final result. Until you receive word that a final choice has been made, you must continue to campaign for the job. I call it polite persistence. Your goal is to make a connection with your target person or audience every seven to ten days until resolution. You need to remind them of your interest and re-emphasize just how perfectly suited you are to the open position. There are a variety of ways you can "stay in contact" and keep your name in front of the decision maker. These include notes, emails, voice mails, association meetings, etc. The idea is to make yourself accessible and memorable, not weird, pushy or awkward. Remember most candidates for jobs, no matter how bad they want the job, sit at home waiting for the phone to ring. They take "don't call me, I'll call you" seriously. Consequently they don't appear to be anxious to land the job and instead look complacent. Not the kind of employee that will work hard to win a new account and not give up until they get the order.

The first step should be obvious: the post-interview thank-you note.

Once your thank you is signed, sealed, and mailed you begin this art and practice of polite persistence. You want to stay in contact with the decision makers and on their collective minds. This can be achieved in many ways.

One of the best is to keep sending notes on a regular basis. These shouldn't be empty gestures that merely show you're still alive and available. They should be indications that you are already, in a sense, working for the company. For example, find an article that you think the hiring manager would find interesting or relevant. Send a note or email with the material attached.

Most often, it will be work-related, but you can also send items that simply reflect something you think the recipient will appreciate.

Perhaps during the job interview, the hiring manager mentioned that she enjoys reading histories of medieval England. Notice I did not say buy a copy of the book and deliver it. HR folks are very sensitive about what might be considered an unseemly gift or even a bribe. The offering of a book might be intended merely as an act of thoughtfulness, but it can be construed as a gift intended to purchase benefits or consideration. It could put the recipient in an uncomfortable position. More than likely, the HR recipient would have to send the book back and that would be awkward for everyone.

It might sound like I'm suggesting you do this only when you stumble across something relevant to your interview. Quite the opposite. Don't let happenstance dictate your career. Go looking for interesting items you can use to reconnect. Visit a bookstore to see what sorts of similar novels are on the market. Surf the internet. Find out what's out there and what people are saying or writing about the subject, then use the fruits of your labor to further your cause. Send along a note with a review attached. It's a nice gesture that can only elevate your status in the hiring manager's eyes—even if she knows why you're doing it (and she probably does).

Written notes are one way to maintain contact, but not the only way. You can call or even drop by, but do so only if you have a good, solid, plausible reason. Dropping by to just say "hi" is not sufficient. It's just wasting time—yours and theirs—and it might be perceived as a little weird and off-putting. But if you are dropping something off then it is reasonable to ask the receptionist or the HR person's assistant if, I don't have an appointment but "per chance" he or she is in and you could say hello. Never hurts to try. And make the receptionist your best friend. She or he can often go around the corner and cajole HR or the owner to come out and meet with you.

Similarly, keep your contacts professional. Sending work-relevant articles or observations is a good thing; sending cookies is not. Remember you are not their personal friend—yet. Keep all of your contacts businesslike and above-board. Never mention families or personal life. Think of it as "professional persistence." How often would you want to be contacted if the roles were reversed? Don't come across as a stalker. You never want to risk making them feel uncomfortable with you.

> *Janette was telling me she really wanted to show her seriousness about a job so she called several times a day for a week. Yeah, she didn't get the job. Polite persistence is not being obsessive. In HR we are trained to hit delete pretty fast.*

> *Doing all of the above doesn't necessarily eliminate the stress and angst of waiting to find out whether you got a job or not, but it just helps. At least you feel like you are engaged and working to make something happen. If you were the decision-maker, wouldn't you be impressed with the candidate that enthusiastically told you that he or she wanted the job and, very professionally, stayed in touch with you? Especially if all the other candidates left the interview never to be heard from again.*

And always keep in mind the old adage about not putting all of your eggs (and effort) in one basket. If you've interviewed for your "dream job," fantastic! Work the angles. Do everything you can to achieve success. But don't stop looking elsewhere. Maintain your networks, line up other interviews, and press forward on multiple fronts.

I've seen too many candidates do the job interview, then sit back to await word. Weeks pass. Then they come to me and say, "It's been two months and the company hasn't made a decision." Yes, they have made a decision; it just didn't involve you.

So when you think your candidacy is not getting the attention you think it deserves, what do you do? Last ditch, and I mean really last ditch, is to contact the hiring manager and tell them very politely and humbly that you have another job offer, followed quickly by "but your position at Company A really interests me and is my first choice. When do you think you will be making a decision?" This approach does one of two things: It kicks companies into gear (for fear of losing you) or gives them an easy out to say "take the other job." That's why

I emphasize last ditch: if you don't want to hear the answer, don't ask the question. But I understand sometimes you just want closure and this is the only way to get it.

If Company A was just putting off telling you that you are not getting the job offer, then the technique worked to finally get closure. If they really want you, then it got them into gear. Either action works for you. The difficult situation is if they say, "Thank you for telling us. You are still a viable candidate for the position but we are not ready to make a decision yet." Tell them that you can hold off for two more weeks; the game continues. They know there is a clock ticking. Offer to get back with them in a week for an update if you have not heard anything.

The other perspective – HR's

I've tried consistently to show that there's more than one perspective to any job-seeking enterprise. There's the viewpoint of the applicant, of course, which is critical. But even more critical is the perspective of the employer who, after all, is the one with the job opening.

Let's talk a bit about how employers view the job offer that they just presented, which for them is almost as big a moment as it is for you, the applicant; maybe more so since they will be investing measurable resources in their new hire.

Odds are the employer has gone through a fairly extensive, rigorous process to find the person they think is right for the job. Someone in HR (maybe many people) has combed through résumés, conducted interviews and research, and done much, much more to find…you.

Now they want to make the job offer and close the deal. A few things may be guiding their thought process at this point:

- Difficulty in filling the position.
- Speed of closure.
- Standard contract.
- No outliers.
- Long-term potential.

What do these things mean to you?

- If finding the right person for the job—you—was the result of a long, hard process, this bodes well for you in negotiating the terms of your employment. On the other hand, if there are a lot of other suitable candidates waiting in the wings, you shouldn't play too hard-to-get.
- Once a job offer is made, most employers want to wrap things up quickly. There are other things to do, other open jobs to fill.
- Most companies have a standard employment contract and prefer to stick to it as closely as possible. It's simpler. It's what they know and understand best. However, most companies also realize that a standard contract is not etched in stone. It's the basis for negotiation and can be changed. They're just likely to want to change it as little as possible.
- No outliers means they don't want to negotiate and approve an employment agreement with you that is dramatically or radically different from agreements with other employees. Don't ask for a higher salary than what your peers make—unless you can validate it. Don't ask for them to hold the job for a lengthy period while you take time off. The company wants a level playing field with equitable benefits so that everybody's equally happy—or unhappy.
- How long will you be with the company? Your answer, naturally, is just short of forever. You are a long-term solution. HR wants to believe that too, so they don't have to find your replacement in six months.

Hold your horses

The moment arrives.
You get the call.
You're offered the job.
You want the job.
You want to say yes.

WAIT! Negotiate!

In the military, you didn't really get to negotiate your orders. If you were lucky, you had a few months to request assignments as they came up. If you weren't so lucky, your new duty station was handed to you based on the needs of your service with no negotiation or even a "let me talk to my spouse about this transfer" before I accept it. As a civilian it is much different. You should never accept a proffered position until you've had time to consider all the pieces of the offer. These include, naturally, issues like salary and benefits but also might include things like flextime, office space, childcare, weekend work, and how much time you'll be away from home or family. Most job offers don't come out of the blue. By the time you've finished a job interview, you should have a pretty good notion of what the job entails, what it pays, and how it's likely to impact your career and life. Remember I told you not to ask about benefits early in the interview process. So now is the time to get very specific in your questions. Nonetheless, these issues cannot be fully evaluated until you have a legitimate job offer or employment agreement in hand.

And to do that, you need time—at the very least a few days, quite often more. And in the private sector we respect applicants who do not kneejerk accept job offers.

Asking for time to consider a job offer is fair and reasonable. You can do so by simply saying you need to discuss the offer's details with your spouse or family. In fact, employers may respect you more for taking time to discuss the job offer with your spouse. No employer should deny you this opportunity, and few would. If a would-be employer does, it's a red flag and you should immediately ask why an immediate decision is required. You might want to seriously reconsider whether you want to work there. A demand that you decide here and now suggests the company places its interests first and foremost, without real regard to employee rights or considerations. No matter what the work, a job offer is a compilation of many parts. It may be fairly simple or extremely complex. It may consist of only a few pages of paperwork that you can work through by yourself or require multiple binders and the assistance of a lawyer or employment professional.

Here are some quick rules of thumb for working out an employment agreement:

- The job offer or employment agreement must be in writing.
- Negotiate after the job offer, not before.
- Read and understand all of the documents involved. Take your time.
- Review documents or agreements with a lawyer, mentor or someone whose judgment you value and trust.
- Review the agreement with HR until you thoroughly understand it.
- Request a reasonable amount of time to review any documents.
- Everything can be discussed, everything may be negotiable.
- Strive for an agreement that is reasonable, clear, brief, and complete.
- Focus on the items most important to you. Negotiate hard for these items. Concede items that aren't important.
- Don't end your job search or eliminate other opportunities until you've actually started your new job.

When you get a job offer, take it home and analyze it. You want to see if it really meets all of your needs. You want to see if it contains elements that cause pause or which you might later regret. You want to balance the positives (big salary, company car) against the negatives (limited medical benefits, working weekends, travel).

You want to understand every aspect of a job offer. Nothing should come as a surprise later on. If you're confused about some part of the offer, ask for clarification from HR or, if appropriate, an outside entity like a lawyer.

The first thing almost everybody thinks about when considering a job is salary. Salary does tend to be the number one issue for most job applicants. In some cases, that's known going in and may be non-negotiable, though you can always inquire if you think there's reasonable room and cause for discussion.

In today's high tech start up world, we are seeing less emphasis on salary and more on stock options. Educate yourself about what this means to you.

The offer you get will likely depend upon a number of factors, some based on you and your qualifications, others on the nature of the company and industry. These include:

- Your work experience. More experience, more money.
- The market rate for your position. Companies keep a close eye on what competitors are paying employees. They want to offer attractive salaries, not excessive ones.
- The nature of the work. Is this job one of a hundred just like it or singular? How many people can do the work? How many have applied for the position?
- The nature of the company. Some businesses and industries have fairly rigid salary schedules. They're locked in by union contracts, business customs or plain old inertia. Young firms may be more flexible and open-minded than older companies that have been doing things a certain way for a long time.

Negotiating your employment package

When a company finally makes a salary offer, always consider making a counteroffer. But be reasonable and have compelling, persuasive arguments to back it up.

It's hard to know how much a company is willing to pay, but almost invariably a first offer is at least slightly less than the maximum. (By the way, if any CEO or HR Manager asks me about this I will deny that I ever said it!)

If you think you're worth more than the first offer and want to counter, do your homework. Find out what your value is in the job market. You might already have a good idea if you've been doing a certain kind of work for a while, but don't hesitate to go beyond that for new information, advice and tips. Look at job board listings describing similar positions. Use salary calculators at various job-related websites, such as CareerBuilder.com or Monster.com. Payscale.

com, for example, offers pay analysis comparing your job profile to the salary and compensation packages of people whose skills and experience match yours. And Salary.com provides on-demand compensation management, information on pay and benefits as well as performance and salary data. Users can research the assessed worth of their position based on job title and ZIP code searches. Cost-of-living calculators and salary differentials are also offered.

If you're inexperienced or fretful about compensation negotiations, don't be reluctant to seek guidance and help. If you have a trusted mentor, ask for advice. Be wary of family or friends, however, who may have your best interests at heart, but no real insight or knowledge about negotiating salary and benefits. This advisor should be someone who is active in the job market and has some experience navigating this world. Maybe they are even in the same career field you would like to transition into.

Most of all, think long and hard about how you make a counter-offer. The last thing you want a new employer to think is that it's just about money—and that you view the offered salary to be inadequate. You worked hard to get this job, to convince your new boss that you will be an exemplary employee driven by real interest in the work, and that you have upstanding values. Don't undermine that perception by immediately asking for more money, unless you know for a fact that you can make a solid, persuasive, fact-based case for bumping it up.

Far better to take the job, work hard, and earn a big, fast pay raise later.

Rebecca, a manager for another Manpower franchise, contacted me about job opportunities at our operations. At the time, she worked at the largest and most respected Manpower franchise, so I was really interested in the possibility of her joining our team. I thought we could learn a lot from her about how to grow our business and become even more successful.

After various discussions and interviews, I thought she seemed like the ideal person to head a new "permanent placement division" and I offered her our normal starting package. She paused, pointed out that her years of experience merited a much higher salary and that the new job she was being asked to do warranted additional compensation. I told her that my offer was our normal package and I wasn't accustomed to negotiating.

Her reply: "Don't you want me to negotiate as hard on your behalf when you hire me as I am now on my behalf?" Wow! She was absolutely right. I suddenly realized that her years of experience were probably worth what she was asking for and that the unprecedented duties deserved unprecedented compensation. The epiphany for me was not to simply rule out counteroffers. Period, no discussion. It's up to job candidates to put forth serious, reasonable, valid reasons for increased compensation packages. It's up to people like me to give them serious consideration. I agreed with her arguments and wound up hiring her because of her negotiating skills. We're both happy.

Salary negotiation

When you do negotiate, strive to maximize your compensation package without appearing unreasonable or inflexible. This can be a tricky process, demanding equal amounts of smarts, finesse, dexterity, creativity, and good faith.

In the military, the concept of negotiating salary and benefits was nonexistent. Your compensation was tied to extremely clear criteria such as rank, time in rank, and few other factors like extra combat pay. There was no negotiation – you took the salary that came with your rank. So it makes sense that salary negotiation is one of the most popular questions that come up in our veterans career seminars. And the topic understandably causes much anxiety for candidates. Now that you've come so far through the interviewing process, you don't want to blow it by holding out for too much. On the other hand, you also don't want to leave money on the table. How do you navigate these choppy waters?

1. Know your number: just like interviewing, salary negotiations also require careful preparation. Hopefully you have an idea as to the compensation range the company can offer. We mentioned ways to delicately ascertain this number near the beginning of the interview process. You should also calculate the absolute lowest figure you could accept for this position, and have that ready before entering into negotiations.

2. Look at the total package: it's not just about cash. Many other benefits in the compensation package have big economic importance: relocation expenses, healthcare, retirement, and other benefits, vacation time, tuition reimbursement for additional education, and flexible working hours/locations are probably the most common. Sales positions may also have a car in the package as well. Make sure you understand everything the employer is including in the comp package before you throw out a salary number.

3. Don't' be too greedy: pushing for anything higher than 20% over the initial offer could price you out of the running. And don't hold out for chump change. If you push for $80,000, and they come back with $75,000 as their best and final, you'd be an idiot not to accept, so long as you can live comfortably on $75K. Besides, a modest raise of just 7% next year will more than close the gap.

4. Have your justifications ready: if you're going to negotiate for more comp, you'll need to be able to justify why the company should hire you at a premium. What extra capabilities and experience are you brining to the role? Can you point to specific accomplishments in your work history as evidence?

5. Hold your fire: it's a classic negotiating tactic, but it's advantageous to let the other person make the first move. If the company's first offer is $75,000, that figure now becomes the floor level, or anchor. Now that a figure is on the table, you are not going to accept anything under that amount. Only higher numbers will be discussed.

6. Know when they can't move: some employers, especially government entities, are actually fairly similar to the military when it comes to compensation. They have set ranges for each position in the organization, and no matter how good you are, there is no way you are going to get a dime more. There may also not be any negotiating with the other benefits either. The good news however is that government agencies are usually very transparent about their salary ranges – if it's not actually on their website, just ask. That information should be readily available.

Employers will sometimes quote salary in annual terms ($75,000 per year) or hourly terms ($36.06 per hour). The quick and easy way to convert back and forth is to assume there are 2,080 working hours in a year: 2,080 x $36.06 = $75,000. So how do you even commence negotiating? First, you have to be fairly confident your salary requirement is close enough to the company's range. Then you ride out the rest of the interviewing process, and wait for the company to issue an offer. Thank them sincerely – you might say something like:

> *"Thank you! I'm really excited to receive an offer, and I look forward to reviewing it. May I have a few days to look it over carefully?"*

You have let the company know that you are excited about joining them, but you haven't committed to anything yet. The momentum is still going forward, and you've bought yourself some time to prepare for your next move. Negotiations are officially open! Most companies are comfortable waiting for a few days, maybe up to a week. However, if they pressure you to accept right then and there, that should be a red flag. Is this how they do business, and is that the kind of organization you want to be a part of? I'm not saying a high-pressure tactic like that on their part would be a total deal-breaker, but it should definitely make you stop and think. In this example, let's assume the company says they'd like to hear back in 72 hours – not unreasonable.

Now let's assume the package is acceptable, but you really feel you're worth an additional $10K. Your next move would be a call to the recruiter or hiring manager:

> *"Thanks again for the offer – the package looks pretty good. However, there is one area I'm hoping you can help me with, in order to get everything locked down."*

From here you can then go in a couple of different directions:

1. "I'm currently at $75,000 in my current position, so $80,000 would enable me to make a move."
2. "Given the additional skills and experience I can bring to the role, I think $80,000 is where I'd like to be." (Be sure to have your evidence ready if you play this card.)

Here are a few last thoughts on salary negotiations:

- Remember, it should be one of the very last steps in the process. Everything about the job itself should just about be finalized: location, scope of work, etc. If you're not sure about the role, don't waste time entering negotiations. It's like waiting for a guy to propose before breaking up with him.
- Sensitive topics like salary negotiations should be done by phone or in-person. Email is too casual for such an important, personal topic. It sounds old school, but it also demonstrates professionalism.
- Keep it positive! Most of us have a tendency to get a little adversarial when negotiations get tough. Don't let this happen – keep the same cheerful disposition you've had all throughout the interview process. Remember how important likeability is. If the company perceives you're becoming a hard-ass, they may decide they can live without you after all, and rescind the offer. Salary negotiations are one of the last conversations you'll have with your new employer prior to your first day on the job. Make sure the tone stays positive, so you set yourself up for success on day 1 of your new career.

You've landed the job and have agreed on salary but may have never had the opportunity to negotiate for a benefits and package. As a veteran you have also taken many benefits for granted. It is always a shock to hear how much the private sector pays for family healthcare. You've taken it for granted. You will also be paying retail for items you were previously able to purchase on base at the exchange. While every compensation package is different, here are some of the likely elements you might find and need to consider:

- Health Insurance. After salary, this is the biggest and most variable part of any compensation package. In the military, you never had to negotiate for this and it can be quite intimidating. Unless you privately insure yourself, your employment agreement should include some type of medical and long-term disability insurance. Ideally, it should also offer dental, vision, life and short-term disability (or at least provide the option of buying into these programs through a group rate plan). The harsh reality, alas, is that many companies only offer medical insurance to full-time employees. (Part-timers and contract employees are often left to their own devices.)
- Whatever your proffered options, pay close attention to them. If you're confused, ask questions. Learn the differences between preferred providers and HMOs, and which is best for you and your family. Is there a pension plan? A 401K? Does your employer provide any kind of matching money? Your hard work now will pay off later.
- Bonus or incentive pay. Is this pay in addition to an acceptable base salary or offered as a way to bulk up a substandard paycheck? If it's the latter, what are the benchmarks for achieving the extra income? Are they reasonable? Are they achievable? If you feel the starting salary is lower that you expected then how quickly do you feel you will be able to get back to parity and what will you have to accomplish and is it reasonable?
- Signing bonus. Unless you're a southpaw with a 100-mile-per-hour fastball, don't expect a signing bonus. They're increasingly rare in the ordinary business world, though you might be able to negotiate something like a bonus if you're

being asked to uproot and move your family across country. Call it a relocation fee.

- Previously scheduled time-off. Let's say you had a long-planned trip with the family to the ancestral homelands. A new job opportunity arises. You go for it. You get it. The new employer is eager for you to start as soon as possible. It's often quite possible to negotiate that time off before you begin the new job—and make sure it isn't deducted from your vacation time with the new company. The request is more common than you think, and most companies will work with new employees if they can. The key is to be upfront and proactive.

- Working from home. Many employees relish the idea. Many companies do too, especially if it helps the bottom line. (A company saves money if it doesn't have to find office space for everybody, every day.) If you want to work from home and it's feasible in your new position, discuss the option. Be clear and specific about why this is a good idea and how it will help the company. Don't forget to ask about reimbursements for costs like your internet connection, long-distance phone calls, office supplies, and postage. But be sure you are at your best working at home and away from the company support and camaraderie. I would be miserable working from home. Be careful what you ask for.

- Stock options. If a company offers these, investigate them in detail. Are they based on performance or paygrade level? Look at their historical market value? Beware of companies that offer you stock options in lieu of salary or benefits. A stock option is only as good as the company offering it. A company that pays with stock options may be giving you worthless paper.

- Severance pay. It seems a little odd to ask about compensation if things go sour, kind of like insisting on a prenuptial agreement with your future spouse. But, hey, this is business. It's not personal. The work world is a tough, volatile place. Things don't always go as you hope and plan. A dream job can become a nightmare. You might find yourself in a depressingly familiar position again—unemployed. If that happens, you'll be grateful that you discussed severance pay when times were young, beautiful and everybody smiled. Many companies have standard severance packages, which range from a guarantee of at least two weeks' pay to several months. The longer you're with a company, the bigger the severance package should be. Asking about severance pay might sound unseemly, but it's really not. You have a right to know what might happen if the worst happens.

- Non-compete agreements. Some industries and companies ask new employees to sign an agreement promising that they will not work for a direct competitor for a specific period of time after leaving a job. Usually it's one or two years. They do it to protect themselves. They don't want ex-employees spilling company secrets. If you're asked to sign a non-compete agreement, think first before you sign. It might be a no-brainer if you plan to spend the next 10-15 years at the same company, but if you imagine yourself leaving much sooner, perhaps working for similar companies, it behooves you to go slow. Read the agreement carefully. Make sure it's reasonable and not overly restrictive. If it's the latter, ask for changes—but only if you can reasonably defend them. And know that non-compete agreements are illegal in many states so it may not be an issue you need to bring up.

- Other perks. Company cars or car allowances, continuing education (thought about getting that MBA?), special loans, paid memberships to clubs, enhanced insurance benefits, discounts to local businesses or attractions.

Always keep in mind when the first compensation package is offered, there are features that may be of real value to you, but don't cost the employer any more money. These might even be features the employer has never offered before. Some examples are flex time— either hours or days. An 8-to-5 shift may be traditional, but it's hardly written in stone. In fact, in the military you probably rarely had a 9-to-5 so you may want it now, but if now, there are all kinds of work week formulations that might do the job and save you time, money, and hassle (like a ten hour day, four days a week saves on daycare). If you and your employer can work out an arrangement that's mutually beneficial and agreeable, go for it.

Vacation and Personal Time Off (PTO) falls into this category. The company's paying you an annual salary. Another week of vacation or PTO won't cost them anything, other than a week of your labor, but it may mean a lot to you. Also PTO blocks your sick days and vacation.

Similarly, telecommuting is a growing option for many employers. They save the overhead costs of housing employees; you save the cost of commute time and expense. With the price of gas regularly surging upward, it's a measurable benefit not to have to drive to work every day.

Making the hard decision

Getting a job offer might seem like a slam-dunk decision, but sometimes it is not. It can be a moment of great importance, especially the first time it happens after you've left the military. I've known countless job applicants who worked assiduously to line up a job, only to balk, the moment it was offered.

A little balkiness is natural. A new job means venturing into the unknown, especially that first private sector job out of your military comfort zone. That gives most veterans some pause. But what about applicants who seem to do and say all the right things to get a job, then suddenly don't seem all that interested when it's offered to them?

Usually the reason is not a surprise: The job was never right for them—or they were never right for the job. Confronted with the opportunity, they suddenly see reasons why they shouldn't seize it. Those reasons were always there. They just didn't recognize them.

Before you take a job, weigh the intangibles. Some of them you should already have pondered earlier in the job-hunting process when you were plotting what kind of work you wanted to do. Earlier in this chapter I talked about what employees said made for a fulfilling job situation. Now, its crunch time for the job offer. Opportunity has knocked. Are you going to answer?

Ask yourself these questions (again):

1. Do you want to learn new skills? Does this job teach them?
2. Is this job a stepping stone on a longer career path?
3. Does this job give you more authority and/or responsibility? Do you want them?
4. Will you be challenged? Do you want to be challenged?
5. Do you want to work alone or as part of a team?
6. Are you looking for a position with less stress?
7. Do you want to work in a fast-moving, high-growth industry?
8. What kind of job security do you need?
9. How important is pay, title or perks?
10. What about overtime, travel, working weekends?
11. How will the new job affect life at home? How does your family view it?

These, of course, are only a few questions you might reasonably ask yourself. And you'll need to take a hard look at comparing those answers in a realistic manner to what they were while you served in the military. Depending upon the particulars of the job and your circumstances, there are many, others too. The point is to have a serious discussion with yourself (and others) so that when you make your decision, it was an educated one and you know exactly why and can live with it.

Your first day

When you get to this point, you've almost arrived. There is always more work to do, which is why there are two more chapters after this one. Your first day of work marks the end of one process and the beginning of a new one.

We'll go into greater detail about what happens after Day One at the new job, but first let's discuss how to tie up a few loose ends and get things off to a fabulous start. The basics are really pretty easy, and mirror some of the things you've learned and done to get this far. They will also mirror some of the things you learned when shifting between units or commands in the military.

A first day at work is a lot like going to a job interview. You want to adequately prepare. If possible, know what will be expected of you when you walk in the door that first time. Be on time. Look good. Dress appropriately. Smile and greet others warmly. These are all things you would've done on your first day at a new command in the military. And much like checking in to a new command, you'll likely be paraded around to several different folks for introductions. These are your co-workers. First impressions count, and relationships often bloom or die based on first impressions.

First days are often a whir of new names and faces, most of which you fear you'll never remember, especially since their names are not on their uniforms out in the civilian world. You will, but more important, remember this: Everybody you meet may play a big part in your unfolding career. The job hierarchy is not nearly as clearly defined in the private sector.

Besides no name tag and no uniform, no one will have their rank on their chest or sleeve. A co-worker you meet today could be your boss tomorrow. Or vice versa. Treat everyone with dignity and respect. No matter how high up you are in the managerial chain, these are the people who can make you or break you. Develop a relationship where they want you to succeed and they respect your time in the military, and don't resent it. Remember you are entering their private sector world, and they are not coming under your command.

As you begin to put faces with names, learn as much as you can. Who are the movers and shakers in your department or company? Who are the best and brightest? Who can help you become a better employee and person? Use them as models and mentors. Basically, these are the same principles you've already learned from your time in service.

Finally, go for it. You may be the new guy or gal, but now is not the time to be shy. Ask questions. Seek responsibility. If your new boss is looking for volunteers, step up. The learning curve might be steeper and harder, but you'll get to the top of the hill faster.

phil-osophy 101   10

This chapter really brings together two overarching thoughts.

The first is a variation on the line from Walt Kelly's celebrated cartoon character Pogo, who wryly opined, "We have met the enemy and he is us."

As I mentioned before, we all have a Career Manager and he is us. Our Career Manager exists not just to help find us a job. He (or she) is also there to guide us when we have a job. My point: Your work doesn't end when you find work. Never stop thinking about your career, both what's happening in the moment and what will happen next. All of the work you did to get your current, fabulous position now transitions into labors to keep and excel at this job. We often forget that as an employee our relationship with our employer is only as secure as how essential we are perceived to that employer's success. If management thinks you're not critical to the equation, then you're vulnerable to being tagged as excess, an overhead cost that can be cut. We are all temps! Never forget it.

Similarly, you're likely to remain with a company or employer only as long as you find the position rewarding, both financially and intellectually. Your personal Career Manager should always have his radar out, looking for new challenges for you. The challenge can be within or outside the company.

Always keep this radar turned on, not only in terms of detecting new opportunities over the horizon, but in staying on top of changing conditions at work. That's not to say every job is an immediate stepping stone to the next, but you should start actively searching for your next opportunity when either you or your employer begin to feel a lack of value in your working partnership. You want to always be in the position of quitting, not being fired.

Watch the caliber of new hires coming into your department. If their skill levels are way above yours, then you may be getting stale. You risk being perceived as the "old way of doing things." This is your red flag to upgrade your skills as fast as you can, to do whatever it takes.

If your company is hiring lower-skilled workers, then be aware that you may be overqualified for the job, probably more expensive, and the work you have been doing is ready to be outsourced or automated. None of this is good for your long-term future in that position.

With your career management radar working 24/7, there should never be any surprises in your career, except perhaps the pleasant kind.

10.0   Keeping the Job

Work is more than just work. It defines who we are.

For one thing, like it or not, it fundamentally determines how we live. I want to be Hoda Kotb, hobnobbing daily with the world's most powerful and interesting people, but that's not my job. Likewise, the fellow who sits behind a desk 9 to 5, Monday through Friday, can believe with all of his heart he has the soul of an explorer, but in fact, he's an accountant and will remain so unless he changes jobs and realities.

A major theme of this book is defining what kind of job you desire and how to get it, recognizing, of course, that in tough times, just getting a cash flow started may be your overriding goal. That's okay in the short term.

What happens, though, once you've landed the job? Your first day at a new job is bound to be exciting, fraught with expectation, high hopes, and maybe a little uncertainty. It's the days that follow, however, that will determine whether your job — and career — are successful.

What does that mean: career success? The answer is completely subjective. For all people some of the time and some people all of the time, it is measured in terms of salary, perks, and acquisitions. A big paycheck, car, and house are obvious benchmarks. Have those, and most folks will think you're doing just fine.

But career success — that is, how you measure the value of your work — is also determined by more personal standards and criteria. It is defined by ideals absorbed and developed from family, friends, education, society, and life experience.

Part of what makes a dream job dreamy is knowing how to recognize, pursue and achieve the elements of a job that provide rewards not measurable by a paycheck or a purchase. These rewards can change with time, experience and outlook. One of your greatest career challenges is determining your definition of success, what it means to you and how to achieve it. Here are some tips and tools to help.

First, success takes hard work. Henry David Thoreau once said, "Success comes most often to people too busy to look for it." Woody Allen said 80% of success was just showing up. There's truth in that joke, but success also means knowing why you've showed up, and why you're there. To define job and career success, you've got to know why you work. How many of these commonly cited reasons apply to you:

- To earn a living
- To become rich
- To help others
- To leave a mark in history
- To travel
- To become famous
- To develop skills
- To learn new things
- To become an expert
- To pursue personal interests
- To make the world a better place

There are lots of smart people out there. You are one of them. You got the job. Now you need to stay smart and get smarter. That means keeping up-to-date on what's happening in your world of work, and using that knowledge to make yourself a better employee. Professional organizations are a great way to do that. You will find no lack of professional associations that you can join that relate to your new job. And each group will have a diversity of thought and background that you would never find within the military. There is always lots to learn and you need to be like a sponge and soak it all in.

Employers want people who can listen as well as talk, have the ability to communicate with others both orally and in writing, who know how to manage themselves, make decisions, solve problems, learn new skills, lead, and more.

These are not just desired attributes, they are essential to continued success and reaching your goals. If the work world was ever easy (and I'm not sure it was), it is not now. The labor force is shrinking and aging, but also hanging onto jobs longer because people can't afford to retire. Post-9/11 veterans are leaving the military and entering the work force. Many land six or seven jobs before they find their new career, so do not be discouraged if that sounds like you. Some industries are experiencing radical restructuring. Jobs are disappearing or changing. Old skill sets are becoming obsolete. Think Lyft/Uber, driverless cars, and artificial intelligence. New skill sets demand abilities unimagined just a few years ago. Job security and employee longevity are virtually gone. Getting a job is hard work. Keeping a job may be even harder.

JobWon! Day one and beyond

You've got the job. It's time to go to work. First days and weeks on a new job are usually a bit nerve-wracking. Like the first day at a new school, everything's new and unknown — from colleagues to specific duties to where the restrooms are. Feeling a bit overwhelmed is natural and probably good. Don't worry about it too much. You got the job. You beat out everybody else. They wanted you!

The trick is to make sure your bosses don't think they've made a mistake. The first few weeks and months of a new job are critical to success. First impressions count, so do second and third ones. All of it combines to build your reputation at work, how people see and think about you.

There are basic elements to making a strong, positive impression on people, first or otherwise. They include appearance, attitude, work habits, attendance, personality, ability to fit in and an evident interest in others and surroundings. More specifically:

- Good attendance. If you're new to a job, shoot for perfect attendance - 100%. No, make that 110%.
- Show your dedication early. In a new job: this is critical. To establish a good reputation, you must put in the time. Arrive early, stay late. Your hours may ease as you begin to understand your responsibilities and find ways to do them better in less time, but in the beginning, it's all about not just showing up, but being there present and engaged.
- Learn names and roles quickly. Everybody likes having his or her name remembered. It indicates they've made an impression on you, that they were worth your devoting a few neural circuits to memorizing them. You may meet a lot of people. It may be hard to remember all of their names, but try.

If you ask people what their favorite word in the English language is, they will always hesitate and become introspective. Research has shown that our favorite word is our own name. When you meet people, use their name repeatedly as a way to help remember it. When you say good morning to someone, add their name at the beginning or end. You will see them visibly perk up. People appreciate the recognition and familiarity of other people using their names. And you will be surprised how rarely people use other people's names when they are talking to them. You will see lots of long-term dividends from this trick.

There are lots of ways and resources to improve your memory for names. A quick surf of the Internet reveals scores of websites with advice. Here are a few quick tips:

- Be interested. Pay conscious attention when first introduced. Don't let the name just wash over and past your brain.
- Verify it. Casually repeat the name back. Ask how it's spelled if the name is unusual. If you're at a conference or place

where people wear name tags, check the tag. Don't be shy to admit you're just trying to fix that person's name in your head. They'll appreciate the effort.

- Imagine their name written on their forehead. That was Franklin Roosevelt's favorite mnemonic device. Use different colors of imaginary ink.
- Write their names in your head. Watch your hand forming the letters.
- Use word associations. If someone's name is Hattie, imagine them wearing a stack of hats on their head. If their name is Jack, imagine them hammering away outside with a big, noisy pneumatic jack. If their name is Arnold, imagine them saying, "Hasta la vista, baby." Whatever works.
- As I said, use names frequently. Once you know somebody's name, use it soon and often. Don't be too obvious or obnoxious about it (you don't want to sound like a salesman), but a few uses should get the name into a groove you'll easily recall.
- Record names in a file you can easily call up, such as a contacts list on your cell phone. Review the file regularly, maybe every time you update it with a new name. Peruse it whenever you anticipate being in a place or situation where you're likely to meet people whose names you should know or remember.
- Know your goals. Know what's expected of you. If you don't get one, ask your boss to go over your job description and understand where you are expected to be in 30, 60 and 90 days. Are there specific benchmarks, such as skills you must learn or goals you must reach?
- Ask questions. Don't assume anything, which as the old saying goes, can make an idiot out of you and me, but also get you fired. It's much easier to ask for instructions now than to explain a mistake later. This is no time for the "easier to ask for forgiveness than permission. Listen carefully to answers. Write them down, if necessary. You aren't expected to know everything immediately. People expect you to ask for help. If you don't, they may think you're just not paying attention or worse, you don't really care.

- Ask for feedback. Don't be afraid to ask, "How am I doing?" Seek input and guidance from others to ensure you're heading in the right direction, that you're doing things correctly. Fix a mistake before it's a fatal one. Your boss and co-workers will appreciate it.
- Remember, it's not the military. The big shock to you may be that, on the civilian side, companies don't operate like the military. The way folks interact is a bit different and accountability may not be the same. It's imperative that you understand and adopt the existing company culture. Even if you've been brought in specifically to change the culture, you need a general understanding of it first.
- Gather information around you. Be inquisitive and observant. Talk to your colleagues about work, about any "unwritten rules." Learn the inside scoop, but avoid gossip. This is not about being nosy or meddlesome. This is about better understanding your workplace so that you can be as productive as possible.
- Stay organized. This means having a system for retaining and using what you know and learn. Create a file system that works for you. I use a leather bound notebook that I keep with me at all times and jot notes down as I talk to people. It will always be a good reference tool that I can scan through to remind myself of important points. Be realistic about what you can and will do. Don't go out and buy a bank of filing cabinets that will end up ignored, empty and gathering dust somewhere. Start modestly and build up as work demands. Keep a calendar—on your computer, cell phone or in your briefcase. Consult and update it regularly. Write down meetings. Make project plans. Do everything you can to stay on top of what's happening. You'll feel better, more in control and fewer things will fall through the cracks.
- Be and stay positive. Leave your personal life at home and (and conversely, leave your work life at work). Be enthusiastic at work. It makes everything easier, for you and your co-workers.
- Fit in. Don't do or say anything that will make you stand out in a negative way. That includes what you wear, when you

come or leave work, when you take lunch, how you behave in meetings and among co-workers. There will be time and opportunity to express your individuality later.

- Be a team player. Make the effort (extra or not) to help whenever you can. People want to see if you can fit into and work in a group. The best way to prove you can is to reach out to others. Remember back in the interviewing chapter when we talked about veterans needing to stop saying "we" when HR asks about accomplishments in your previous work? I encourage you to start thinking "I" accomplished certain projects. Well now is the time to file that away and become the team player that was drilled into you for 20 years. Be flexible. Follow the lead of others and be as supportive as you can. You must become part of the pack before you can become the leader of it.

- Avoid or minimize personal business. Your job is where you do your job, not where you buy stuff online, surf the internet, call family and friends or make party plans for the weekend. Do these things on your own time after work, during lunch, or on scheduled breaks.

- Practice the 80/20 rule. Listen 80% of the time, talk 20%. If you talk too much, you're likely to find others tuning you out, especially if you're too free with irrelevant opinions. In fact, avoid opining if at all possible. Stick to research and facts versus feelings and unsubstantiated observations and hearsay.

- Don't act like you know it all. You may have been hired because you possess a rare and impressive set of skills, but don't put it all out there immediately for everybody to appreciate. They won't. In fact they will resent you. A few days or months aren't nearly enough to establish you as the consummate expert, unless of course you were hired precisely to fill that position. But even then, be modest. Offer your knowledge and expertise confidently, and with some humility. We can all learn from others.

- Read company literature and rules. It may be boring. There may be a lot of it. But it's important for you to be a student of your company. Just like in the military, the written documentation contains the key to the castle. You should understand what your company does and how it seeks to position itself among competitors and in the world. Annual reports and sales brochures are good sources of information and insight. If any of it doesn't make sense to you, ask to have it explained.

A good book to read about this topic is Michael Watkins's *First 90 Days*. He covers all of this and a lot more.

Surviving and thriving in the workplace

No two places of employment are alike. That's obviously true when comparing an auto body shop to a hair salon, but it also applies to companies and businesses in the same line of work. Your job in the military will not likely be similar to your new civilian job. A bank is not a bank is not a bank. Bank of America is not the same working environment as Credit Suisse. Every workplace has its own rules, types of people, and challenges. The quicker you figure out how your new workplace works, the better you will do. Be a good observer and a better participant. The first few months are all about blending in. You can spread your feathers when you feel comfortable that you are on firm ground.

Let's start with a consideration of "corporate culture." What precisely does that mean? Wikipedia describes it as "the psychology, attitudes, experiences, beliefs, and values (personal and cultural) of an organization." It has been defined as "the specific collection of values and norms that are shared by people and groups in an organization and that control the way they interact with each other and with stakeholders outside the organization."

Corporate culture is "how things get done around here." And that clearly affects you. Corporate culture in the private sector world can often be 180 degrees different than in any branch of the military.

A company's culture/system/routine will dictate or influence:

- The number of hours you work per day or per week, and whether you're required to put in traditional eight-hour days or can choose options like flextime or telecommuting.
- The environment in which you work, whether it's competitive or collegial, formal or relaxed, nose-to-the-grindstone or fun.
- The dress code, what's acceptable, whether there are casual days. What exactly defines "casual?"
- The way you communicate with colleagues. Are there lots of regularly scheduled meetings or are decisions made ad hoc in hallways? We all know companies whose style is to email the person in the next cubicle. How do you interact with management? Is there an open door policy? Is there a hierarchy, with lots of gatekeepers between you and the top managers?
- In our Manpower offices we have a "door policy." Most of the time all of our managers' doors are wide open, encouraging fellow workers to come in at any time to interact. If the door is partially closed that means the occupant is involved in something or with someone but it is okay to stick your nose in if it is an important issue. But if the door is closed and latched (the infamous click), then the building better be on fire and you are breaking in to save our lives!
- Your office space. Will you have an office, a cubicle or just a desk in a sea of desks? Can you display personal items? If yes, bring in a framed picture of your family (not in uniform) so your coworkers can learn more about you and it looks like you are settling in for the long haul—literally nesting.
- Your development opportunities. Does the company run training programs for advancement? Can you attend professional conferences? Are there ways to improve yourself to make you a better employee and more marketable for future jobs and employers?
- The perks available. Some companies are rich with them: onsite gyms, daycare facilities, and such. Often the abundance and variety of perks is a reflection of how well an industry and companies are doing, or how competitive and creative it must be to attract and keep high-quality employees.

Think about corporate culture like you think about buying a car. You want a car that's comfortable, matches your personal style, and lasts long enough to get you where you want to go. A car that keeps breaking down doesn't meet these requirements, and obviously it isn't a good fit. A company culture that doesn't match your needs is probably one where you just won't fit in, which means it's not likely to take you very far.

No matter what the job, there are certain qualities that all top-performing employees share. These are skills applicable to almost any kind of work. They're portable. You can take them with you from job to job. You probably already have some of these from the military. Master them and you are master of your fate:

- Time management. Making the most of your time boosts productivity and efficiency. Make to-do lists. Keep your schedule up-to-date. Prioritize projects and goals. Meet deadlines.
- Be dependable. You want to be the go-to person in your office. That doesn't mean you have to be a pushover, the guy everybody dumps work upon. It does mean that when you agree to do a job, you do the job. On time and on or under budget.
- Look and act promotable. You've got a job, but unless you plan to make it the last job you ever have, think long-term. Act like you're a man or woman on a mission, always prepared to take the next step, to take your career to the next level. Dress accordingly. In fact, dress for the job you want, not the job you have. Showcase your work when you can. Go above and beyond.
- Create value in everything you do. Don't just cross things off a to-do list. If you have a job to do, do it well. Commit your best effort to all tasks, large and small. That might be challenging at times, but people notice. Always exceed expectations and follow the trite saying to under promise and over deliver.

- Be resourceful. Think outside the box. If you're doing a job and you see a better way to do it, speak up (in a polite, respectful way). Anticipate problems and find answers before they're needed. In the military, you probably heard that it was better to be a solutions person than a problems person, and the same goes here. Don't be afraid to do a little legwork, a little sweating before its necessary. If you have to bring the boss or the department a problem then always also bring a potential solution. It will always pay off.

- Get noticed. There's nothing wrong with stepping up and stepping out: Volunteer for extra duties. Look for chances to be part of a team. Likewise, look for chances to work with other departments, both to learn about that department but also to meet new people. Offering to manage the United Way campaign for your company is an example of a good way to work with many of the other departments and have the opportunity to make companywide presentations and to exceed goals and set new records.

- And always offer to work with key customers. They are your magic carpet to being invaluable to your company. If the company's largest customer loves you, your boss will love you too. Amazing how that works. Your visibility and success will rise as others think of you when the next big, exciting project comes around.

- Stay informed. Become an expert in your field. That includes staying on top of industry news and trends, company policies, department memos, etc. Read the company newsletter. Talk to others in the know. The more information you have at hand, the better prepared you will be when opportunity comes knocking. Be seen as the go to guy in your department: it will be noticed.

- Stay positive. No matter what's going on, remain level-headed, upbeat, with your eye on the prize. There are always ups and downs but focus on the long-term. Be the person who brings energy into any room they enter. You know my feelings about sighing and yawning. They both suck all the energy out of any room. If you have a temper, it is your—and only your—responsibility to never show it at work.

- Be a team player. This is about more than just getting along with others or telling a good joke. In meetings or group efforts, you want to be seen as a valued contributor who offers feedback, meets deadlines, and gets things done— all for the common good. Know your teammates, their strengths and strive to make them look good too.
- Conduct effective meetings. The best way to avoid getting anything done is to call a meeting. That's a little harsh, but meetings truly are the most abused aspect of the workday. The best meetings are short, sweet and to the point. If you're calling the meeting or running it, make sure you have an agenda and stick to it. Make sure only the people that need to be at the meeting are there. Stay on point. Allow everyone to speak who wants to speak, but keep them focused on the subject. Try to complete all of the tasks of the meeting before the meeting ends. If that's not possible, assign action items with due dates. And you will always be a hero if you cancel a meeting that was scheduled but found to be unneeded. You become the one who gave back to employees an hour or two of their day.
- Be a leader. You don't need an impressive title to be a leader. You remember the folks in the military who lead despite their titles. Even though you may be the boss, your job is to bring your staff and co-workers along with you on a project. Never appear to be commanding them to follow you blindly because of your higher rank. You need the requisite attributes: Initiative. Persuasiveness. A sense of responsibility. Creativity. Fearlessness. Want more details: Read John Wooden's 1997 book (with Steve Jamieson), *Wooden: A Lifetime of Observations and Reflections On and Off the Court.* One of the all-time greatest basketball coaches and an even greater molder of young men, Wooden reflects upon what he learned in a lifetime of teaching about basketball and life. It's heartfelt and brilliant. (There's also a 2005 follow-up by Wooden and Jamieson called *Wooden on Leadership: How to Create a Winning Organization.*)

All forms of communication are important. You know you need to speak clearly, concisely, and get to the point as quickly as possible. If you have a heavy accent that others struggle to understand, it is your obligation to speak slowly and enunciate. In a professional environment, do your very best to speak without the accent. This is not to hide your ethnicity or background. It is your problem if people cannot understand you. In the long run you will be the loser, not them. There are also "Accent Modification/Reduction" courses available, online and in person, to help you to lose or soften your accent.

And then there is email. In some ways, email has supplanted the phone as the most common form of business communication. However, be aware of when it is or is not appropriate to use email in place of a phone call or face-to-face meeting. Email is impersonal and might be counterproductive. When you do email for business, follow these basic rules:

- Pique the recipient's curiosity with a descriptive subject line. If it's not, there's a decent chance the recipient won't even open up the email.
- Begin with a greeting and end with a close. Include contact information. Do not use V/r or whatever you use in the military. Remember to civilianize.
- Watch your tone. Don't use all UPPERCASE letters, which is commonly perceived as a sort of digitized yelling. Use proper grammar and punctuation.
- Be brief. People get lots of emails. If yours are like books, people will learn not to open them or will wait to read yours when they have more time. That time may never come and you need an answer now.
- Only use "reply all" when absolutely necessary.
- If you have attachments, mention them in the body of the email so that the recipient will know to look for them.
- Proofread before you transmit. A badly written email with misspellings is not the image you want to send. And watch out for spell-check. It can be your enemy. Double-check spell-check. I have a terrible time spelling "inconvenient."

My spell-check often changes it to "incontinent," Which can change the context of the email. Not exactly the meaning I intended!

Dare I ask for a raise?

So you're doing great. Heck, better than great. What's next? Well, that's actually the subject of the last chapter, but let's finish up here talking about asking for a raise. It's a tricky subject.

Nobody likes doing it. It's hard to tell a boss that you think you're worth more than you're being paid, but frankly, there are often times and situations when doing so makes absolutely perfect sense. In the military, you never asked for a raise because that's not how it worked. You were promoted if they had slots available and you were viewed as a top contender. Often, your bosses had little control, aside from the evaluation they signed every year. The rule of thumb is that you should be in a job for at least six months before asking for a raise. This first year is key-when you demonstrate the value of your work.

Before you step into the boss' office and say, "I'd like to discuss my current compensation package," do a few things first and make a plan. This is very much like an attorney preparing his case to go to court. Keep in mind that your boss may have lots of employees and not be aware of the extra work that you have been doing or how key you are to the success of many of the department's projects.

To make your plan:

- Gather supporting evidence. Build a case of facts. Collect any positive emails, letters, or other documents extolling your work from clients, co-workers, or others. Keep a list all year long of your accomplishments so you can share them with the boss during the discussion.
- Review your skills, responsibilities, and accomplishments. Assess them honestly. Look for weaknesses or places where your boss might question you. Figure out your answers in advance.

- Know your market value. How much is someone in your position typically paid? Where does your current salary fit into this picture? Salary sites like and www.salary.com can help.
- Be willing to negotiate. You want to have a figure in mind for a raise, but it might not legitimately be possible for the company to meet that expectation. Negotiate in good faith and expect the same good faith from your boss. If your boss can't satisfy your requested raise, perhaps you can get other perks sweetened: additional vacation days or permission to work from home one day a week, for example. Go into the meeting with a list of options other than cash that mean a lot to you but don't cost the company money. Also be aware of budget constraints. The best time to have this discussion is before the boss sets his or her staffing budget for the year and before they come up with your salary adjustment. I don't want you to have to appear unhappy with what they are offering. Instead have the discussion before they see the amount and let the increase look like their idea.
- Be professional. Make an appointment. Don't corner your boss in the elevator or ambush him at lunch. Make a formal presentation, with all of the necessary bells and whistles. And give the boss time to consider your requests and to get back to you. He may have to get permission from his boss or just get comfortable with the changes you asked for. He will also have to see how your increase falls in line with your co-workers. Maybe everyone deserves a bump and he can't give one to one you.
- And conversely, here are a few things you *should not* do:
- Don't say you "need" a raise. No boss wants to hear about your rent increase or mortgage. Do show why you deserve one.
- Don't be afraid. If you can prove you're worth it, then you are worth it. Your boss is likely to welcome the chance to reward you.
- Don't make threats. Scare tactics don't prove anything and are clearly counterproductive, except that maybe you're not the right person for the job. If you threaten to leave if you don't get the raise you will disenfranchise the boss, and he

or she may well call your bluff and show you the door. At best they will remove you from the team player list in their department and write you off for future promotions.

- Don't beg. You want to appear confident in yourself and in your value to the company.
- Don't ask for a raise just because someone else got one. Unless you have earned it or it is an issue for the Equal Employment Opportunity Commission, every employee should be compensated in relation to his or her own value to the company.

If you've done your homework and the timing is right, a requested raise will likely be yours. Congratulations! But if it doesn't happen or you don't get everything you asked for and there are lots of legitimate reasons why you didn't—do not be disconsolate. It's not the end of the world. Ask your boss for reasons why a raise was not possible. Ask if there is something you can do to better your chances of earning more in the future. Accept any feedback with a professional demeanor and a determination to use the knowledge to improve your value to the company. After you've gotten the feedback, take action!

Playing nicely with others

It takes a lot of different types of people to create a workplace. The office environment is like any other place where people gather together: There will be natural leaders, followers, motivators, slackers, overachievers, and ne'er-do-wells. Every office is different, but every office has some basic personality types. It's a big change in approach from what you may be used to. In the real work world there are few commands that must be obey because you are the boss and "I out rank you." In the private sector that behavior is counterproductive and no employee worth having will stand for it. To be effective and successful, you'll need to work with all of them. That means learning what makes each type tick, and how to interact with their different styles.

Invariably, there will be people who you will struggle to work with. Some folks are simply jerks, lazy, chronically angry, obnoxious, or worse. No difference here than in the military. As much as you can, identify them quickly and try to stay clear. But if you can't, do the following (even if it's hard):

- Treat them like customers
- Be genuine
- Smile
- Don't get angry yourself
- Recognize that an attitude problem exists
- Help them take responsibility
- Acknowledge the underlying cause for the negativity, if you can
- Be tough
- Be positive
- Be a good team player

But if it someone is affecting your work, or the perception of your work, then you need to do something about it. It is probably affecting the work effectiveness of the department in ways that the boss is not even aware of. If the boss does not see it as a problem and the situation is intolerable for you, then you need to call up your Career Manager and make some things happen.

phil-osophy 101   11

The great comedian George Burns once said, "I look to the future because that's where I'm going to spend the rest of my life." Since the guy once played the role of God in the 1977 movie, Oh, God!, presumably he knew what he was talking about.

The goal and theme of this book has been to help you find yourself, at least in the sense of helping you find yourself a career. But the work doesn't end with work. Or the last page of this book. Feel free to read it again at different stages of your career.

Once you've settled into a new place of employment, it's easy and natural to turn off the jets, close down the networks, heave a sigh of relief and just focus on the work at hand.

And to a great degree, that is exactly what you should do. The preceding chapter was all about how to establish yourself in your new job—and how to excel: Goal setting, team playing, and staying organized. These are just some of the things you should actively put effort into and pursue. You need to take them seriously!

On the other hand, unless you've just landed the dream job of a lifetime, defined as a job you literally would enjoy doing every day for the rest of your work life, and your employer has given you an iron-clad contract guaranteeing permanent employment (including regular, acceptable cost-of-living adjustments, pay raises, etc.), no matter how poorly or inadequately you perform now or in the future, it's wise to think about your next job, the one you haven't yet imagined or begun pursuing.

That's because no job lasts forever. We are all temps, and don't' forget it. Just look around. Everybody knows the story of somebody who lost a job through no fault of his or her own. Maybe he was usurped by a younger, tech savvy co-worker. Maybe she was fired as part of a corporate cutback or restructuring. Maybe they messed up and deserved it.

If you are reading this now and say none of this applies to me, I love my job, I love my boss, I love my industry, I love my company...and they all love me and I am essential to the success of the company, they can't live without me...then consider this your wake up call. Life changes, new competitors appear every day, new technology appears every day, and the boss's daughter appears on the horizon and he thinks she is more loved than you. Have your radar on at all times, watching your company, your competitors, management changes in your company, and any other extraneous changes that might affect your job. Don't ever be complacent and assume conditions that affect your career will never change. Instead be proactive.

For our purposes, the particular reason doesn't matter. If you're out of work now because you were fired, laid off or quit isn't the point. The point is that you're out of work. Or you were out of work. Or you woke up and hated your job and you did something about it. Now you've got a job that you really enjoy. Cherish it, but also start thinking about what happens next in your working world. Always be preparing for anything to happen.

11.0
Managing for Change in your Career

Stuff happens. Things change. We just don't always notice it until—BOOM! I like to compare this notion to the tectonic plates that are shifting beneath our feet. They move small distances each year until so much pressure builds up that CRACK! RUMBLE! POW! We have a huge earthquake that no one saw coming or could have forecast.

Let's discuss two basic ways of thinking about this.

The first is the most obvious: You have developed a long-term career plan that involves a series of jobs that serve as stepping stones to an ultimate aspiration. That's good. Everyone should have a plan. It should be flexible enough to accommodate new factors or unforeseen change. Either that or you're willing to regularly revisit the plan and amend it as needed.

If you don't yet have a career plan in hand, do it now. Unlike some of the other lists I've asked you to create, this list is about goals, short- and long-term, stuff you haven't done yet. Short-term goals are generally those that can be achieved within a few months or a year. They're often stepping stones to longer- term goals, which may take three to five years to achieve.

Your career plan describes the steps you'll take to reach your goals. Usually the goal is a particular career objective: You want to be president of a company, own your own business, or earn a certain income. Here are some questions to ask yourself as you shape your career plan:

1. What do I love to do?
2. What do I want to do?
3. What motivates me?
4. How far do I want to go?
5. How will I get there?
6. Who will help me?
7. Am I willing to make any sacrifices? What kind?
8. What do I do next?

Your career plan is a roadmap, but there is no single way to get to your objective. Your plan can be a basic checklist, a time schedule, or a 100-page, detailed document, complete with footnotes and annotations. Whatever works for you.

If you're stuck on how to start, start simple. Here is an example of one of my clients who wanted a career in the banking industry. Make a list with four headings:

POSITION	TIMELINE	STEPS TO TAKE	RESOURCES NEEDED
Bank Teller	June 2018	Finance BA	Scholarships
Vault Manager	July 2019	Certification	
Education Reimbursement Loan Manager	September 2020	CRE Credentials	
Savings Reimbursement Branch Manager	January 2022	MBA	
Regional Manager	January 2026		
Pacific School of Banking Area Manager	January 2031		

Once you've filled it out, don't file it away somewhere to be forgotten. This is a living document. You should review it at least twice a year to evaluate where you are and make necessary revisions. Remember everything to do with career management should be written in pencil.

The second mode involves maintaining an internal conversation with yourself about what you're doing for a living now. Are you following your Career Plan? Are you meeting your timeline? How's work going? Are you satisfied? Are there things you'd like to do, or do differently? Is it in your power to make changes? Are there changes that need to be made?

On the flip side, how are you perceived by your boss, upper management, and your co-workers? Do they think you're doing a great job? Are you exceeding their expectations or just meeting them? The latter happens more often than you might think. I've met, worked with, and helped many people who firmly believed they brought something unique and invaluable to their jobs, that they were so highly prized and admired by their companies and colleagues that nothing untoward would ever happen to *them*.

Then they got laid off.

Know when to go

One key to knowing when it's time to begin looking for a new job is an honest evaluation of your current employer's condition. What are your company's vital signs? Is it healthy and thriving, with a good revenue stream, steady expansion, and reinvestment in new technology and research? Or is it struggling, overextended, on the verge of bankruptcy or closure? In your industry, are larger companies circling, ready to swoop down and buy companies like the one where you are now working? If not, will they be soon? Is that a good thing for your career or a bad thing?

These questions may or may not be easy to answer. The workers in the last buggy whip factory probably knew their days were numbered. Heck, they probably drove to their last day at work in horseless carriages.

Companies in trouble don't often broadcast their struggles if they can avoid it. Bad news generally begets more bad news. Customers shun businesses they fear won't be around tomorrow. Employees flee companies in trouble or turmoil. Nobody, especially you, wants a co-worker beating them to a scarce job opportunity. Nobody wants to be the last guy to turn off the lights.

After an honest evaluation, if things are good, then stay right where you are. If things are bad, as in you are a duplication that will not survive, then red lights should be flashing and your radar should be in second gear.

There are always signs of doom and disaster, and you need to be able to recognize them. *Get Hired Fast! Tap the Hidden Job Market in 15 Days*, Brian Graham describes 15 situations that might be signs your career security is at risk. Keep them in mind and keep your eyes open:

1. Did the person who hired you leave? (There goes your patron.)
2. Are other key players leaving? (What do they know that you don't?)
3. Is a change of ownership in the office? (New owners, new rules, new employees.)
4. Is there a change in reporting structure? (Bad news?)
5. Is the company's stock moving downward? (Death spiral?)
6. How is your industry doing as a whole? (Does anybody make typewriters anymore? No.)
7. How is your division or department doing? (Are you expendable?)
8. How are your major clients faring? (Sometimes you get dragged down by others.)
9. Are managers often locked away in secret meetings? (Clueless employees are happy employees.)
10. Is there a "black hole" when it comes to new contracts or projects? (Black holes are never a good sign.)
11. Do you see evidence of cash flow problems? (Where's the bleeding? Where's the fix?)

12. Are you being excluded from meetings you used to attend? (Never good news.)
13. Are your requests for help being denied? (It might be a lack of resources. It might be a lack of interest in helping you.)
14. Are you sensing strange vibes? (You'll know them when you feel them.)
15. Are you being asked to prepare for outsourcing?

There's a flip side to this coin. There are signs, too, that tell you when to move on, even if your employers love you. Graham suggests asking yourself these two questions, particularly if you're aware of opportunities elsewhere.

- Am I getting stale (or bored) in the job? Have I peaked in terms of company advancement?
- Is my current job an unpleasant place to be? Has something changed for the worse?

The new and improved you

Each day on the job, you have an opportunity to get better at what you do, to learn something new, and then apply it to your work. It's called experience. Unless you're asleep at the wheel, you naturally exploit past experience and build on it to get ahead.

Ed Vargo once joked about his chosen profession: "We're supposed to be perfect our first day on the job, and then show constant improvement." That's remarkably insightful for a major league umpire. So what exactly constitutes the perfect employee?

But that's not enough now days. You need to constantly reinvent yourself into a shinier, newer model. You need to actively seek out new knowledge and learning. One of the smartest things you can do is pursue any opportunities available through your current company for training or professional education. An employer-paid education allowance is something that should never go unused.

This can be done formally, in the sense of seeking an advanced educational degree. If you have a bachelor's degree, consider getting a master's. If you don't have any degree, get one now. Having a spoonful of alphabet soup after your name is no guarantee of full-time employment — there are plenty of PhDs out of work — but education never hurts and almost always helps improve your marketability and attractiveness as a job candidate.

Dave found himself caught in a sticky wicket. He lived in the Los Angeles area and survived several mergers in his industry until the last one. (Isn't that always the case?) He became redundant after the latest merger, but his skills were still good and he found a similar job in Phoenix. He and his wife had young children whom they did not want to move in the middle of the school year. So Dave moved alone to Phoenix and commuted home every weekend. He and his wife's ultimate goal, however, was to live and work in San Diego, his wife's hometown.

Now, as the plot thickens, the school year ended and Dave's bosses assumed Dave would be moving his family to Phoenix — a reasonable expectation from a committed management employee, right? But Dave is not a committed employee. He is bored with the new job and wants to live in San Diego.

Issue one: How does he seek employment in San Diego when he doesn't live there, knowing he is competent in his industry with equally qualified job seekers who already live there. By the way, we employers like hiring people in our communities, rather than moving them here. Doing so is more complicated and expensive. Locals almost always have an advantage over out-of-towners.

Issue two: How does Dave answer questions from his boss about how the Phoenix house hunt is going?

Issue three: How does Dave make good use of all his free time while he is sitting alone in an apartment in Phoenix all week?

What would you tell Dave? The condensed version of our chat was that he should spend every free moment in San Diego networking and using family connections, which is how he met me. Yes, the school year is out, but they have not been able to sell their house and can't move until it sells. Also, use his time to start working on an MBA degree. It will help him in any career, but it will especially impress any interviewer.

Also consider certification programs. If your chosen field of work is one in which skills can be advanced and recognized through formalized training programs, by all means pursue them. Again, they don't guarantee a pay raise or a better job, but they almost always help and set you apart from others who haven't shown similar initiative. I suggest people develop one skill that they become the "go to guy." And everyone in the department or company knows that. Maybe it's software like Salesforce, or the home office computer system. It makes you much more valuable to the company.

Finally, there are informal and indirect ways to improve your employability, such as staying on top of the latest computer skills or learning a new language. If your employer doesn't offer such programs, look into taking classes at the local community college, extension course programs, professional groups, or industry associations. Other options are online programs, personal tutors, and self-help books.

How do you know what kind of class to take or language to learn? For instance, you might consider where are most of your company's off shore clients or employees? That's easy. Stay informed. Read everything: newspapers, magazines, websites, blogs, trade journals. Soak up information like a sponge. You never know what tidbit you learn today will be useful tomorrow.

In terms of your specific career, ask your boss:

"Mr. Jones, I really enjoy working here at Acme Industries. I certainly enjoy the accounting department. Where else could you see me being able to utilize my other talents and grow within the company, and add more value? Hmmm.... interesting. What skills and education would I need to succeed in that department?"

Serious kiss-up? You bet! Was the boss wowed? Probably. It may be the first time an employee has ever talked to him that way. Did you get some great insight into what your boss thinks about the job you are doing and your future with Acme? You may not like what he had to say and now it is your time to react. You obviously did not talk about any options outside of Acme, but depending on what the boss said, it may be time to rev up a new job search. This search will be at your leisure while you have a job, rather than after being surprised and let go.

Very different than the military it's always smart to know what's happening not just in your company and your industry, but also in other industries. This will let you anticipate what your boss or company will be looking for in their next hire. One way to do this is to peruse job boards and postings on a regular basis. Even if you're not actually looking for a job, it's beneficial to see what employers want. Ask yourself a couple of questions as you scan the listings: Are there any commonalities among the jobs being offered? Do they seem to all want qualities like good communication skills, presentation experience, or expertise with a particular kind of software, tool, or technique? If they do, and you don't think your abilities or experience quite fit or meet the need, maybe these are areas you should pursue in terms of additional training or education.

Keep your network active

As I have said throughout this book, it's important to keep your network open and operating. It's like building a house. You labor mightily to lay the foundation, put up the walls and roof, paint and furnish it. Once you move into the house, it's all about maintenance, keeping your new home in good shape.

Your network of business-related contacts, sources, colleagues, and friends are no different. You must nurture this network because it is the foundation upon which your career rests. The job you have — or the job you will have next— is quite likely not the last job of your life. You'll need your network again.

So "circle back," take the time and effort every few months or so to email or phone members of your network. Arrange to get together for lunch or catch up on the news. Update phone numbers and addresses. It's important to create an efficient, simple, easy way of keeping track of your network. You can do that any number of ways, but the relevant information you want to keep in your online career notebook is:

- Name
- Title
- Employer
- Hobbies
- Industry
- Professional associations
- How you know this person
- Where you met
- And anything else that might be of interest in the future. You might also note when you last spoke or met, what you talked about, if you asked anything of them or they of you.

That may sound like a lot of work — and maybe it is — but keeping your network viable and up-to-date is a lot less laborious than reviving or starting a network when you need to look for a new job.

And besides, these people are supposed to be important to you, so why wouldn't you want to stay up-to-date with them? Which brings up a related point: Don't call the people in your network only when you need a favor or assistance. You want people to know you value them for themselves, that you're interested not only in whom they're LinkedIn with, but who they are. Birthdays are always a good way to stay in touch. Also make them aware of job openings that might be of interest to them.

Conversely, members of your network should know you're there for them as well if they need a hand. Be proactive about it. If you can help, help. Indeed, look for opportunities to be of assistance, even if it takes some effort on your part. Good deeds pay off, in all ways. Pay a good deed forward.

When do I use my network?

You've worked hard to keep your network of friends and colleagues up and running like a finely tuned racecar. That's great. The question is, when do you actually hop into the car and drive it? Odds are, you'll know the answer when you need it, but here are some times when you might want to tap into your network:

- You're thinking about a new career
- You're investigating a particular career field
- You're working through a professional challenge or crisis
- You're requesting references or referrals
- You're spreading word that you're seeking new career opportunities
- You're looking for a new job

Craig was happy with his job, happy with the firm he worked for, and happy working in the industry he was in. And Craig was a star. Recruiters (lovingly known as Headhunters; sounds a bit cannibalistic to me) were calling Craig all the time and he politely took their calls to see what was out there. And then along came a merger, he didn't want to move to the headquarters and he was out in the cold because the job did move. Well guess how long it took Craig to pull out all those business cards and emails from past headhunters to tell them he was now seriously in the market. A huge fan base started working on his next job (and their next fee) immediately. A great head start for Craig.

And that's the way it is

I always tell my military and private sector audiences that if I ever make a job search or long-term career planning seem easy, they have the right to call me out on it. The process is not easy, never will be, and if it ever is then we have a host of new problems. We will be living under the cloud of very slow job growth for many years to come. That's the reality of our "new economy."

But thousands of people are getting new jobs in our country, and in your community, every day: Why shouldn't you be one of them? Why shouldn't you be among the 10% who love their jobs or at least the next 40% who really like their jobs? There is no reason. If you are willing to put the work into managing your job search and continually managing your career, I guarantee you that you will be among those of us looking forward to going to work every day.

There are really two themes in this book: how to manage a job search as and how to manage your long-term career. Now I want you to look back through the book and see if there is anything I suggested you do that you are not capable of doing. I doubt there is. Probably the most common pushback I get is people saying they are uncomfortable approaching strangers for help. They are not comfortable networking. But life takes us on some twists and turns that we never expected. We need to approach these twists as interesting opportunities and not fi them. Once they know strangers would not hesitate to approach them, it all seems alright. And trust me, you get used to it. Remember I was a shy kid, and, boy, did I get over that!

I am convinced networking will have the biggest influence in your future job searches, planned or unplanned, for many years. Why? Because as my fellow HR professionals use more and more automation and technology in conducting candidate searches, we will fall back even more on who we personally know and who comes personally recommended to us. It's almost like we are running away from too much technology in the HR world and reaching out for real people. And real people come recommended to us because of all our new friends, like you, that we meet networking.

What makes the job search and career management doable is the "Career Manager" I talked about. You! It sometimes feels like Sybil, the lady with multiple personalities. Sometimes you are the client and sometimes you are the counselor. Just like sometimes you are the pigeon and sometimes you are the statue! Remember, as you are watching out for yourself, you are inherently watching out for your family too. That thought alone is very motivating.

If you are searching for a job or a career or currently working and want to make sure you are not on a dead end path, then listen to your Career Manager, heed the advice, know it will be good for you and then make it happen. I have complete faith in you and just wish that I could be there to hear all of your success stories, and help you celebrate when you hear "You're Hired!"

But it does take work. I hope you have found value in reading *Job Won! for American Veterans*, maybe even enjoyed it. Life is too short to take ourselves too seriously — I hope we never lose our sense of humor, including being able to laugh at ourselves. But when it's time to get serious and plan a goal for ourselves, we have to have a map to get there. We also must be empowered to get out of our comfort zone. For most of us, searching for a new job is definitely out of that comfort zone. I have found, though, that once I am confident that I know what I am doing, why I am doing it, and have the tools to do what I need to do, my comfort zone really expands. I hope yours does too. And I hope *Job Won! for America's Veterans* empowers you as you transition to this next big adventure.

Appendix

Somebody's got to do it

In our lives, we will all have many jobs—and likely many careers. The days of a gold watch after 50 years with the same employers are over, assuming they ever really existed. I mean, really, have you ever met anybody who worked for the same company for generations and has a timepiece to prove it?

You'll probably do a lot of things to earn a living, and some are likely to have little to do with your interests or long-term aspirations. Before you become rich and famous, you might have to follow in the footsteps of these celebrities and their one-time occupations:

- Jim Carrey, security guard
- Sean Connery, milkman
- Simon Cowell, mail room clerk
- Michael Dell (the computer guy), dishwasher
- Danny DeVito, hairdresser
- Walt Disney, paperboy
- Harrison Ford, carpenter
- Hugh Jackman, clown
- Mick Jagger, ice cream salesman
- Madonna, doughnut shop worker
- Demi Moore, debt collection agent
- Brad Pitt, refrigerator mover
- Sylvester Stallone, lion cage cleaner
- Rod Stewart, gravedigger
- Barbara Walters, secretary

Insider scoop: The recruitment process

Below is a very typical process for a company that may or may not use an outside recruiting agency. Although, each organization has its own hiring procedures, you will most likely encounter most of these components as part of the recruitment and hiring process. In the event they do not use a professional recruiting agency, then the steps listed under recruiter would probably be handled by an HR staff person, the owner of a small business or the manager of a department in a medium sized company:

1. Candidate capture (candidate networks their way to the recruiter, is referred from a business contact, responds to a job posting, or is contacted directly by a recruiter).
2. Résumé screen – recruiter reviews the candidate's résumé against the job criteria, compares with other résumés already received.
3. Email contact – recruiter contacts candidate to set day, time for phone call.
4. Phone interview. Even if it is just to set the time for the phone interview, every call is part of the interview process so be on your toes.
5. Face-to-face interview with recruiter or HR staff (or via Skype, FaceTime, or other teleconferencing software, if candidate and recruiter are located in different cities).
6. Recruiter submits résumé to the Hiring Manager or Client.
7. Hiring Manager or Client screen your résumé – if they like what they see, client gives OK for the recruiter to arrange a meeting.
8. Client interview #1 – face-to-face if local or via teleconference with the Hiring Manager. (a company usually pays for the candidate's travel expenses).
9. Psychometric or skills-based assessment (some companies use these, although many don't).
10. Client interview #2 - face-to-face or via teleconference with different members of the executive team.
11. Client interview #3 - face-to-face with the CEO.
12. Client interview #4 - face-to-face with members of the staff (your potential direct reports) and team (your potential

colleagues/peers). This is as much for you to meet them as for them to meet you.

13. Client interview #5, - face-to-face with the CEO and several board members.

14. Reference checks (recruiter or hiring manager contacts the candidate's previous supervisors or work-related points of contact provided by the candidate).

15. Background checks: candidate signs authorization form, company hires agency to run report.

16. Drug screen and possible physical evaluation.

17. Offer issued.

18. Candidate takes a few days to review.

19. Negotiations – items include salary, benefits, vacation, bonuses, start date, etc.

20. Formal offer letter detailing final terms agreed sent by company to candidate.

21. Candidate signs and returns letter.

22. Candidate provides two weeks' notice to current employer (if working).

23. Start date at new job (may include probationary/trial period of up to 90 days).

24. Completion of probationary period, full benefits kick in.

How do companies really recruit?

- Here's a few additional inside observations I'd like to share with you:

- It's always a little bit different. The recruitment process will differ tremendously between organizations, and even between different positions within the same organization. Some move very quickly, and will post a job, screen candidates, conduct interviews, select a finalist and make an offer in a matter of just a couple weeks. For other organizations, particularly anything in the public sector, the process will be long and drawn out, with many steps, some of which might seem redundant. It's not uncommon for some organizations to take 6+ months to make a decision.

- It ain't over 'til it's over. Smart candidates know that a position isn't closed until an offer letter is signed and even until the candidate shows up for work the first day. That means you need to keep checking back with the recruiter or hiring manager until you are finally advised the job was filled with another candidate, closed, or canceled. I've seen dozens of candidates come back from the dead to ultimately land an offer. Here is where polite persistence comes in again. You want the recruiter to know you are serious about the position but no a pest. Most candidates just disappear after their interview. More on that later.

    o *Dana really wanted to work for this very innovative public relations and marketing firm because they were on the cutting edge of what she wanted to do. They did not select her and she was very disappointed. The agency offered the job to someone else, who accepted but alas, when the candidate gave notice the current firm countered and the candidate decided to stay where she was. The fat lady had not sung! I had Dana stay in touch with polite persistence and when she called to see if the new person was working out (hey, things happen) they told her to start the next day. Later they told she was the only one to stay in touch and evidently wanted the job more than all the others.*

- *Recruiters and HR are at the mercy of their clients.* If you are working through a recruiter or the HR Department, please know that we can only move as fast as our client is willing, and we can only share as much information and feedback as the client gives us. I'm a big fan of timely, candid, and actionable feedback. If you don't get the job, I want to be able to share with you the reasons why, so you can use those data points to improve your game for the next job. Unfortunately, our client doesn't always provide us with that information.

Believe me, nothing frustrates us more than when the client says "they just weren't the right fit", or "I just didn't get the right feeling about him". Those comments don't help you improve for your next interview, nor do they help me get any closer to finding the ideal candidate who *will* give them that "right feeling". So if you feel your recruiter isn't getting back to you, it's not that we're avoiding you, it's just that the client hasn't given us anything to share...and please know that we're every bit as frustrated as you are!

- *Stay in touch.* Let's say you apply for a position through a recruiter, but ultimately aren't selected for the role. If you had a positive experience working with that recruiter, stay in touch. New positions come up all the time, and you want to stay front of mind for that recruiter when they become available. I routinely contact folks I've interviewed years ago.

Craig was happy with his job, happy with the firm he worked for, and happy working in the industry he was in. And Craig was a star. Recruiters (lovingly known as Headhunters; sounds a bit cannibalistic to me) were calling Craig all the time and he politely took their calls to see what was out there. And then along came a merger, he didn't want to move to the headquarters and he was out in the cold because the job did move. Well guess how long it took Craig to pull out all those business cards and emails from past headhunters to tell them he was now seriously in the market. A huge fan base started working on his next job (and their next fee) immediately. A great head start for Craig.

Activity Tracker

Date Last Contact	Company Name	Position Applied For	Location	Contact Person	Email	Phone	Title	Source	Action	Follow-up Date
/2/17	Manpower	Staffing Spec.	Downtown	Trevor Blair	tblair@...	619 237 9900	Workforce Development Manager	Spoke at SDFF	Sent f/up email to set up call	6/9/17
/10/17	Qualcomm	HR Assistant	Sorrento Valley	Linda Adair	ladair@...	620 237 9900	Regional Director	Monster.com	Sent resume and application	6/17/17
/15/17	UPS	HR Assistant	Kearny Mesa	Steve Redding	sredding@...	621 237 9900	HR Director	Google search	Sent intro email	6/22/17
/20/17	Kyocera	Admin Assistant	Kearny Mesa	Dara Kauftheil	dkauftheil@...	622 237 9900	Recruiter	Adecco	Walk-in	6/27/17
/20/17	AAA	Customer Service Rep	Mission Valley	Vanessa Reid	vreid@...	623 237 9900	Recruiter	Manpower	Walk-in	6/27/17

266

Bibliography

Ziglar, Zig & Ziglar.. Born to Win: Find Your Success Code. SUCCESS Media, 2012. Print

Jansen, Julie. *I Don't Know What I Want, But I Know It's Not This: A Step-by-Step Guide to Finding Gratifying Work.* Penguin Random House: New York. 2016. Print.

Bolles, Richard N. *What Color is Your Parachute?* Ten Speed Press: Berkeley. 2009. Print.

Frankl, Viktor E. *Man's Search for Meaning.* Beacon Press: Boston. 2006. Print.

Cameron, Roger. *PCS to Corporate America.* Odenwald Press. 2013. Print.

Collins, Jim. Good to Great. Harper Collins Publishers: New York. 2001. Print.

Ries, Eric. *The Lean Startup: How Today's Entrepreneurs Use Continuous Innovation to Create Radically Successful Businesses.* Crown Business: New York. 2011. Print.

Christensen, Clayton M. *The Innovator's Dilemma: The Revolutionary Book That Will Change the Way You Do Business.* Harper Business: New York. 2000. Print.

Grice, Mike. *Orders to Nowhere: The after action report from a career Marine's transition back to the civilian world.* CreateSpace: Charleston, SC. 2015. Print

Beshara, Tony. *Unbeatable Résumés: America's Top Recruiter Reveals What REALLY Gets You Hired.* Amacom Books: New York. 2011. Print.

Kador, John. *201 Best Questions to Ask on Your Interview.* McGraw-Hill: New York. 2002. Print.

Watkins, Michael. *The First 90 Days: Proven Strategies for Getting Up to Speed Faster and Smarter.* Harvard Business School Publishing: Boston. 2013. Print.

Wooden, John (with Steve Jamieson). *Wooden: A Lifetime of Observations and Reflections On and Off the Court.* McGraw-Hill: New York. 1997. Print.

Graham, Brian. *Get Hired Fast! Tap the Hidden Job Market in 15 Days.* Adams Media: Avon, MA. 2005. Print.